St Antony's Series

General Editor: **Richard Clogg** (1999–), Fellow of St Antony's College, Oxford

Recent titles include:

Steve Tsang (*editor*)
JUDICIAL INDEPENDENCE AND THE RULE OF LAW IN HONG KONG

Karen Jochelson
THE COLOUR OF DISEASE
Syphilis and Racism in South Africa, 1880–1950

Julio Crespo MacLennan
SPAIN AND THE PROCESS OF EUROPEAN INTEGRATION, 1957–85

Enrique Cárdenas, José Antonio Ocampo and Rosemary Thorp (*editors*)
AN ECONOMIC HISTORY OF TWENTIETH-CENTURY LATIN AMERICA
Volume 1: The Export Age
Volume 2: Latin America in the 1930s
Volume 3: Industrialization and the State in Latin America

Jennifer G. Mathers
THE RUSSIAN NUCLEAR SHIELD FROM STALIN TO YELTSIN

Marta Dyczok
THE GRAND ALLIANCE AND UKRAINIAN REFUGEES

Mark Brzezinski
THE STRUGGLE FOR CONSTITUTIONALISM IN POLAND

Suke Wolton
LORD HAILEY, THE COLONIAL OFFICE AND THE POLITICS OF RACE AND
EMPIRE IN THE SECOND WORLD WAR
The Loss of White Prestige

Junko Tomaru
THE POSTWAR RAPPROCHEMENT OF MALAYA AND JAPAN, 1945–61
The Roles of Britain and Japan in South-East Asia

Eiichi Motono
CONFLICT AND COOPERATION IN SINO-BRITISH BUSINESS, 1860–1911
The Impact of the Pro-British Commercial Network in Shanghai

Nikolas K. Gvosdev
IMPERIAL POLICIES AND PERSPECTIVES TOWARDS GEORGIA, 1760–1819

Bernardo Kosacoff
CORPORATE STRATEGIES UNDER STRUCTURAL ADJUSTMENT IN ARGENTINA
Responses by Industrial Firms to a New Set of Uncertainties

Ray Takeyh
THE ORIGINS OF THE EISENHOWER DOCTRINE
The US, Britain and Nasser's Egypt, 1953–57

Derek Hopwood (*editor*)
ARAB NATION, ARAB NATIONALISM

Judith Clifton
THE POLITICS OF TELECOMMUNICATIONS IN MEXICO
Privatization and State–Labour Relations, 1928–95

Cécile Laborde
PLURALIST THOUGHT AND THE STATE IN BRITAIN AND FRANCE, 1900–25

Craig Brandist and Galin Tihanov (*editors*)
MATERIALIZING BAKHTIN

C. S. Nicholls
THE HISTORY OF ST ANTONY'S COLLEGE, OXFORD, 1950–2000

Anthony Kirk-Greene
BRITAIN'S IMPERIAL ADMINISTRATORS, 1858–1966

Laila Parsons
THE DRUZE BETWEEN PALESTINE AND ISRAEL, 1947–49

M. K. Flynn
IDEOLOGY, MOBILIZATION AND THE NATION
The Rise of Irish, Basque and Carlist Nationalist Movements in the
Nineteenth and Early Twentieth Centuries

Karina Sonnenberg-Stern
EMANCIPATION AND POVERTY
The Ashkenazi Jews of Amsterdam, 1796–1850

Shane O'Rourke
WARRIORS AND PEASANTS
The Don Cossacks in Late Imperial Russia

St Antony's Series
Series Standing Order ISBN 0–333–71109–2
(*outside North America only*)

You can receive future titles in this series as they are published by placing a standing order.
Please contact your bookseller or, in case of difficulty, write to us at the address below with
your name and address, the title of the series and the ISBN quoted above.

Customer Services Department, Macmillan Distribution Ltd, Houndmills, Basingstoke,
Hampshire RG21 6XS, England

Judicial Independence and the Rule of Law in Hong Kong

Edited by

Steve Tsang
Director, Asian Studies Centre
Reader in Politics
and Louis Cha Senior Research Fellow
St Antony's College
Oxford

palgrave

in association with
St Antony's College, Oxford

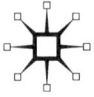

First published 2001 by
PALGRAVE
Houndmills, Basingstoke, Hampshire RG21 6XS and
175 Fifth Avenue, New York, N. Y. 10010
Companies and representatives throughout the world

PALGRAVE is the new global academic imprint of
St. Martin's Press LLC Scholarly and Reference Division and
Palgrave Publishers Ltd (formerly Macmillan Press Ltd).

ISBN 0–333–93052–5

This book is printed on paper suitable for recycling and
made from fully managed and sustained forest sources.

A catalogue record for this book is available
from the British Library.

Library of Congress Cataloging-in-Publication Data
Judicial independence and the rule of law in Hong Kong / edited by Steve
Tsang.
      p. cm. — (St. Antony's series)
    Includes bibliographical references and index.
    ISBN 0–333–93052–5
    1. Rule of law—China—Hong Kong. 2. Judicial power—China—Hong
Kong. 3. Due process of law—China—Hong Kong. I. Tsang, Steve Yui-
Sang, 1959– II. Series.
    KNR169.7 .J83 2000
    340'.11—dc21
                                                        00–049155

10   9   8   7   6   5   4   3   2   1
10   09 08 07 06 05 04 03 02 01

Printed and bound in Great Britain by
Antony Rowe Ltd, Chippenham, Wiltshire

To Don Liu

Contents

Preface and Acknowledgements

The Crown Colony of Hong Kong became a Special Administrative Region (SAR) of the People's Republic of China (PRC) on 1 July 1997, under an unusual constitutional arrangement which the Chinese call 'one country, two systems'. The governing principles for this experiment are codified into a legal document, the Basic Law of the Hong Kong SAR. The survival of the existing way of life in Hong Kong requires the upholding of this law and therefore hinges, to a very considerable extent, on the maintenance of the rule of law and judicial independence.

This is a matter of great importance not only to the nearly seven million people of Hong Kong. The successful maintenance of the rule of law and judicial independence in a Chinese SAR, as distinct from a British colony, will mark the entrenching of these Anglo-Saxon concepts in a Chinese community, which despite special constitutional arrangements, falls under the jurisdiction of a Leninist party-state. It can serve as a shining model for other Chinese communities, particularly the PRC itself and Taiwan, whose cultural and legal traditions are different from those of the Anglo-Saxons.

A cosmopolitan financial and commercial centre dedicated to free trade, a hub for global communications, and the unofficial capital of the vast Chinese diaspora, Hong Kong in an important sense belongs not only to the Chinese but to the world at large. Fundamental to its ability to play these multiple roles in its British period was the existence of an independent judiciary and the rule of law. The continuation of these basic conditions now that Hong Kong is part of the PRC is therefore of great interest and significance to the rest of the world.

However much one may believe in the sincerity of the Chinese leaders in their pledge to keep their promises summed up in the policy of 'one country, two systems', the survival of the rule of law and an independent judiciary in the SAR cannot be taken for granted. After all, major political upheavals in the fifty-year history of the PRC have been such that even a Chairman of the state, three General Secretaries of the Communist Party and an overwhelming majority of top leaders had at various times been removed from power by extra-constitutional means. The continuation of the rule of law and judicial independence in Hong Kong will depend not only on its courts behaving impeccably in the common law tradition but also on the behaviour of its government and of the PRC government, the attitude and activism of the local people, interest groups and the media, as well as the general political situation in the PRC.

The rule of law is as much a way of life as an institutional or constitutional arrangement. This is a matter that deserves careful study and requires constant vigilant attention both inside and outside Hong Kong.

A year after Britain handed Hong Kong over to the PRC, the Asian Studies Centre at St Antony's College, Oxford University, organized a workshop focusing on this crucial subject. Out of the brainstorming among scholars from Hong Kong, the PRC, Australia, Ireland and the United Kingdom this volume was conceived. It is based primarily on the papers presented. However, it is more. Just as the discussions and debates at St Antony's College provoked new thinking and ideas, events in Hong Kong – most notably a threat to the integrity and authority of its Court of Final Appeal over the right of abode for the children of recent immigrants – not only caught the headlines in newspapers but also provoked further reflection and new research. Much of this volume which was conceived at the workshop was subsequently revised, in some cases fairly substantially, to take into account new developments towards the end of June 1999, two years after the handover and when the implications of the right-of-abode case are sufficiently clear.

In organizing the workshop I was deeply indebted to my colleague David Faure who co-organized it, and to friends and colleagues who led discussions. In this connection Johannes Chan, Richard Cullen, Anthony Dicks, Hualing Fu, Leo Goodstadt, Daniel Fung, Cheuk-yan Leung, Christopher Munn, Mike Palmer, Lord Thomas of Gresford, Byron Weng, and Peter Wesley-Smith deserve a special note of thanks. I am also grateful to Darius Edler and Ann Delahaye for all kinds of practical help. Last but emphatically not the least, I would like to underline my gratitude to Adrian Fu, whose generous support to the Asian Studies Centre had made this event possible.

In putting this volume together I am obliged to all the contributors for their co-operation in making this endeavour an enjoyable one. I am also grateful to Berry Hsu, Peter Wesley-Smith and Ming K. Chan for their advice in the process. Collette Caffrey has also provided excellent help for which I am thankful.

STEVE TSANG

List of Abbreviations

AJL	*Australian Law Journal*
ATV	Asia Television
BBC	British Broadcasting Corporation
BL	Basic Law
BORO	Bill of Rights Ordinance
BSP	Beijing Statement of Principles of the Independence of the Judiciary in the LAWASIA Region
CCC	Canadian Criminal Cases
CE	Chief Executive
CFA	Court of Final Appeal
CFI	Court of First Instance
CJ	Chief Justice
CJC	Chief Justice of Canada
CJHC	Chief Judge of the High Court
CPG	Central People's Government
CPPCC	Chinese People's Political Consultative Conference
DCO	District Court Ordinance
DPP	Director of Public Prosecution
DPS	Directorate Pay Scale
FEER	*Far Eastern Economic Review*
FLR	*Federal Law Review*
GIS	Government Information Service
HCO	High Court Ordinance
HKCFAO	Hong Kong Court of Final Appeal Ordinance
HKJAAR	*Hong Kong Journalists Association Annual Report*
HKLJ	*Hong Kong Law Journal*
HKLRD	*Hong Kong Law Report and Digest*
HKSAR	Hong Kong Special Administrative Region
ICAC	Independent Commission Against Corruption
ICCPR	International Covenant on Civil and Political Rights
J	Judge/Justice
JCPC	Judicial Committee of the Privy Council
JLG	Joint Liaison Group
JORC	Judicial Officers Recommendation Commission
JORCO	Judicial Officers Recommendation Commission Ordinance

Legco	Legislative Council
MECAB	Minor Employment Claims Adjudication Board
MPS	Master Pay Scale
NCNA	New China (Xinhua) News Agency
NPC	National People's Congress
NPCSC	National People's Congress Standing Committee
NYULR	*New York University Law Review*
NZLJ	*New Zealand Law Journal*
OSA	Official Secrets Act
PC	Preparatory Committee (for the SAR)
PEI	Prince Edward Island
PRC	People's Republic of China
PUC	Provisional Urban Council
PWC	Preliminary Working Committee
POO	Public Order Ordinance
RTHK	Radio Television Hong Kong
SAR	Special Administrative Region
SCMP	*South China Morning Post*
SO	Societies Ordinance
SPC	Supreme People's Court
TO	Judicial Officers (Tenure of Office) Ordinance
UK	United Kingdom
UNSWLJ	*University of New South Wales Law Journal*
USA	United States of America

Notes on the Contributors

Johannes Chan is Professor and Head of the Department of Law, University of Hong Kong. His main publications include: *General Principles of Hong Kong Law* (with Albert Chen and others) (1999); *Media Law and Practice* (with Kenneth Leung) (1995); *Human Rights and Public Law: a Hong Kong Sourcebook* (with Andrew Byrnes) (1993); *The Hong Kong Bill of Rights: a Comparative Approach* (with Yash Ghai, 1993); and *Human Rights in Hong Kong* (1990).

Richard Cullen is Professor and Head of the Department of Business Law and Taxation at Monash University. He was a Visiting Fellow in the School of Law at the City University of Hong Kong in 1998. His main research areas include media law, comparative public law and taxation law. Among his more recent publications are: *Media Law in China* (1996) (with H.L. Fu); 'Seeking Theory from Experience: Media Regulation in China' (1998), *Democratization*, 155 (with H.L. Fu); and 'Freedom of the Press in Hong Kong' (1997) *Internationales Asienforum*, 29.

Hualing Fu is Assistant Professor in the Department of Law, University of Hong Kong. His research interests include the criminal justice system, constitutional law, and human rights in China. He has published widely on these topics in journals including *The China Quarterly*, *Democratization*, *Policing and Society*, and *The Journal of Chinese Law*.

Leo F. Goodstadt was the Hong Kong government's chief policy adviser as Head of its Central Policy Unit (1989–97). He previously served as a consultant economist to several financial institutions with substantial Asian assets, as Deputy Editor of the *Far Eastern Economic Review*, and as a Lecturer at the University of Hong Kong. He has published widely on economic and political trends in China and Hong Kong. He is author of *China's Watergate: Political and Economic Conflicts* (1979), and *Mao Tse Tung: the Search for Plenty* (1972).

Christopher Munn holds a doctorate from the University of Toronto. He had taught at the University of Toronto and at the University of

Hong Kong. He has published a number of articles on politics and the law in early colonial Hong Kong. His book *Anglo-China: Chinese People and British Rule in Nineteenth-Century Hong Kong* will be published in 2000.

Steve Tsang is Reader in Politics and Louis Cha Senior Research Fellow at St Antony's College, Oxford University, where he is also Director of its Asian Studies Centre. His main publications include: *Democratization in Taiwan: Implications for China* (with Hung-Mao Tien) (1999); *Hong Kong: an Appointment with China* (1997); *Government and Politics: a Documentary History of Hong Kong* (1995); *In the Shadow of China: Political Developments in Taiwan since 1949* (1993); and *Democracy Shelved: Great Britain, China and Attempts at Constitutional Reform in Hong Kong* (1988).

Byron S.J. Weng was until 1999 Professor and Chairman of the Department of Government and Public Administration, the Chinese University of Hong Kong. He has published extensively on the politics, law and foreign policy of the PRC, Taiwan and Hong Kong. He had also served on the Law Reform Commission and the Central Policy Unit in the Hong Kong government, and on the National Unification Council and the Mainland Affairs Council in the ROC government. His current research focuses on relations among the PRC, Taiwan and Hong Kong.

Peter Wesley-Smith was until 1999 Professor of Constitutional Law at the University of Hong Kong. His best-known work is *Unequal Treaty 1898–1997* (revised edn 1998), and he has also authored *Constitutional and Administrative Law in Hong Kong* (2nd edn 1994), *An Introduction to the Hong Kong Legal System* (3rd edn 1998), and *The Sources of Hong Kong Law* (1994). He is now living in rural New South Wales.

1
Commitment to the Rule of Law and Judicial Independence

Steve Tsang

In spite of its cosmopolitan character Hong Kong remains essentially a Chinese city. What sets it apart from the People's Republic of China (PRC) more than anything else is the existence of the rule of law and an independent judiciary. They are generally accepted in Hong Kong as the most important legacy of 156 years of British imperial rule.[1] They are also seen as the cornerstone for the future of Hong Kong as a Special Administrative Region (SAR) in the PRC which retains a Leninist political system.[2] The inherent contradictions between the latter, in which the supremacy of the Communist Party cannot be challenged, and Hong Kong's liberal and capitalist system are real. In an important sense whether Hong Kong can maintain its own system and way of life, as provided for in the Sino-British Joint Declaration of 1984 and enshrined in the Basic Law for the Hong Kong SAR (1990), will depend on the survival of what underpin them – the rule of law and an independent judiciary. Equally significant is the commitment on the part of the SAR – the government, the judiciary and the people – to upholding these two principles once they are no longer guaranteed by the built in supremacy of the British legal and judicial systems before July 1997.

The importance of the rule of law and an independent judiciary as the cornerstone for Hong Kong's future is such that most people tend to take it for granted that they had always worked perfectly well in British Hong Kong. As Christopher Munn makes clear in Chapter 2, this is a gross simplification. The development of both in the crown colony of Hong Kong has to be put in historical perspective. The great emphasis which has been laid on them by senior officials of the SAR government since the handover also needs to be put into context. Leo Goodstadt is right in highlighting in Chapter 8 the reality that the

1

continuation of the rule of law and judicial independence have been hailed by the SAR government not least because Hong Kong has not developed democracy and, in its absence, it is advantageous to, and politically astute for, the administration to focus public attention upon them rather than on the issue of democratization. There is also a question of how Hong Kong's common law tradition and judicial system can coexist or dovetail the socialist and Chinese legal system in the PRC.[3] This is strictly speaking a matter to be governed by the Basic Law. However, as Byron Weng aptly explains in Chapter 3, it is unrealistic to expect the Basic Law alone to safeguard the rule of law and judicial independence in the SAR since the Basic Law is a piece of legislation in a country with a different legal tradition. It is also a country where the respect for the constitution has been haphazard at best and where the Maoist axiom of 'politics in command' remains a fact of life.

An uncertain beginning

The record of China's handling of relations with Hong Kong since the handover appears to suggest it has basically respected the maintenance of the rule of law and judicial independence in the SAR. Indeed, since July 1997 the Chinese authorities have been much less vocal and interventionist over events in Hong Kong than previously. This was the result of an order issued by Jiang Zemin, Chairman of the PRC and General Secretary of the Communist Party, by which he prohibited heads of government ministries, their equivalent departments in the Communist Party, provinces and special municipalities from interfering into affairs of the SAR.[4] The issuance of this order and its being enforced are useful to illustrate the actual implementation of the 'one country, two systems' policy. The enforcement of this order was greatly assisted by the careful positioning of the Chief Executive of the SAR in the hierarchy of the state bureaucracy and the Communist Party in China as a whole. As soon as the SAR was founded, its Chief Executive was given the rank of a Vice-Premier or State Councillor, one bureaucratic grade above that of a minister in Beijing or a governor in the provinces.[5] Even in the all important party–state relations a similar special arrangement was made. In terms of its importance, the SAR ranks equal to the special municipalities of Beijing, Tianjian and Shanghai whose party chief is of Poliburo rank. In order not to put a party man senior in rank to Tung Chee-hwa in the SAR Beijing deliberately appointed a mere member of the Communist Party's Central Committee, and not of the Poliburo, to head the Party's Work

Committee in Hong Kong. This party head, Jiang Enzhu has also been instructed to operate under the cover of his public duties as Director of the local branch of the Xinhua News Agency rather than like a normal party secretary in a special municipality. This anomaly is undoubtedly intended to prevent lower ranking PRC cadres from putting pressure on the higher ranking SAR Chief Executive and thus minimize any attempt by them to further their selfish personal, provincial or departmental interests. This is also in line with Beijing's established policy towards Hong Kong which is to exercise maximum flexibility within the rigid framework of protecting the sovereignty of the PRC and the supremacy of the national interests as defined by the Communist Party leadership.[6] The continuation of this basic policy represents the commitment on the part of Beijing to give the SAR reasonable scope to uphold the rule of law and judicial independence.

The survival and prospering of the rule of law and judicial independence do not depend solely on Beijing's policy and actions, however. They are also dependent on the commitment of the SAR. This is reflected in the protection against abuse in the name of national security which is examined by Hualing Fu in Chapter 4, the state of institutional protection which forms the focus of Peter Wesley-Smith's inquiry in Chapter 5, respect for upholding the due process which Johannes Chan scrutinizes in Chapter 6, and an independent and free press which is analyzed by Richard Cullen in Chapter 7. They are further affected by events within the SAR, such as the approach and behaviour of its judiciary, law officers and the executive branch. In this regard Hong Kong has a mixed record in its first two years as the SAR.

In the celebrated and controversial case concerning the SAR courts' handling of the right-of-abode of illegitimate children born to at least one parent who has such right in Hong Kong, the Court of Final Appeal (CFA) ruled on the basis of the law in January 1999 and ignored the very serious political and other practical problems which its ruling would cause. Under the Basic Law children born to Chinese citizens who are permanent residents of Hong Kong are deemed to have the right of abode.[7] What is not clear are whether children born out of wedlock or before their parents acquired the right of abode can enjoy the same right, and whether the Court should secure an interpretation from the National People's Congress (NPC) or its Standing Committee on the relevant provisions in the Basic Law, which will be binding on the Court.[8] On the first two questions the Court ruled in favour of the children. With regard to the last the Court decided that it did not need an interpretation from the NPC. Indeed, it worked on the basis that it had the authority 'to examine whether any legislative acts of the NPC are consistent with the Basic Law and to declare them to be invalid if found to be inconsistent.'[9] By its ruling the Court disregarded the prevailing local public opinion and the views of the SAR government which opposed letting in hundreds of thousands of mainland migrants.[10] It also faced a torrent of criticisms from the Chinese authorities which accused it, above all, of attempting to challenge the NPC's authority to interpret all ambiguous provisions in the Basic Law.[11]

The strong reactions from Beijing raised the prospect for either a constitutional crisis involving the jurisdiction of the CFA or a decision of the Court being overruled, subverted or otherwise set aside by the PRC or by the SAR executive branch acting under instructions from Beijing. This potential constitutional crisis was averted in February 1999 by a compromise worked out between the governments of the SAR and the PRC. Under this arrangement the SAR government asked the Court to 'clarify' its ruling. In response the Court declared that it accepted the NPC as the supreme law-making body of the land and did not question that authority though it did not alter its ruling.[12] Whether the CFA ruling is sound according to the law or not, it was widely and rightly accepted in Hong Kong as a positive landmark development in protecting the rule of law and judicial independence.[13] Since Beijing accepted the compromise and the ruling of the Court was allowed to stand, this dispute did not in a strictly technical sense undermine the rule of law or the independence of the judiciary in Hong Kong.

The SAR government's albeit pragmatic intervention to defuse the situation did raise the question whether this may reflect a pattern of executive actions that will eventually undermine the rule of law, however.[14] This issue is examined further in Chapter 3 by Weng.

To begin with, the SAR government suggested sometime in 1998 to the CFA that before the latter rendered its final judgment it should seek a binding interpretation of Articles 22 and 24 of the Basic Law from the NPC Standing Committee.[15] This action was no doubt taken to protect what it saw as the best interest of the SAR, as it realized the political sensitivity of the case and deemed it politically advantageous to pre-empt a development which could lead to a confrontation with the PRC authorities. However well intentioned this might have been it still casts a shadow over the priority set by the Justice Department and the government as a whole – do they put the law or political considerations of the day first?

What is more worrying is that about two months after the danger of a constitutional crisis was removed, the SAR government reversed course and sought to set aside the decision of the CFA when it calculated that this decision could result in up to 1.67 million mainland Chinese being able to exercise the right of abode and settle in Hong Kong over a period of seven years and thus put what it called 'a very heavy – even unbearable – burden' on the SAR.[16] In order to pre-empt this worst case scenario the Chief Executive Tung announced in May 1999 that he would try to reduce what he saw as the negative impact of the Court's decision, by either seeking an amendment to the Basic Law or asking the NPC Standing Committee to reinterpret the Basic Law.[17] Whether the SAR government's calculation of the likely number of immigrants is sound or not, there is no doubt that the Court's decision will result in at least hundreds of thousand Chinese being able to claim the right to live in the SAR and thus generate enormous pressure on housing, education, health and other social services.[18] This is a daunting challenge for a metropolis of 6.5 million already suffering from one of the highest population pressures in the world. The magnitude of this problem is not the real cause for worry, however.

It is the manner by which the SAR government handles the issue which may pose a serious challenge to the rule of law. Instead of devoting itself to devise policies and make plans to deal with the implications of the decision of the CFA, as is normal in a common law jurisdiction, the SAR government seems to have dedicated itself to seek ways to circumvent what it no doubt believes to be an ill conceived decision of the Court. Hence, the government has chosen to scare the population into rejecting the implementation of the decision of the Court by hailing the worst possible scenario as if it were a certainty. It dismissed out of hand the possibility of making arrangements to regulate the settlement of those people concerned in a reasonable manner, which will on the one hand recognize their right of abode and on the other hand allow the SAR scope to deal with a large and steady inflow of people.[19] The alleged need for the SAR to overturn in effect the decision of the CFA also seems to be based on dubious premises. The government has apparently not taken into account several crucial considerations. First, the movement of people from the PRC to the SAR is regulated not only by the SAR but also by the border control exercised on the PRC side. Given the PRC authorities' hostility to the CFA decision and long established policy in controlling internal migration it is doubtful that all the illegitimate offspring of Hong Kong residents will be allowed to leave the mainland freely for the SAR. Second, it is questionable that a decision of the SAR Court is legally binding on government organizations in the PRC. Third, the PRC simply does not have the institutional infrastructure to deal with a massive migration of this kind since this is a new demand generated only as a result of the SAR Court's ruling at the end of January. Unless the PRC government will devote significantly more resources to deal with the issue, about which there is no indication, there will almost certainly be a long delay for applications to leave to be processed. Fourth, the estimated figure is highly problematic as it includes, for example, those who are not yet born or conceived but are believed to be eligible on the basis of the fertility rate of the prospective immigrants.[20] Likewise, the SAR government has reportedly compiled data on those eligible but indicated that they have no intention to relocate to Hong Kong, but suppressed the data and simply worked on the assumption that all who are entitled to will in fact migrate.[21] Finally, the illegitimate offspring will also need to establish proof of parentage. With so many imponderables the SAR government's projected pressure on Hong Kong's society and resources seems exaggerated. If the pressure were not such that it would be a matter of survival, why had the SAR government proposed to take such an extraordinary course which would undermine the rule of law? Does this not reflect the basic attitude of the government and a lack of commitment to uphold the rule of law?

Of the two options which the SAR government initially put on the political agenda in Hong Kong – to amend the Basic Law or ask the NPC to reinterpret the Basic Law – the Chief Executive chose the latter.[22] This is highly problematic. According to Article 158 of the Basic Law the power to interpret does rest with the NPC Standing Committee but it is supposed to do so on the basis of a request from the SAR Courts – not from the SAR government. The really controversial issue is whether the CFA had the right to decide not to seek an interpretation on the issues at hand. Whether the Court was right or not in this matter it adjudicated without requiring interpretation. (The rule of law does not imply the Courts never make mistakes, but if they do such mistakes should be rectified through the due process – not by executive fiat.) This being the case it is questionable if the SAR government has the constitutional right to request an interpretation clearly with an intention to side-track the decisions of the Court. In the common law tradition the only situation for the CFA to change its mind (or, in this case, request an interpretation) is for a new case that presents new and significant evidence to justify a change of judgment being put to it – not a matter within the remit of the Chief Executive. The other option, amendment of the Basic Law, is at least constitutionally viable, though it can only be done by the full NPC, which is not scheduled to meet until around March 2000. In any event the Chief Executive's proposal amounts to subverting, or at least setting aside, a decision of the Court duly arrived at on the basis of the law. By choosing to invite Beijing to relieve it from its obligations under the Basic Law the SAR government is, despite its rhetorical commitment, resorting to an expedience with little or no regard to upholding the rule of law.[23]

The irony in this incident is that there is no evidence to suggest the SAR Chief Executive has acted under pressure from Beijing. He almost certainly took the initiative on his own accord, or on the advice of his law officers, though the views of Beijing had undoubtedly been taken into account as well. What is particularly worrying is one of the considerations which the Justice Department appears to have based its advice to the government. In the *South China Morning Post*, Deputy Law Officer R. Allcock made the following disconcerting comment on this matter:

> Under the common law, the ultimate power to interpret the law is vested in the judiciary. However, Hong Kong is part of the People's Republic of China, which has a civil law system. Under the mainland's system, the ultimate power to interpret statutes is vested in the NPCSC.[24]

However incredible it may seem this view of the Deputy Law Officer does appear to represent that of the SAR government, as the Justice Secretary herself publicly states that the replacement of the Letters Patent and the Royal Instructions by the Basic Law has resulted in 'an earth-shaking change in the most fundamental part of this legal system'.[25]

This development raises the question of whether the SAR government has the intention to uphold all the rights given to the SAR by the Basic Law, including Article 8 which specifically stipulates that the common law – not the civil or socialist legal – system should be maintained. It is ironic that in the first two years of Hong Kong as the SAR the threat to the rule of law has come more from failings of the SAR government than from interference from the Leninist party in control of the PRC. If the SAR government's bowing to political and socio-economic considerations in the illegitimate migrants case is but an isolated exception, it will not constitute a pattern of executive actions and its significance should be assessed accordingly. By setting this incident against the record of the SAR government's handling of a few other cases a pattern does appear to exist, however.

To begin, there was the widely reported case concerning the trial and execution of a gangster leader Cheung Tze-keung, popularly known as Big Spender, in the PRC in 1998. Cheung was a Hong Kong citizen who committed, among various serious offences, the kidnapping of two business tycoons, Walter Kwok of the Sun Hung Kai group and Victor Li, son of Li Ka-shing, in Hong Kong. Neither Kwok's nor Li's family reported the kidnapping to the Hong Kong Police. However, they apparently asked for help from Chairman Jiang Zemin, which led to the arrest by the PRC police of Cheung and his gang.[26] Together with his gang Cheung was put on trial in the Guangzhou Intermediate People's Court, in spite of the fact that he was a Hong Kong citizen who was alleged to have committed crimes against other Hong Kong citizens in Hong Kong. Given the almost certain outcome of such a trial in a PRC court – conviction and swift execution – Cheung's counsel and family asked the SAR government to seek his return to face trial in Hong Kong. However nasty a criminal Cheung might have been he undoubtedly had the right as a Hong Kong citizen to expect to face justice in a Hong Kong court for crimes he was alleged to have committed locally. The SAR government ignored the pleas of Cheung's lawyer, family and human rights advocates and declined to seek his return.[27] The government had apparently chosen not to press the issue in order to avoid confronting the PRC. Although this was probably an astute political move in the context of maintaining good PRC–SAR relations, it raised two serious questions. Does this case imply Hong Kong citizens who commit criminal offences within the SAR can – contrary to Article 18 of the Basic Law – be subjected to the Chinese Criminal Code should they be arrested in the PRC? Furthermore, does the politically astute move on the part of the SAR government mean that, in cases where it is politically expedient, it in effect concedes it cannot be expected to stand up for the human rights of SAR citizens who may have incurred the wrath of the Chinese government or top leaders and thus find themselves in trouble with law enforcement agencies in the PRC?

The 'Big Spender' case should also be seen in the context of how the SAR government dealt with another somewhat similar case. This one concerns a PRC citizen Li Yuhui (Lee Yuk Fai in Hong Kong usage). Li worked as a Feng Shui master and allegedly committed five murders in Telford Gardens in the SAR but was apprehended in the PRC. Similar to the Big Spender case the SAR government refused to secure his return to face justice in Hong Kong. What happened to Li subsequently was no surprise. He was convicted and executed in Guangdong.[28] Whether he should have been tried in the PRC instead of in Hong Kong is debatable. The case for trial in the PRC is essentially based on the extraterritorial reach of the Chinese Criminal Code, which gives PRC Courts the right to try a PRC citizen who committed an indictable offence overseas.[29] However, under Article 18 of the Basic Law the Chinese Criminal Code should have no application in the SAR since the Code is not one of those PRC national laws specifically listed in Annex III of the Basic Law.[30]

Any doubt that this provision of the Basic Law can override the extraterritorial jurisdiction of the Chinese Criminal Code should be dispelled by the very special nature of the Basic Law which was promulgated to found the SAR. The Basic Law is clearly meant to resolve anomalies or discrepancies in law between the PRC and the SAR inherent in the 'one country, two systems' principle in favour of the SAR practice. This is based on the same principle upon which the constitutionality of the Basic Law itself is established. Under various provisions of the PRC Constitution the existence of anything like a SAR is prohibited. Article 1, for example, stipulates specifically and clearly that the PRC 'is a socialist state under the people's democratic dictatorship' and the 'sabotage of the socialist system by any organization or individual is prohibited'. This is reinforced by Article 5, which 'upholds the uniformity and dignity of the socialist legal system' and adds that 'no law or administrative or local rules and regulations shall contravene the Constitution'. Since the capitalist Hong Kong SAR committed to the common law is neither socialist nor conducive to upholding the socialist legal system in the PRC, it would have been logical that the creation of the SAR is prohibited by the Constitution. However, this problem is, according to all Chinese legal authorities, resolved by Article 31 of the Constitution.[31] This article authorizes the establishment of SARs in which their systems 'shall be prescribed by law enacted by the National People's Congress in the light of the specific conditions'. In the same spirit that Article 31 can override the other articles of the Constitution and make the establishment of the Hong Kong SAR constitutional, Article 18 of the Basic Law ought to take precedent over the applicability in the SAR of the extraterritorial scope of the PRC Criminal Code. Li should therefore have been prosecuted and tried in the SAR only for the crimes which were wholly committed there. Similar to the Big Spender case, this incident raises the questions of whether, and indeed why, PRC courts have the authority to try a person for crimes committed in the SAR and whether the SAR's Justice Department prefers to abdicate its responsibilities in a criminal case if it might lead to a negative political reaction from the PRC?

Another case which is equally problematic concerns the decision by the Secretary for Justice Elsie Leung not to prosecute Sally Aw, Chairman of the Sing Tao Group which publishes an English language newspaper the *Hong Kong Standard*. (See also Chan's analysis in Chapter 6.) Three senior executives of the Sing Tao Group were prosecuted and jailed for fraud, for inflating the circulation figures of the *Hong Kong Standard* in order to boost advertising revenue in 1998, but Aw herself, named as a co-conspirator, was not prosecuted. This caused an outcry in the SAR. Speculation circulated as to the reasons for her special treatment. They include allegations that she was spared because she is a member of the Chinese People's Political Consultative Conference, an advisory body to the PRC government, or because the Chief Executive had previously served on the board of Sing Tao. Reacting to public pressure Secretary Leung explained that Aw was not prosecuted because it was not in 'the public interest' to do so since prosecution might lead to the collapse of her business empire. Leung elaborated on her reasoning by saying that 'apart from the staff losing employment, the failure of a well-established, important media group at that time could have sent a very bad message to the international community.'[32] Whether the Secretary for Justice acted entirely on the basis of her own judgement or not, her decision and reasoning have raised two important questions. First, does this not set a precedent which will encourage the super rich to ignore the law in Hong Kong provided they are major employers with an international profile and, thus, raise the prospect that the legal system will treat the rich and the poor differently? Second, does this not make a mockery of Article 25 of the Basic Law, by which 'all Hong Kong residents shall be equal before the law'?

While the four cases above have shown a pattern of behaviour which raises doubt as to the determination of the SAR government and its ranking law officer to uphold the law rather than yield to political considerations, except for the illegitimate immigrants case there is no evidence that the PRC government has put pressure on the legal or judicial process in Hong Kong. Even in the illegitimate immigrants case what pressure Beijing applied at the time of the Court of Final Appeal's ruling was put on the SAR government rather than on the judiciary directly. Does the record of the PRC government in the first two years of the SAR therefore provide reasonable grounds to suggest it demonstrates sufficient commitment to the maintenance of the rule of law and judicial independence in the SAR?

Although the self-restraint which the PRC government has exercised so far should be recognized, it also needs to be put in context. In three out of the four cases examined above, the SAR government had gone out of its way to avoid any development which might provoke the PRC into taking actions against the judicial system in the SAR. The exception was the Sally Aw case, for which there is no tangible evidence to suggest the Secretary for Justice had acted to placate the PRC government. The reluctance of the SAR government to do anything about the Big Spender and Telford Gardens murder cases were clearly meant to neutralize any concern the PRC government might have in terms of any challenge from Hong Kong about the legality of its actions. Even in the illegitimate migrants case, once the PRC authorities indicated its displeasure over the alleged challenge by the CFA to the sovereign authority of the NPC, the SAR government promptly took the initiative to broker a compromise which Beijing accepted. However, as Wesley-Smith argues in Chapter 5, the public criticism of the Court's decision by quasi-government officials in the PRC 'came perilously close to infringing judicial independence' and the whole incident did 'a good deal of damage ... to the dignity and independence of the court'.

Nevertheless, in a strictly technical sense, neither was infringed upon. The PRC's record so far confirms that its policy towards Hong Kong has continued to be governed by the principle of exercising maximum flexibility within a rigid framework. While this remains true, the lack of direct interference into the legal and judicial processes in the SAR from the PRC is also, above all, because the PRC government has no reason or need to interfere. The SAR government has studiously made sure of that. The assumptions which the PRC authorities took in the Big Spender and the Telford Gardens cases remain a cause for concern. In neither case did the PRC authorities appear to feel restrained by Article 18 of the Basic Law which excludes the application of the PRC Criminal Code to the SAR. The fact that the SAR government has never raised this issue with Beijing does not mean it is not important.

All in all the record of Hong Kong in its first two years or so as the SAR is a mixed one. On the one hand the independence of the judiciary has continued. The CFA has proved its mettle by resisting the temptation to bow to political and other considerations, even in the particularly controversial case of the illegitimate immigrants. On the other hand the SAR government and its Justice Department have on balance demonstrated a lack of determination to uphold the rule of law though they essentially respected the independence of the judiciary. The real commitment to the rule of law and judicial independence from the people of Hong Kong has just been put to the test. Their responses to the Chief Executive's move to circumvent the decision of the CFA over the illegitimate migrants case will provide good indication of their sense of commitment. The SAR government has so far disguised the issues and most people in Hong Kong have not yet realized that if they want to maintain the rule of law as the cornerstone for their future, they will have to be prepared to pay a price, which is that if the Court has ruled strictly in accordance with the law its decision must be respected, even if it should have undesirable social or economic consequences.

Continuity and changes

How does this mixed picture of the SAR's commitment to the rule of law and judicial independence compare to the record of British Hong Kong? What do the differences amount to in reality? Does this mixed picture mean the rule of law and judicial independence still form the cornerstone of Hong Kong's future?

A useful starting point for looking at these questions is Munn's meticulously researched critical survey of the imperfection in the rule of law in the early years of British Hong Kong (see Chapter 2), which helps to put things in better perspective. It is important to remember that while Munn has documented several different ways by which the rule of law was circumvented, or set aside, in the first half-century of British administration, he nevertheless concludes that 'the rule of law still set the standards for government and justice in the colony'. One should also not lose sight of the fact that since the nineteenth century the world has changed and so have the standards and the public expectations of the standards in the rule of law, whether in Hong Kong or in the common law world at large. Despite the somewhat bleak account of early justice given by Munn, an imperfect start to the rule of law does not necessarily mean it cannot take root and flourish later. The rule of law can eventually thrive provided there is an institution or an authority higher than the local government which will provide a redress to abuses. In the colonial period it was the existence of supervision from London, where its democratic government often checked excesses or rectified specific failings by colonial officials or judicial officers, that had resulted in, for example, administrative meddling and the miscarriage of justice.

In this new era when Hong Kong is a Chinese SAR, for which a high degree of autonomy is guaranteed in writing, the higher authority for this purpose is neither Britain, the old colonial master nor Beijing, the new sovereign power. It is or, at least, ought to be the Basic Law. Although the Sino-British Joint Declaration also provides for the rule of law and judicial independence in Hong Kong to be protected it is the Basic Law which ultimately matters. It is not only the legal instrument to turn the agreed principles in the Joint Declaration into reality but is also the constitutional instrument for the SAR – the ultimate point of reference for any dispute between the executive, legislative and judicial branches in Hong Kong. How effective it can be in replacing the role played by Britain before 1997 remains to be seen. In Chapter 3 Weng highlights the limitations which the Basic Law has for this purpose. In addition to a careful examination of the inadequacies of the Basic law, for example, in only preserving the independence of the courts and not of individual judges, he carefully analyzes in some detail the first major test of the Basic Law as the ultimate defender of the rule of law and judicial independence. As explained briefly earlier this involves the case of the right of abode for the illegitimate immigrants from China. On the basis of his research he concludes that while Hong Kong's government system was 'entrenched in the tradition of the rule of law and the principle of judicial independence … there is little ground to assert that the principle of judicial independence will be upheld in the SAR as it was in the British period'.

As the constitutional instrument protecting the rule of law and judicial independence in the SAR, one issue which can cause serious reservation concerns its provision on national security – a cause which can be used to justify undermining these two principles on the ground of exigency. The relevant provision in the Basic Law is Article 23, which Fu examines in depth in Chapter 4. He not only gives the historical context for the inclusion of Article 23, which was essentially Beijing's response to the Tiananmen incident of 1989, but highlights the fact that even under British Hong Kong there was a body of law which could have met practically all the legitimate requirements for national security under Article 23 in a common law jurisdiction. It is worthy of note that despite the long existence of some fairly draconian pieces of legislation, such as the Emergency (Principal) Regulations (1949) which could make it 'possible for the Hong Kong government, at least in principle, to abuse its extensive emergency powers in conditions which elsewhere would not have justified the use of such powers',[33] checks from London and self-restraint exercised by the government in Hong Kong had prevented serious abuse under the British. It is possible, as Fu argues cogently, to reconcile concerns over national security and the protection of human rights. A basic change that has happened in this connection inherent in the handover of sovereignty is the replacing of democratic and human rights respecting Britain by the authoritarian PRC where neither the rule of law nor respect for civil and political rights can be taken for granted. This difference is fundamental to the concern that Article 23 can neutralize the other elements protective of human rights in the Basic Law. It underlines the need to ensure the rule of law and the independence of the judiciary in the SAR. The fact that despite the modification of Article 23 and the passing of the Crimes (Amendment) Bill in 1997 incorporating 'secession' and 'subversion' as criminal offences into Hong Kong's body of law, the SAR government has not given notice to bring this amendment into effect and has not come under pressure from Beijing to do so is significant. It is further testimony to Beijing's adherence to the principle of exercising maximum flexibility within a rigid framework in matters dealing with the SAR.

Compared to the early years of British Hong Kong when it was treated by many of its residents as a kind of a colonial frontier town at a time when the rule of law in Britain itself was less well developed and entrenched than now, the SAR has the great advantage of having inherited a wealthy and sophisticated community in which an independent judiciary functions healthily and the rule of law is well established after 156 years of practising the common law. As Wesley-Smith explains in considerable detail (see Chapter 5) an entire infrastructure exists to buttress the institutional and individual independence of the judiciary and the rule of law, which were so much more tenuous in the nineteenth century. In his careful, detailed and perceptive study of the many different factors that affect the independence of judicial personnel and institutions, Wesley-Smith brings out clearly both the continuity and the changes between Hong Kong as a Crown Colony and a Chinese SAR. A basic issue which stands out in his inquiry is the simple fact that few, if anyone, questioned the many and various arrangements in place before the prospect of a transfer of sovereignty loomed because they were deemed to be consistent with

British experiences, but that they have become subjected to more searching standards as that prospect became a reality. The differences in the legal and judicial traditions in China and in a British jurisdiction, and the lack of confidence in the former, account for this shift.[34]

How well will the common law culture of Hong Kong, slowly but steadily acquired under British rule, survive and develop now that it is a Chinese SAR? A critical test of Hong Kong's commitment is the respect for the due process in the courts and by the government. Chan reviews in Chapter 6 a few particularly interesting and significant cases in the SAR. He points out that at first the Courts seem to have taken a restrained view of their role in cases where major government policies appeared to be at stake. They include the court's handling of the illegitimate migrants case before it eventually reached the CFA which, as explained earlier, took a much more robust stance than its lower courts. If Chan's concern over the courts' assertion over their independence can basically be laid to rest by the CFA's bold ruling over this case in January 1999, the same cannot be said of the SAR government. Chan's dispassionate and judicious study of various cases, including that of the non-prosecution of Sally Aw and the Xinhua News Agency (a PRC state organ that serves as cover for Communist Party's Work Committee) for what appeared to be a clear breach of the law, provide serious cause for reflection and concern.

The future of the rule of law and judicial independence also depends on the community's commitment, which is most effectively reflected in the existence of a free press. The role of the media is particularly important in Hong Kong since it still does not have a democratic political system and, in accordance with Annex II of the Basic Law, cannot have one before 2007. As Cullen explains in Chapter 7, Hong Kong had a free and very vibrant media under the British, which has survived the change of sovereignty. Nevertheless, the issues of press freedom and self-censorship in the formative period of the SAR are not simple ones. They are more than just a matter of whether the courts uphold the freedom of the press or whether the SAR government starts to infringe upon it, or if the PRC government has started to put pressure on the local media tycoons, though they are all important and relevant questions. They also depend on economic, financial, business or management calculations in the media world. Here, as Cullen highlights, even senior members of the press can prove a problem. The attack launched by the publisher of the *Mirror* magazine on Radio Television Hong Kong in March 1998 is a case in point. It is important to recognize that the judiciary is a key agent in maintaining the freedom of the media, and a free press, in turn, has a vital role to play in supporting the rule of law and the independence of the judiciary. Whether this somewhat symbiotic relationship can develop into a virtuous circle in the new political environment of the SAR remains to be seen.

This brief survey of Hong Kong's commitment to the rule of law and judicial independence suggests that while the community as a whole is keen, often taking it as an article of faith, the same cannot be said of its government after the change of sovereignty. Despite its public rhetoric the SAR government seems to support them more for pragmatic calculations than as a matter of principle. As Goodstadt aptly observes in Chapter 8, expressing verbal commitment is useful to the SAR government as it distracts public attention from the retrogression in democratic development following the handover, helps to maintain business confidence, and reassures the general public that their way of life has not changed. The PRC government has likewise accepted this state of affairs out of utilitarian considerations. Beijing is keen to make a success of the takeover for prestige and for practical reasons. It sees the existence of a stable legal order as the key to the economic miracle of postwar Hong Kong. It is prepared to keep this going, as Hong Kong makes a vital contribution to the success of economic reform on the mainland, and its legal order serves as a useful point of reference to Chinese reformers who want to build up a legal system which will ensure political stability amid rapid, major economic changes in an authoritarian political order. The extent of Chinese pragmatism in this matter was reflected in the negotiations which they had with the British in setting up the CFA in the twilight years of British rule. However, the PRC government's handling of the Big Spender and the Telford Gardens murder cases as well as the ruling by CFA over the illegitimate migrants demonstrates the harsh reality. Despite its policy of non-interference, the PRC government does not understand what the rule of law in Hong Kong means; certainly not the principle that it is there to protect the rights of individuals rather than to further government policies. Thus, the continuation of the rule of law and an independent judiciary in the first two years of the SAR is no ground for complacency. As Goodstadt aptly highlights vested interests and the SAR government, if not the PRC government itself, must join with the general public in Hong Kong and display a commitment beyond rhetoric and expediency which is rooted in genuine respect for the principles before the rule of law and judicial independence can really entrench themselves in the SAR.

Notes

1. See, for example, Ming Chan, 'The Legacy of the British Administration of Hong Kong: A view from Hong Kong', *The China Quarterly*, no.151 (1997), pp. 567–82.
2. For the defining characters of a Marxist–Leninist system as a distinct subset of the world's political system see Archie Brown, *The Gorbachev Factor* (Oxford: Oxford University Press, 1996), p. 310.
3. *Yiguo Liangzhi Chongyao Wenxien Xuanbian* (Beijing: Zhongyang wenxian chubanshe, 1997), p. 306 (speech by Qian Qichen).
4. *South China Morning Post (SCMP)*, 2 July 1997 (Jiang's speech at the SAR establishment ceremony); Guo Shiping and Qian Xuejun, *Jiuqi hou Zhonggang Xinguanxi* (Hong Kong: Taipingyang Shiji chubanshe, 1998), p. 53. The head of state in the PRC is in Chinese 'Chairman of the state' though it is often translated into 'President' in English.
5. Steve Tsang, 'Changes in Continuity: Government and Politics in the Hong Kong Special Administrative Region', *American Asian Review*, Vol.XV, no.4, Winter 1997, pp. 51–2.
6. For a detailed examination of this policy, see Steve Tsang, 'Maximum Flexibility, Rigid Framework: China's Policy Towards Hong Kong and its Implications', *Journal of International Affairs*, Vol.49, no.2, Winter 1996, pp. 413–33; and Steve Tsang *Hong Kong: An Appointment With China* (London: I.B. Tauris, 1997), especially pp. 132–55.
7. *The Basic Law of the Hong Kong Special Administrative Region of the People's Republic of China* (Hong Kong: Government Printing Department, undated), p. 23 (Art. 24).
8. *Immigration Department Annual Report 1997/1998* (Hong Kong: HKSAR Immigration Department, undated 1999), pp. 55–6.
9. Quoted in Frank Ching, 'Judgement Call', *Far Eastern Economic Review (FEER)*, 18 February 1999, p. 21.
10. Ibid., pp. 20–1.
11. Albert H.Y. Chen, *The Court of Final Appeal's Ruling in the 'Illegal Migrant' Children Case: Congressional Supremacy and Judicial Review* (Law Working Paper no.24), (Hong Kong: Hong Kong University Law Faculty, 1999), p. 1.
12. Alkman Granitsas, 'Compromising Issue', *FEER*, 11 March 1999, p. 20.
13. Albert H.Y. Chen, *The Court of Final Appeal's Ruling in the 'Illegal Migrant' Children Case: A Critical Commentary on the Application of Article 158 of the Basic Law* (Law Working Paper no.23), (Hong Kong: Hong Kong University Law Faculty, 1999), p. 1. Chen is a leading advocate that the Court was wrong in its judgment.
14. Granitsas, 'Compromising Issue', op. cit.
15. Frank Ching, 'Inviting Trouble', *FEER*, 21 January 1999, p. 23.
16. Frank Ching, 'Scare Tactics', *FEER*, 13 May 1999, p. 18.
17. Rachel Clarke, 'Tung to seek law change to beat $71b migrants bill', *SCMP*, 6 May 1999.
18. For a sceptical view of the SAR government's calculation see, for example, 'True test of the SAR's mettle', *SCMP*, 7 May 1999.
19. *Right of Abode: The Solution*, paper tabled by the SAR government at the

Legislative Council House Comittee special meeting on 25 May 1999, paragraph 7.
20. Ching, 'Scare Tactics', pp. 18–19.
21. Ibid., p. 19.
22. Jimmy Cheung and Angela Li, 'NPC likely to intervene', *SCMP*, 7 May 1999.
23. The NPCSC duly accepted the SAR government's request to reinterpret sections under Articles 22 and 24 of the Basic Law at the end of June 1999. Chris Yeung, 'NPC lays down the law', *SCMP*, 27 June 1999.
24. R. Allcock, 'NPC's Standing Committee must decide', *SCMP*, 19 May 1999.
25 Angela Li, 'Justice chief's view of law branded "terrifying"', *SCMP*, 22 July 1999.
26. Frank Ching, 'Another Place, Another Crime', *FEER*, 5 November 1998, p. 26.
27. Cheung was executed shortly after his appeal was dismissed. The execution verdict was returned not for the kidnapping but for firearms and smuggling offences for which he was also charged and prosecuted.
28. 'Regional Briefing', *FEER*, 29 April 1999, p. 17.
29. See Richard Cullen and H.L. Fu, 'Some Limitations in the Basic Law Exposed', *China Perspectives*, no.22, March/April 1999, pp. 54–7.
30. Margaret Ng puts her case on a different basis. M. Ng, 'Fundamental Questions Raised by the Trial of Cheung Tse Keung and Others', *Policy Bulletin,* no.9, February/March 1999 (Hong Kong), p. 3.
31. See, for example, *The Basic Law*, p.94 (Decision of the NPC on the Establishment of the Hong Kong SAR); and Xiao Weiyun (ed.), *Yiguo Liangzhi yu Xianggang Tebie Xingzhengqu Jibenfa* (Hong Kong: Wenhua Jiaoyu chubenshe, 1990), pp. 63–5.
32. Quoted in *The Financial Times*, 5 February 1999.
33. Steve Tsang (ed.), *Government and Politics: A Documentary History of Hong Kong*, Volume 1 (Hong Kong: Hong Kong University Press, 1995), p. 53.
34. For an excellent exposition of the Chinese legal tradition, see Philip C.C. Huang, *Civil Justice in China: Representation and Practice in the Qing* (Stanford: Stanford University Press, 1996).

2
The Rule of Law and Criminal Justice in the Nineteenth Century

*Christopher Munn**

> But by England's laws,
> Than which none can be finer,
> You can't assault a man,
> Because he's born in China-r.
> Tol de rol de rol
> Tol de rol de rido.[1]

Officials, lawyers and journalists in nineteenth-century Hong Kong made much of the potency of English law, although they rarely used the term 'rule of law'. In their more florid moments they might throw up phrases like 'the Reign of Law', or 'the mild but incorruptible majesty of British Law'.[2] More often they spoke of 'English Law', or simply 'The Law', almost always with a capital 'L'. Despite the vagueness, they usually had a clear idea of what they meant by the terms. By the time of the British acquisition of Hong Kong in 1841, English Law had come to embrace a cluster of principles. All men were held to be equal before the law. The government acted according to the law. Justice was administered by an independent judiciary. And, in a crown colony such as Hong Kong, both legislature and executive were accountable to the Crown and parliament. In the administration of criminal law, a number of further principles gave protection to the accused. Among these were the remedy of *habeas corpus*, the right to a fair and open trial, access to trial by jury, the presumption of innocence and the right to silence.

The English doctrine of the rule of law was an important theme in the rhetoric of colonial rule throughout the British Empire, whether it was a question of doing justice to natives or of protecting the rights of 'freeborn Englishmen' from the 'unEnglish' tendencies of some colonial governors. In nineteenth-century Hong Kong the doctrine had a special relevance. The apparatus of English law was introduced into Hong Kong more quickly than in Britain's larger Asian possessions of India or Ceylon. Colonists frequently contrasted the liberal principles of English law with what they saw as the absence of these principles in the Chinese system. Still more important, successive governors saw the rule of law as one of the greatest attractions to the Chinese settlers who were essential to the colony's viability. From Governor Davis's early vision of 'property and person secure under the protection of equal laws' to Governor Patten's recent image of a population of refugees who 'swam, walked, ran and climbed over barbed wire' to 'enjoy here the peace and safety guaranteed by the rule of law', the magnetic pull of Hong Kong's rule of law has always been a prominent feature of gubernatorial rhetoric.[3]

At an early stage in Hong Kong's history, Chinese inhabitants began to echo and absorb the doctrine. Some of the first Chinese petitions praised the government for its desire to place Chinese and Europeans on an equal footing. At the end of the century, the 'splendidly embroidered address', presented by leaders of the Chinese community to mark Queen Victoria's golden jubilee, contained 'a striking recognition of British justice'.[4] Reformers based in Hong Kong, like Wang Tao, Ng Choy and Ho Kai, advocated the British system as a model for China. Equally, Chinese leaders were prepared to confront the colonial government when it failed to live up to its own claims. A mass petition of 1871, for example, complained about the social damage caused by Governor MacDonnell's racially discriminatory policy of licensed gambling, and reminded the government of the impartiality of British laws, whether applied at home or to colonial subjects.[5]

The rule of law in nineteenth-century Hong Kong was something more than just rhetoric or wishful thinking. It determined the structure and procedures of the colony's legal system. It restrained some governors from pursuing policies that ran counter to its doctrines. And it helped to secure the acquittal of many men and women wrongly accused of committing crimes. A vigilant and often libellous press was keen to expose any miscarriage of justice. An increasingly competent legal profession kept the idea of the rule of law alive in the higher courts. Judges were sensitive about their independence from the executive. Hong Kong's greatest Chief Justice, Sir John Smale (1866–81), used the bench as a platform for a controversial campaign against slavery and oppression in one of the region's largest industries, the trade in human beings.

Yet the rule of law in nineteenth-century Hong Kong was a precarious institution. It was compromised by poor resources. It was challenged by the enormous gulfs in communication between the European minority who administered it and the mostly Chinese defendants and witnesses who were subjected to it. It was frequently circumvented by the various alternative systems of justice operating in and around the colony. When legal principles came into conflict with the colonial imperatives of maintaining order and protecting trade, it was frequently undermined by the very men – the governors, judges and attorney-generals – who sang its praises most loudly. This chapter examines these problems. The first part explores the difficulties that arose in the early years of the colony when the British attempted to extend trial by jury to a wide range of offences arising both within Hong Kong and in a large maritime region beyond. The second part seeks to explain the extraordinarily heavy caseload of the Magistracy, then, as now, one of the busiest branches of government in Hong Kong. The third part discusses the government's tendency to circumvent the rule of law by relying on other jurisdictions for the handling of many criminal cases. The fourth part examines erosions of the rule of law by executive interventions in sentencing.[6]

The decline of the Supreme Court's criminal jurisdiction

The fountain-head of the rule of law in nineteenth-century Hong Kong was the Supreme Court, where the Chief Justice and a jury tried the more serious criminal cases. It was the one court in the colony that came close to administering 'the laws of England in all their purity'.[7] In Norton-Kyshe's 1300-page history of the early courts of Hong Kong the Supreme Court occupies a central position in British rule. During the darkest days of the colony's early history it stands out 'as the one and probably only monument of integrity and uprightness', and its stature increases as the century progresses.[8] Yet, whatever growth might have taken place in the Supreme Court's prestige, its criminal caseload declined dramatically. In 1848, when the population of the colony stood at only 22 000, Hong Kong's higher courts, the Supreme and Admiralty Courts, tried a total of 228 defendants charged with criminal offences. Fifty years later, when the population had increased to nearly a quarter-of-a-million, the Supreme Court (which had in 1850 absorbed the criminal jurisdiction of the Admiralty Court) tried a mere 54 defendants on criminal charges.[9]

Norton-Kyshe explains this decline by improvements in policing and a greater 'acquiescence' by the Chinese population 'in the laws by which they are governed'.[10] These are no doubt important factors. But a more compelling reason is perhaps to be found in the dramatic shrinking of the scope of the Supreme Court's criminal work, as the jurisdiction of the Magistracy grew and as executive decisions increasingly threw even serious criminal cases into the hands of jurisdictions that were largely beyond the reach of English law. A comparable expansion of summary justice took place in England over the course of the nineteenth century, as the introduction of milder punishments made it less necessary, and less desirable, that defendants charged with minor property offences should be tried by jury. In Hong Kong the process began earlier and was accomplished more quickly for a very different reason: the general acknowledgement that the Supreme Court, this 'monument of integrity and uprightness' was lamentably ill prepared to try most of the criminal cases that arose within its jurisdiction.

It is hardly surprising that the British in Hong Kong should have encountered difficulties in extending English criminal law to a troubled region inhabited by people accustomed to very different forms of justice. The early colonial government had the option of a form of reciprocal extraterritorialism for Hong Kong, by which Chinese offenders on the island would be handed over to Chinese officials for trial according to Chinese law: indeed, the Chinese government's insistence throughout the nineteenth century that this was an obligation and not an option played some part in shaping criminal justice in the colony (see below). Largely for reasons of sovereignty, the early Hong Kong government decided on an extensive application of trial by jury, not just to the crimes committed on the island, but also to the piracies taking place in a vast maritime region, whether or not those piracies involved British subjects. A judicial system that had emerged out of a desire to protect and control British subjects in Hong Kong and China, quickly became a tribunal in which European juries decided the fate of defendants who were usually Chinese, and who in many cases had little or no contact with the colony prior to their trial.

According to a typical colonial explanation, 'the difficulties which beset the path of British jurisprudence amidst a people like the Chinese' arose from the 'proverbial bad faith and chicanery which distinguishes them, the "unknown tongue" through which Justice is interpreted, our total inability to ascertain the past character and pursuits of the arraigned, coupled with the utter impossibility of binding the conscience of the witness by any sort of sacred obligation.'[11] This incomprehension, and the deeply entrenched suspicion that went with it, seriously impaired the practical workings of the higher courts and undermined the justice they sought to deliver. Nearly all criminal trials in nineteenth-century Hong Kong required interpretation for the various Chinese dialects and other languages spoken by defendants and witnesses appearing before the courts. While it is impossible to assess how far the frequent complaints about the incompetence or corruption of interpreters affected the quality of justice, it is clear enough from the trial reports that the reliance on interpreters was a serious obstacle to a fair trial. 'We seem to be merely groping about for meanings', commented one newspaper, 'and this is not a very pleasant sensation when we think how much criminal justice depends on translation.'[12] On the questionable assumption that Europeans were less prone than Chinese to corruption, government policy favoured the employment of European interpreters in the Supreme Court, which sometimes required the employment of officials with multiple responsibilities. The most notorious example was the assistant police superintendent, Daniel Caldwell, who interpreted in cases that he and his network of informants had played a leading role in bringing to court. Caldwell's system was exposed in the late 1850s as a dangerous and pervasive protection racket. Interpretation was also intended mainly for the benefit of the English-speaking judge, jury, prosecutor, reporters and defence counsel (if present). The Chinese defendant usually heard and understood only the questions put to him, and (if he understood the dialect) the evidence given by witnesses. Some defendants were reportedly unaware of the sentences passed on them.[13]

Incomplete interpretation was only one of the difficulties that Chinese defendants encountered under an alien and complex trial process. Although from 1872 onwards defendants on capital charges were assisted by counsel subsidized by the government, the great majority of defendants, including those on capital charges, received no professional assistance before or during their trials. The trial of Wong-awah for piracy and murder in early 1857 is an extreme example because it took place at a time of colonial emergency. But it illustrates the incomprehension that dominated the experience of many defendants. In a petition to the Governor following his conviction, Wong protested that he had himself been taken prisoner by the pirates for whom he had been seen loading plunder. Two missionaries insisted that Wong's Haifeng dialect had made it impossible for him to understand most of what had happened in court.

Wong recounts in his petition, 'On the first day when I was tried ...'

four witnesses were brought against me, and I was charged with piracy. The next day there were six witnesses and I was accused of murder. I protested against these charges, and requested the inter-preter to make known my wish to call the members of the Hong-thai-hong [a firm which had briefly employed Wong in Hong Kong] as witnesses to my character, but this was not granted to me and I was told that the Judge had already decided my case.[14]

The Governor-in-Council rejected the petition and Wong was hanged.

Most defendants who put forward defences claimed that they were the targets of malicious prosecutions, brought either out of revenge or for the purposes of extortion. These claims received short shrift from the court, despite considerable evidence that false accusations were rampant. The Chinese system of justice took a dim view of witnesses and relied more on the forensic skills of the magistrate and the confes-sion (by force if necessary) of the accused. It also imposed severe punishments on those who brought false charges. The lack of effective remedies for this problem under the English system, and the English dependence on witnesses for the proving of a charge, offered an entirely opposite approach to prosecutions. Bringing malicious prose-cutions was made easier in Hong Kong by the existence of a public prosecutor (the Attorney General), who prosecuted all criminal cases in the Supreme Court. This contrasted with the practice in England, where, until late in the century, the majority of criminal cases were still prosecuted privately by the complainant.

Official concern, however, was directed not so much at wrongful convictions as at the embarrassingly low conviction rate caused largely by the unpredictable behaviour of prosecution witnesses. The Supreme Court's conviction rate of 25 per cent in 1848 (its lowest ever) was due partly to prevarication by prosecution witnesses unused to the exact-ing demands placed on evidence, but mainly to the simple failure of witnesses to turn up at the trial. Officials attributed much of the problem to widespread tampering with witnesses by criminal groups, and numerous cases appear to support this conclusion. But the long gap between committal and trial, the sojourning nature of the popu-lation, and a general lack of faith in the system were probably equally responsible. Various cases suggest that victim and accused had come to terms outside of the trial.

Statutory remedies to the problem of uncooperative witnesses enacted in the 1850s were, by the standards of the time, extreme and increased the jeopardy in which the accused was placed. The controversial Ordinance no. 1 of 1851, for example, did away with the problem of absconding witnesses by permitting depositions taken from witnesses by the magistrate at the committal stage to be used as evidence in the main trial, a measure which negated important principles of English law because depositions were taken in private and because the defendant was unable to confront his or her accusers. Numerous cases show that Chinese men and women were convicted solely on depositions without any of the main prosecution witnesses appearing in court. In 1851, for example, the following case was brought against Yee-aon, a watchmaker charged with piracy:

> The only witness in Court was the policeman into whose hands the prisoner was given by some Chinaman or other, and who said that on examining a box pointed out by the prisoner as his, a jacket was found and claimed by the informer; two glass plates were also found, which witness did not say had been claimed by any one. The Attorney General then begged that the Depositions of the other witnesses might be read, but without attempting to prove that the witnesses had been removed by either force or bribery (so that the accusation might have been brought out of revenge for aught he knew). Strange to say, the Judge acquiesced.[15]

Unable to come to a unanimous verdict, the jury was dismissed after several hours. A second jury tried the case the following day and found Yee guilty on the same dubious evidence. Yee was sentenced to 15 years' transportation and drowned in a shipwreck on his way to the penal settlement in Singapore.[16] Convictions were made still easier by the introduction in 1851 of majority jury verdicts (except for capital cases), and majority verdicts were guaranteed in 1858 by the slight enlargement of the miniature Hong Kong jury from six to seven men: this meant that a defendant, having been prosecuted on the decision of the Attorney General, could now be found guilty of a serious offence by as few as four members of the colonial community.

These and other procedural reforms in the 1850s reflected a growing belief among colonists that English law was not appropriate to the conditions in and around Hong Kong. English justice, it was accepted, worked well enough for the tiny minority of European offenders who were given special treatment at all stages in the judicial process. But, colonists increasingly argued, it was not working for the mainly Chinese defendants who came before the Supreme Court. Some explanations noted the 'strain of English laws upon the Chinese inhabitants' and the 'vexatious, unsatisfactory, and to the Chinese unintelligible administration of justice.'[17] Most, however, were harshly racist. It became axiomatic among colonists that the Chinese were an unruly population with criminal tendencies. Crime and disorder in the region, already severe in the 1840s, had indeed grown in the 1850s with the spread of rebellion and piracy. The response of officials in Canton had been to increase the severity of an already harsh penal system by mass summary executions of rebels, pirates and other criminals. The mass executions on the mainland only deepened the concerns in Hong Kong. Critics of the judicial system in Hong Kong argued that neither the careful procedures of English law nor the punishments imposed by the Supreme Court were any deterrent to a people whose sensibilities had become brutalized by the growing violence in their own country. English justice, so dependent on truthful evidence given on oath, was also, the critics argued, systematically compromised by 'heathen' Chinese witnesses, who were incapable of telling the truth, even where it might help them to do so. Worse still, the Supreme Court in Hong Kong had allegedly become an object of fear among law-abiding people subjected to the extortions of traffickers in evidence, and a laughing stock among the hardened criminals who had made Hong Kong their regional headquarters. Exposing the Chinese so suddenly to trial by jury and all the protections of English law was, one characteristic letter to the newspapers complained, a recipe for anarchy.

'The social liberties of the Chinese in Hongkong, are too extended, ... they find themselves here, too suddenly emancipated – they will require time, and contact with Europeans to enable them to handle such dangerous weapons with safety.'[18]

Civilizational stereotypes about 'the Chinese character', shared by many influential colonists, provided ideological justifications for the reorganization of the criminal justice system that was already underway. Practical necessity supplied the impetus. The resources of the small and cash-strapped colonial government, of which the judiciary formed one of the largest heads of expenditure, were simply inadequate to its proclaimed role as a regional centre of justice. Under current prosecution policies, the *China Mail* complained in 1852, 'pirates from the whole coast of China, and even from other countries, might be brought here in hundreds by their own countrymen, to be dealt with according to our laws and at our sole expense.'[19] Manpower was also at a premium. Despite the removal of property qualifications in 1851, the small number of male European jurors were complaining about the impositions placed on their time by complex piracy cases or trivial property cases that had no connection with British interests. Shortages of interpreters and widespread sickness in the mid-1850s forced the Supreme Court to adjourn its criminal sessions on several occasions.

The greatest constraint lay in the government's limited ability to give effect to the punishments awarded by the Court. Most judges and governors were reluctant to see too many capital sentences implemented. Hangings were, in the words of Governor Bonham, 'contrary to the spirit of the present age', and jurors tended to be reluctant to have the deaths of too many prisoners on their consciences.[20] During the Supreme Court's early years a solution was found in the sentence of transportation, which in many cases was an automatic commutation of the death sentence on the recommendation of the judge for crimes (such as piracy or robbery with violence) that still carried a mandatory death sentence. Between 1844 and 1858 nearly 600 convicts, most of them Chinese, were transported to other British colonies for terms varying from seven years to life.[21] From the point of view of the colonial government, transportation was an ideal punishment: it was economical and it was understood to be viewed by the Chinese population as a punishment worse than death. But by the late 1850s transportation destinations closed down, as other colonies became concerned about the rebellious character of many Hong Kong transports. The Hong Kong government was now forced, at a time of war and increasing piracy, to fall back on its own resources, to replace transportation with penal servitude and to hold more and more prisoners sentenced to longer and longer terms.

Imprisonment was the worst of all options for the colonial government. It imposed a recurrent and growing burden on colonial expenditure. This became especially apparent in the late 1850s, when officials calculated that current prosecution rates and the end of transportation would add an average of 50 long-sentence convicts (most of them convicted of piracy) every year to a prison population that was already 70 per cent in excess of capacity.[22] Victoria gaol was notoriously insecure. Persistent overcrowding, lack of funds and the language barriers between European or Indian turnkeys and Chinese prisoners ruled out the elaborate policies of reformation increasingly pursued in England and in colonies such as Singapore. A succession of spectacular escapes made it increasingly undesirable for prisoners to be put to hard labour outside the gaol. Worst of all, imprisonment was understood to be no deterrent to the average Chinese criminal. Annual reports by successive superintendents depict Victoria gaol as a noisy sitting-out area for professional criminals, many of whom allegedly preferred imprisonment to paying the fines that they were well able to afford. Starving paupers reportedly cut down government-owned trees in order to gain entry into Victoria gaol, where the longer-term inmates grew so fat that the gaol committee of 1877 recommended photographing prisoners twice, once at the time of trial and once on their release.[23] Yet all trends pointed towards imprisonment as the staple punishment in British criminal justice. In Hong Kong periodic controversies interrupted and progressively limited the imposition of flogging, the preferred judicial punishment, while the proliferation of regulatory offences and the inability of thousands of people every year to pay the smallest of fines filled the gaol with petty offenders.

The effectiveness of English criminal law in early colonial Hong Kong was, then, undermined by three main problems. In a society divided by race, culture and language, the Supreme Court was increasingly seen by colonists to be inadequate to the task of either doing justice or deterring crime: procedural reforms might relieve the court of some of its problems with evidence, but only by undermining principles still held by many to be vital to the rule of law. Second, the resources available to the government, whether for supplying jurors and interpreters or for giving effect to the heavy sentences imposed by the Supreme Court, were increasingly limited, especially after the suspension of transportation. Third, English punishments, particularly imprisonment, were no substitute for the capital and corporal sentences widely implemented in China during a period of rising crime and conflict, and at a time when colonists believed Hong Kong to be beseiged by 'a moving mass of crime and vagabondage, caused by its immediate proximity to millions of the worst population of the Chinese Empire.'[24]

The solutions to these problems were discovered and implemented at an early stage in Hong Kong's history. They included, first, enlarging the jurisdiction of the executive controlled Magistracy; second, leaving many serious crimes to be dealt with by the Chinese government or by quasi-judicial Chinese agencies within the colony itself; and third, a tendency by governors to interfere with the sentences of the Supreme Court, usually with the aim of reducing imprisonment and increasing the deterrent effects available through other punishments. Not all of these trends were necessarily detrimental to the interests of justice. Their general direction, however, took the administration of criminal justice in Hong Kong further away from its English roots than many historians have been prepared to admit.

Summary justice, preventive justice, and state-created crime: the Magistracy

The Magistracy has always been the bedrock of Hong Kong's judicial system. Yet, despite its enormous caseload, it features hardly at all in historical works on the relations between government and people in Hong Kong. The Magistracy is one important department of government to which the paradigm of 'indirect rule', by which historians traditionally characterize early colonial government in Hong Kong, cannot be applied. Indeed, the high annual prosecution rate raises serious questions about the value of this paradigm. A series of ordinances, beginning in 1847, enlarged the range of offences that could be tried at the magistracy level and progressively increased the sentencing powers of magistrates so that by the 1860s magistrates were able to sentence prisoners to gaol terms of up to six months (two years for some crimes), extensive flogging and fines of up to $50, or the equivalent of about a year's income for the average Chinese resident. While (with the exception of flogging and other degrading punishments) these powers fall somewhat short of the powers enjoyed by Hong Kong magistrates today, they were well in advance of the more cautious expansion of magisterial jurisdiction in England. They were also condemned by early critics who saw the process as an 'unconstitutional and dangerous nature of legislative interference with the courts of law.' The main concern of the Colonial Office in London was to ensure that the reforms did not place Europeans in jeopardy.[25] The aim, and the effect, of the reforms was to remove from the Supreme Court the everyday thefts and acts of violence that would, with the population explosion in the late 1850s, otherwise have entirely submerged the Supreme Court. In addition, as in any other English jurisdiction, the Magistracy dealt with a much larger, and growing, body of regulatory offences designed to control public behaviour, protect the revenue and prevent serious crime before it happened.

By the last decade of the nineteenth century 99.5 per cent of all defendants on criminal charges were tried by the Magistracy and of these defendants 86.5 per cent received some form of punishment. There were, at most, only two magistrates at work at any time in the nineteenth century, hearing, usually through an interpreter, an annual caseload rising to more than 18 000 in the mid-1890s, when a single magistrate also doubled up as Coroner and Superintendent of the Fire Brigade. An equivalent, on average, of between 6 per cent and 10 per cent of the colony's population (rising to 12 per cent and 13 per cent in some years) appeared as defendants before the magistrates in most years of the nineteenth century. Although about three times the rates in nineteenth-century England these ratios are remarkably similar to more recent experience in Hong Kong. A far greater proportion of defendants in the nineteenth century, however, were committed to prison (31.5 per cent in 1900, compared with 2.5 per cent in 1994). Just over half of the prisoners sentenced to imprisonment in 1900 (2691 out of 5263) were imprisoned in default of payment of fine, and more than 40 per cent (2267) were committed for gambling and breaches of the opium monopoly, offences which, in the opinion of the gaol superintendent, were 'not of a criminal nature'.[26]

The principles inherent in the rule of law did not often intrude into the daily workings of the Magistracy. Indeed, the nature of much of its work turned many of these principles on their head. Far more than its equivalents in England, the Magistracy was an integral part of the executive and, until 1862, in control of the police force and gaol. A large proportion of the laws it administered made distinctions between Chinese and non-Chinese, whether in the definition of crime or in the prescription of punishments. Some offences reversed the presumption of innocence by placing the burden of proof on the accused. A preoccupation with what Governor Davis called 'preventive justice' and a proliferation of what Governor Hennessy referred to as 'state-created crime' brought the threshold of criminality far closer to the daily lives of Hong Kong's Chinese inhabitants than any understanding of the rights and liberties under English law ought to have allowed.

The magistrates who presided over this system can be divided into three broad categories. An assortment of 'men on the spot', with no formal legal training, shouldered most of the work of the Magistracy up to the late 1870s. These men were strong advocates of the rattan cane and prided themselves on their 'experience in the subtleties of Chinese character' more than on their knowledge of the law.[27] A second category began to appear in the late 1850s, when Governor Bowring insisted on the recruitment of a qualified barrister to serve as Chief Magistrate. One member of this category, Ng Choy, served as the only Chinese magistrate in nineteenth-century Hong Kong for a few months in 1880. The third category consisted of cadet officers, recruited from the universities in England and (largely through observing cases before the Magistracy) trained in Cantonese. Their terms as magistrates alternated with other postings as officials in other departments. Qualified barristers and Cantonese speakers ought, in theory, to have improved the administration of justice in the Magistracy, and, over all, they probably did. But this cannot always be taken for granted. The early barrister–magistrates had little staying power and seem to have left most of the work to their unqualified assistants. Later barrister–magistrates were also criticized for their hurrying of cases in order to free themselves for their private practice in the afternoons.

By the time when barristers and cadets had become established as magistrates, the administration of criminal law in Hong Kong had anyway accumulated so many local practices and assumptions that the colony's penal system was recognized by the Colonial Office to be necessarily 'different from that adopted in other parts of Her Majesty's dominions'.[28] Among these assumptions were the notion that the colony's Chinese population needed to be carefully controlled; that, because of its immigrant and 'fluctuating' nature, this population was not entitled to the legal protections normally available to British subjects; and the axiom that the colony needed to avoid the 'danger of attracting criminals from the Province of Kwangtung by a system of comparative leniency'.[29]

Peter Wesley-Smith has drawn attention to the considerable body of racist legislation in nineteenth-century Hong Kong that differentiated between Chinese and non-Chinese.[30] Much of this legislation created criminal offences which, by definition, only Chinese could commit, or prescribed punishments, such as caning and queue cutting, which could only be applied to Chinese. Some of the more extreme provisions were introduced at times of war or other emergency yet were retained for decades after the emergencies had subsided. The racially based legislation included: a nightly curfew on Chinese inhabitants introduced (by law, at least) shortly after the outbreak of the Second Opium War (1856–60) and retained until 1897; anti-triad provisions; controls on Chinese public assemblies and processions; extensive registration and licensing schemes applied only to Chinese inhabitants or trades; vicarious liability on Chinese landlords for certain crimes committed by their Chinese tenants; and extensive powers of search into Chinese homes, vessels and businesses. After a scandalous tendency among early magistrates to apply caning for practically any crime, the use of harsher 'Chinese punishments' (at least as judicial punishments) declined as the century progressed. Magistrates were increasingly constrained in the amount of flogging they could impose; and, despite suggestions that it should be reintroduced, queue cutting was discontinued as a 'Chinese punishment' in the late 1840s. The constraints on flogging culminated in 1881, when Governor Hennessy confined the punishment to three offences, roughly corresponding with the provisions then current in England.[31] Hennessy's measures coincided with (and no doubt contributed to) a dramatic increase in imprisonment for petty offenders. Colonial opinion, with qualified support from leaders of the Chinese community, found this unaccept-able and magistrates complained that it was beginning to make their work impossible. In 1887 flogging was again made available for a variety of offences (though not for petty larceny) and for repeat offenders with two or more previous convictions.[32]

The new flogging ordinance followed the growing practice, encour-aged by the Colonial Office, of phrasing criminal legislation in non-racist terms. Like a great deal of existing legislation of an appar-ently non-racist nature, much of this simply disguised the fact that, in application, it was directed mainly, if not exclusively, at the Chinese population. The offence of unlawful possession of property (an English offence, under which a defendant could be punished for failing to explain property found in his possession) was applied exten-sively against men of 'the coolie class' found on the streets with planks, tools, screws, or unusual clothing. During a blitz on crime in 1868, another offence, that of being 'a suspicious character', enabled the police to convict 427 persons believed to be connected with crimes but who could not be prosecuted because 'the main charge through the absence of witnesses or non-production of property, would have broken down.'[33] A perusal of the 150 or so main categories of offences in the magistrates' returns for 1890 (10 772 defendants: a relatively light year) reveals a long list of both explicitly racially constructed offences and disguised class offences, which, in the social conditions of the time, applied only to Chinese. The largest single category for this year (and for most other years in the 1890s) was the offence of breaching the recently reconstructed opium monopoly (1468 defendants, or 13.5 per cent of all defendants), on which the government relied for a substantial and increasing proportion of its revenue.

One reasonable objection to an analysis of this kind is the simple point that Chinese people committed so many of these offences because they formed the majority of the population and because they alone pursued the occupations (hawking, plying chairs or boats for hire, boiling or retailing opium and so on) or the pastimes (street gambling, letting off firecrackers) to which they apply. This objection perhaps underestimates the combination of social inequalities and economic imperatives which 'encouraged' certain types of crime. The government's dependence on revenue from land and the low incomes among the labouring population promoted property price inflation, desperate overcrowding and a spilling out of household activities into the streets that came up against unrealistic sanitary regulations. At the same time, a policy of free immigration, designed to provide a ready supply of cheap labour, maintained a large floating community of impoverished, underemployed 'street coolies', available for hire by the hour, whose frequent idleness subjected them to charges of vagrancy, obstruction, street gambling and various other offences. The government's determination to milk the opium monopoly for as much revenue as it could, and the extensive afforestation projects pushed by governors at the expense of traditional foraging practices, created new categories of economic and ecological crimes.

A further problem with the objection is that police enforcement of the law, even of the most universal offences, was often racially determined. In 1856 editorials complaining about the detention overnight of nearly 200 Chinese men for breaching a proclamation against letting off fireworks after sunset during Chinese New Year noted that large numbers of Europeans letting off fireworks outside the Hong Kong Club and along Queen's Road had been left unmolested by the police.[34] Selective enforcement of the law against urinating in the streets, in the opinion of the *China Mail* in 1871, not only caused injustices but encouraged crime: law-abiding Chinese new to the island or unfamiliar with its detailed laws, seeing foreigners relieving themselves in the street and the police turning a blind eye, were given to believe that the activity was quite legal, yet, under a law of 1856 which applied only to Chinese, they rendered themselves liable to flogging for the offence.[35]

Alternative justice

One of the most striking features of the decline of the Supreme Court's criminal caseload is the sudden drop in piracy cases from around the early 1860s onwards. A variety of factors explain this decline. The nature of piracy changed during the course of the century, from extensive opportunistic raids in the 1840s and 1850s to more carefully planned attacks on prize targets later in the century. With the reconsolidation of government after the troubles of the 1850s, Chinese naval patrols were more active. From the late 1860s, following concerns from the Foreign Office about naval intrusions into Chinese waters, Chinese shipowners were given the message that colonial and naval gunboats would no longer chase pirates beyond the boundaries of British jurisdiction.[36] In addition, the colonial and naval authorities implemented a progressive change in prosecution policy, which increasingly took the form of relying on the Chinese authorities to try and punish pirates. In some ways this was a realistic adjustment of responsibilities in a sphere in which jurisdictional boundaries over-lapped and in which rights and obligations were still being worked out under international law.

The functions, however, assumed by the British authorities in supplying the Chinese courts with alleged pirates raise larger questions about the rule of law in Hong Kong. From almost the beginning of British rule the colonial authorities and the Royal Navy had followed the practice of delivering large numbers of alleged pirates to the Chinese authorities, despite concerns expressed by Lord Palmerston that it was 'scarcely consistent with European feeling that British Ships of War should be capturing large numbers of Chinese, and should be handing them over to the Chinese Authorities to be punished invari-ably by death.'[37] The policy was also frequently applied to cases already within the Hong Kong judicial system. In 1844 Governor Davis handed over for summary execution by the Chinese authorities the notorious Chintae and several other pirates alleged to have robbed a British army treasure boat near Stanley on the ground 'that there would be no sufficient evidence according to the technicalities of English law to condemn him.'[38] In 1849 the *China Mail* cited two cases in which alleged pirates, having been examined and released by the magistrate in Hong Kong, were handed over to the Chinese author-ities, when, by law, they should have been set at liberty.[39] Chinese officials were reported to be waiting at some Supreme Court trials to apprehend defendants acquitted of piracy.

The policy of 'giving justice a second chance', as one early news-paper described it, seems most often to have been applied to piracy cases, where suspects might well be wanted by both the Hong Kong and Chinese governments. But the colonial government also handed over to the Chinese authorities many Chinese accused of other crimes. Apart from the common practice of deporting vagrants and 'suspicious persons', some of whom were allegedly required to buy their freedom from the Chinese authorities, criminal suspects or plain 'delinquents' were often handed over without any application from the Chinese government. Among the latter category were members of the Triad Society, outlawed in China and, from 1845, made liable to criminal charges in Hong Kong. The Hong Kong legislation (which provided for the punishment of branding) was deeply unpopular in the colonial community, partly because it seemed to threaten freedom of association among colonists themselves, and partly because it suggested that Davis was truckling to the despotic Manchu government. Realizing that no jury would convict under such legislation, Davis quietly instructed the Magistracy to hand over triad members 'with their treasonable papers' to the Chinese government.[40]

The greatest clash between colonial expediency and 'European feeling' came during the crisis of 1857, when Governor Bowring was faced with war, terrorism and a harbour effectively blockaded by pirates. In February Bowring despatched two naval ships to capture eight pirate junks obstructing access to the harbour one day after the pirates had reportedly murdered ten of their prisoners. Seventy-three pirates were captured and taken before the Chief Magistrate for committal for trial in the Supreme Court. Fearing that the gaol, the courts and the gallows could not cope with so many prisoners, Bowring ordered that the 73 men be handed over to the Chinese authorities, 'who received them in a most satisfactory manner'.[41] Bowring's explanation to the Colonial Office of this controversial measure neatly summarizes the inadequacies of the Supreme Court. The pirates spoke at least three different dialects, he pointed out:

> they were to be tried by a Judge and a Jury and prosecuted by an Attorney General who understood no Chinese dialect whatsoever and who had the facts conveyed to them by other Chinese who could not make themselves understood to all the prisoners but required still further interpretations for their own information, and with these facts before me I could not but hesitate before sending these men to be tried for their lives in this Colony.[42]

The local press condemned Bowring as 'the greatest monster on the face of the earth; a disgrace to the government he serves – a disgrace to the name of Englishman.'[43] The Colonial Office was equally unsympathetic. The trial of piracy cases, the Secretary of State pointed out, was 'one of the most important purposes for which the Supreme Court at Hong Kong is established.' Bowring's logic, a Colonial Office official observed, was tantamount to arguing that Chinese were 'never to be tried at all' by the colony's courts.[44]

The surrender of pirates to the Chinese authorities continued throughout the century. The policy was not reciprocated by the Chinese government, which, in strict observance of its treaty rights, continued to refuse to surrender Chinese suspects wanted for trial in Hong Kong. The result was that defendants in the same piracy cases were often divided between two jurisdictions, depending on whether they had been captured by British or Chinese security forces. The most celebrated case of this kind was the brutal piracy of the *S.S. Namoa, en route* from Hong Kong to Swatow, in December 1890, in which the British captain and several crew members were murdered. Twenty-five of the culprits were captured by the Chinese authorities and publicly beheaded. In contrast, the seven suspects arrested in Hong Kong were eventually released because of lack of evidence.[45] The policy of non-cooperation by the Chinese authorities rendered it necessary for some Chinese suspects to be tried in China for serious crimes taking place within the colony itself. A prominent example was the murder of W.W. Holworthy, the Assistant Superintendent of the Military Stores, on a secluded hill road on Hong Kong island in 1869. Despite the offer of a $500 reward and the repeated cross-examination of three suspects, the evidence was insufficient to send the case to trial. Meanwhile, other suspects were tracked down to their native village on the mainland: 'two prisoners were subsequently convicted, and sentenced to decapitation in Canton by the Chinese authorities, as there existed no means, under any treaty, of claiming the rendition of Chinese guilty of any crime on British soil.'[46]

Earlier in the century governors had often sanctioned the use of gunboat expeditions or kidnapping plots to capture men wanted for crimes committed in or near Hong Kong, particularly where the victims had been Europeans. In the long run, however, there was little that the colonial authorities could do about the Chinese government's refusal to surrender Chinese suspects wanted in Hong Kong. Although governors were strict in their actions against Chinese officials caught seizing wanted persons within the colony, some seem to have welcomed having the responsibility for trying and executing fugitive criminals taken out of their hands and off the consciences of judges and juries. Executions in Canton of criminals wanted in Hong Kong were officially publicized in Hong Kong; and the Hong Kong government officially thanked the Chinese admiral responsible for 'tracking and bringing to trial and condign punishment the "Namoa" pirates.'[47]

A parallel, and perhaps more constructive, divestment of some of the formal legal system's responsibilities seems also to have taken place in other fields of life. The District Watch Committee, formed in 1866 by Chinese merchants with the encouragement of the colonial government, was a practical recognition of the inadequacy of the colonial police, despite the fact that Hong Kong was one of the most densely policed cities in the British Empire. Within months of their establishment the salaried Chinese watchmen employed by the Committee were active in bringing a variety of offenders, including some Europeans, before the magistrates.[48] It also appears likely that the district watchmen were resolving on their own a large number of cases without any reference to the courts: in 1870 the magistrate, Charles May, complained that 'the police are in ignorance of half the robberies that are reported to the District Watchmen'; and a senior policeman cited a case in that year in which district watchmen had retrieved $500 worth of property stolen from a Chinese merchant without making any formal report to the police.[49]

Informal resolution of cases by various unofficial agencies had a long tradition in both Britain and China. The informality necessarily makes it impossible to assess how extensive the practice was in Hong Kong, though various cases before the courts show clear evidence of attempts at alternative forms of dispute resolution in the background. Both official policy and the unsuitability of the Supreme Court for trying purely Chinese cases had encouraged informal resolution of civil disputes. In addition to the mediation performed by neighbourhood headmen, elders, compradors and other prominent figures, the Man Mo Temple and the early Tung Wah hospital became centres of dispute resolution for the Chinese community: the cases that came before them were predominantly civil but must inevitably have included some strictly criminal cases, the distinctions perhaps being all the more blurred by the absence of any division between criminal and civil jurisdiction in formal Chinese law.[50]

The establishment by Chinese merchants of the Po Leung Kuk in 1878, for checking kidnapping and other abuses against women and children, was an explicit recognition of the failure of British justice to tackle these problems and a defensive measure against Chief Justice Smale's attack on the *mui tsai* (or bonded female domestic servants) system, then prevalent in Hong Kong, as a form of slavery under the definitions of English law. In what amounted to one of the most extensive and persistent erosions of the rule of law, successive governors compromised with the Chinese élite, who mounted a successful campaign against the Chief Justice's attempts to criminalize what they saw as a form of charity for the daughters of distressed families. Under this compromise, 'respectable' forms of bonded female domestic servitude were in practice decriminalized; the policing of kidnapping and other abuses associated with it was placed in the hands of the Chinese

élite who managed the Po Leung Kuk. It was, argued the founders of
the Po Leung Kuk, hardly reasonable for the colonial government to
single out the selling of women and girls by impoverished families into
domestic servitude when it tolerated brothel slavery on an extensive
scale.[51] The rapid growth of the Chinese population in the colony
might well, they admitted, have been attributable to the 'equitable
administration of the criminal law on the part of the English courts of
law', but they complained, 'the principle of liberty of the person' on
which the laws of Hong Kong were founded made it too easy for
kidnappers to hire a lawyer, 'turn the crooked into straight', and
'escape through the meshes of the law'.[52] Working in collaboration
with the Registrar General, the Po Leung Kuk fed the colonial courts
with the more serious cases but reserved for itself a large jurisdiction
over what is perhaps best summarized as customary Chinese family
law: deserting or adulterous wives, abusive husbands, borderline cases
of kidnapping or enticement, ill treatment of *mui tsai* and so on.[53]
Colonial suspicions about the powerful role of the Kuk culminated in
an official enquiry in 1892 to investigate, among other things, allegations that the Kuk was administering a 'secret system of espionage'
over the Chinese population that was 'repugnant to the principles of
British Government'.[54]

   The increasing social and economic prominence of the Chinese élite
brought with it exemption from many of the repressive laws designed
to keep the labouring masses in their place. The better off could afford
the low fines that put many poorer people in prison, and could, and
did, buy immunity from vexatious police interference. In addition,
some exemptions for the socially privileged were built into the legislation. A variety of passes could be obtained to enable their Chinese
holders to be on the streets after curfew on the condition that they
carried lanterns: nearly 19 000 such passes were, for example, issued
quarterly in 1891.[55] The Chinese Extradition Ordinance (no. 26 of
1889) contained special protections for persons who had lived in the
colony for a year or more. The government also increasingly sought
advice on penal policy from its Chinese legislators and justices of the
peace. Much of this (particularly the persistent opposition to expenditure on new gaol accommodation) was in support of the hardline
advice given by their colleagues among the colonial élite. But some
tended towards applying reason and restraint to the more extreme
proposals on corporal punishment put forward by some European
advisers.[56]

Executive interference in sentences

Governors had the power to revise judicial sentences by pardoning convicted prisoners or reducing their sentences. The Royal Instructions also required them to confirm or remit all capital sentences. Given the large number of miscarriages of justice in the early Supreme Court and the erratic sentencing of some judges, it was fortunate that governors and their executive councils took this duty seriously. Early governors used the Queen's birthday, the most import-ant festival of the colonial year, as an opportunity to pardon large numbers of prisoners whose sentences were excessive or whose convic-tions had subsequently been found to be unsafe. Prisoners might also be pardoned separately, particularly where press campaigns drew attention to unreasonable verdicts or severe sentences, or where imprisoned European sailors needed to rejoin their departing ships.

Pardons were sometimes granted when malicious prosecutions came to light. In 1848, for example, a number of prisoners sentenced to transportation for the piracy of two large opium ships were pardoned when it became clear that Caldwell's chief informant, Too-apo, had been framing men who were refusing to give him money. Many of the interventions by the Governor-in-Council were prompted by petitions from the Chinese community. In the notorious Shaukeiwan murder case of 1869–70, the master and three of the crew of a trading junk were narrowly saved from the gallows after a petition from one of the colony's principal Chinese merchants, Li Tak-cheong, alleged that the evidence on which they had been convicted of the murder of a European police sergeant was false. A series of perjury cases instituted by Li revealed an extensive conspiracy, encouraged by heavy official rewards, to which the police investigators had turned a blind eye. After the four innocent men had been pardoned, the Chief Justice, Sir John Smale, confessed to having 'shuddered' at the possibility that the death penalty had in other cases been inflicted on innocent men, especially during a decade in which he believed the number of executions in the small colony of Hong Kong to have been equal to more than half the number of all the executions in England for that period.

Cases like the Shaukeiwan murder case caused periodic agitation in the colonial community about the state of justice and policing. Chief Justice Smale hoped that the outcome would encourage 'other respectable Chinamen' to help the government in the suppression of crime. But such investigations into judicial decisions were equally likely to give rise to objections that interventions by the Governor-in-Council interfered with the workings of justice or paid too much attention to protests from the Chinese community. These interventions clearly served the interests of justice. But other, more doubtful forms of community and executive influence on sentencing policies began to appear in the mid-1860s and became an important feature of the penal system under governors MacDonnell and Kennedy. In 1865 a new ordinance, inspired by a recent English enactment, empowered the Supreme Court to impose public whippings on prisoners found guilty of offences involving violence. In 1866 the acting Chief Justice, Henry Ball, began to apply the ordinance to European as well as Chinese offenders. An American seaman, Austin Melville, was convicted of wounding a fellow seaman with intent to do grievous bodily harm after a hard drinking session on board ship. Having heard of the new ordinance, Melville requested a sentence of flogging in lieu of imprisonment. This was unwise: Ball sentenced him *both* to two years penal servitude *and* to two public whippings of twenty-five lashes each, and pointed out that 'he would not make any distinction between one man and another, whatever country they might belong to.'[57]

Two months later, Ball added flogging to the prison sentence of another European, John Thompson, convicted of robbery and of having administered a stupefying drug to a Chinese woman, Lea-akow, who was under the protection of various respectable European men. The sentence imposed on Thompson provoked outrage in the colonial community, which petitioned the Governor against the sentence, and drew attention to 'the disgrace that would attach to the European community by the public flogging of one of their number in the presence of Chinese.' It is not clear what became of Thompson's sentence, although this does appear to be the last time a European was sentenced to flogging. In the case of Melville, the Executive Council received a petition from the US Consul requesting that the flogging portion of the sentence be remitted. The Governor decided that the spirit and the letter of the English act on which the Hong Kong ordinance was based had been misapplied because its intention was that the crime should be accompanied by robbery or attempted robbery.[58] The Hong Kong ordinance (no. 12 of 1865), in fact, contained no such condition. The English act also appears to have been entirely forgotten in the subsequent imposition of flogging on Chinese prisoners convicted of a wide variety of crimes involving violence.

Whatever consideration may have been given to European offenders, the trend in the 1860s and 1870s was to increase the amount of corporal punishment imposed on Chinese prisoners. The number of hangings increased dramatically in the early 1860s, partly in order to increase the deterrent effect of punishment, but perhaps also because governors knew that, in the absence of transportation, the commutation of every death sentence added a life prisoner to the rapidly expanding gaol population. During Governor MacDonnell's blitz on crime in the late 1860s, the number of floggings increased dramatically. Much of this was achieved by 'extra-judicial' and often plainly illegal methods. Section 15 of MacDonnell's 'maintenance of order and cleanliness' ordinance (no. 8 of 1866) provided that Chinese persons deported from the colony and returning without permission might be branded and flogged. MacDonnell got round the subsequent disallowance of this provision by the home government by introducing a policy under which prisoners still serving sentences could voluntarily petition for early release. In return they were to subject themselves to branding and to deportation on the condition that if they returned to Hong Kong they would be flogged and reimprisoned on the orders of a magistrate.[59] Although still illegal, this policy remained in force, with the reluctant acquiescence of the Colonial Office, until, during MacDonnell's absence from the colony in 1870, some officials exposed what amounted to a private system of justice administered under the provision by the governor of Victoria gaol.[60] Following an opinion from the Attorney General that the whole scheme was illegal, the Colonial Secretary gave orders that branding be discontinued.[61] The scheme was legalized, with Colonial Office sanction, in 1872, after MacDonnell and his police officials engineered a crime scare on the basis of what later turned out to be spurious crime statistics.[62]

The exact number of prisoners subjected to this 'optional' scheme is unclear, though it probably ran into some hundreds.[63] As Governor Hennessy (who abolished the scheme in 1877) pointed out, in enabling magistrates to impose short prison sentences and leave the rest of the sentencing to the governor of the gaol, the scheme prevented many serious cases from going up to the Supreme Court.[64] It also made nonsense of the prison sentences imposed by the Court, since many prisoners were released and deported long before their terms expired.[65] At the end of April 1867 MacDonnell could claim that, in combination with the Supreme Court's flogging sentences, the policy had brought the gaol population down from 876 in October 1865 to under 500.[66] By restoring to their native province 'the scum and crime of the worst criminal population of China' the scheme would, MacDonnell reported, 'leave with the Vice Roy the future superintendence and charge of a large proportion of criminals whom it has hitherto been impossible to keep long out of Gaol here.' He was able, in 1866, to dispense with a large and expensive gaol under construction on Stonecutters' Island. He was also able, he claimed, to maintain a prison regime that was healthy, disciplined and free of the suicides and other forms of death so prevalent under earlier crowded and unsanitary conditions.[67]

MacDonnell's claim has to be balanced by the fact that between 1867 and 1876 a total of 1945 floggings of prisoners took place, some from judicial sentences, but the vast majority for offences committed within the gaol. Most went unrecorded in the bland prison reports sent back to London and only came to light during investigations initiated by Hennessy in 1877.[68] The aim within the prison, MacDonnell explained in response to later questions from London about suicides in Victoria gaol, was to produce 'a system of discipline and labor as without actual inhumanity may have a deterrent effect on the thousands in the vicinity of the Gaol, who are quite ready to run the risk of becoming inmates of it, if there be the least relaxation in the disagreeable penal character of its discipline.'[69] Whatever the mis-behaviour of prisoners, it is difficult to view this policy as anything other than an attempt by the executive to boost the deterrent effect of judicial sentences, which, owing to increasing limitations imposed by the Colonial Office, could not legally have included flogging. Flogging on such a large scale was abolished by Hennessy. But the view prevailed among officials that flogging was the only satisfactory way of dealing with Chinese offenders. This was apparent not just in the advice they and their political colleagues consistently gave on the subject, but also in their response to emergencies. In January 1887, for example, the gaol authorities took advantage of a strike among the chain gang (in protest against a reduction in diet) to impose whipping on 69 prisoners. The punishment, reported the acting gaol super-intendent, 'proved most successful in the Gaol, and I may mention incidentally that the number of prisoners fell from 658 to 585 and that the Captain Superintendent of Police remarked, as I am informed, of the quiet state of the town after its infliction.'[70] A comparable deter-rent was invoked in 1911, when the government feared that celebrations and demonstrations following the Chinese Revolution might get out of hand: the Legislative Council passed a brisk amend-ment to the Peace Preservation Ordinance empowering magistrates to impose whipping for a wide variety of offences.[71]

Did the rule of law matter?

In focusing so much on executive meddling and miscarriages of justice, this chapter may have given the impression that the rule of law in nineteenth-century Hong Kong was a dead letter. Such a view would be mistaken. Despite its manifest shortcomings, the rule of law still set the standards for government and justice in the Colony. Even where it was most overshadowed by emergency legislation, executive manipulation, or callousness on the part of judges and juries, it survived in the background as a point of reference and as a resource on which courts, officials and public opinion could occasionally draw. Supervision from London, though uneven and inconsistent, ensured that the extremists among the officials in early Hong Kong did not get away with *all* of their more outlandish legislative proposals. The safeguards and values inherent in English law enabled officials, judges and jurors who put principles before expediency to insist that justice should be done, even in the face of considerable opposition. They allowed, for example, the men charged with the attempted poisoning of the European community in 1857 to be acquitted by a jury, when many colonists and some officials had called for their summary execution. They also allowed Chief Justice Smale to release Kwok A-Sing, charged with piracy on board a French coolie ship in 1871, on the grounds that he had been held on the ship under coercion, when the trend in the many previous cases of this kind had been to uphold the authority of the ship's captain, whatever laws he might have broken.[72]

The detailed circumstances surrounding the poisoned bread and Kwok A-Sing cases, and particularly the executive's efforts to frustrate the workings of justice in both these cases, also reveal that they were far from being the triumphant confirmations of the rule of law that they might seem. Like the miscarriages of justice described elsewhere in this chapter, they point to the fragility of the rule of law in a society like early colonial Hong Kong. The rule of law was frequently undermined, set aside, and turned on its head. It was systematically eroded by racist legislation, procedural short-cuts, and a growing dependence on summary jurisdiction and alternative justice. Its ideology and rhetoric masked what became, for the most part, a system of discipline and deterrence directed at the colony's poorer Chinese inhabitants and designed to protect the colonial community and their property from the depredations of what was depicted as a dangerous and criminal populace. This can hardly be surprising in a rapidly growing colony deeply divided by race, class and language, located in a difficult region, and run by a government that lacked the knowledge, resources and popular legitimacy necessary to administer genuine justice. But it suggests that, in attempting to understand the experiences of people who came before the British courts in Hong Kong, historians would do best to turn their attention away from such hypothetical notions as the 'rule of law' and to concentrate more on the divisions, inequalities and insecurities that shaped the development of justice and government in the colony.

Notes

* This chapter has benefited greatly from advice received from Allyson N. May, Jerry Bannister, Kenneth Chan, Derek Roebuck, Robin McLeish, Steve Tsang and Peter Wesley-Smith.
1. *China Mail*, 15 October 1846, pp. 142–3.
2. *Friend of China*, 4 September 1844, p. 492; Robert Montgomery Martin, 'Minute on the British Position and Prospects in China, 19 April 1845', in *Reports, Minutes and Despatches on the British Position and Prospects in China* (London, 1846), p. 79.
3. Davis to Stanley, 21 December 1843, CO 129/4, p. 278; Patten's 1996 policy address to the Hong Kong Legislative Council, *South China Morning Post*, 3 October 1996.
4. Sir G.W. Des Voeux, *My Colonial Service* (2 vols., London: John Murray, 1903), II, p. 204.
5. Petition from the Chinese community of Hong Kong, February 1871, CO 129/149, p. 227.
6. For a more detailed discussion see Christopher Munn, *Anglo-China: Chinese People and British Rule in Nineteenth-Century Hong Kong* (London: Curzon Press, forthcoming 2000).
7. *Friend of China*, 4 September 1844, p. 492.
8. J.W. Norton-Kyshe, *The History of the Laws and Courts of Hong Kong, Tracing Consular Jurisdiction in China and Japan, and including Parliamentary Debates, and the Rise, Progress, and Successive Changes in the Various Public Institutions of the Colony from the Earliest Period to the Present Time* (2 vols, London, 1898, repr. Hong Kong: Vetch & Lee, 1971), II, p. 57.
9. The statistics here and elsewhere are from court returns in the Hong Kong Blue Books (CO 133) and *Hongkong Government Gazette*.
10. Norton-Kyshe, *History*, II, p. 554.
11. *Hongkong Register*, 13 November 1849, p. 182.
12. Ibid., 29 June 1852, p. 102.
13. Gaol Commission Report, March 1857, CO 129/64, pp. 348–9.
14. Executive Council minutes, 9 February 1857, CO 131/4, pp. 39–44.
15. *China Mail*, 6 March 1851, p. 39.
16. Transport list, CO 129/36, 114, 14 April 1851; *Friend of China*, 7 June 1851, p. 184.
17. *China Mail*, 20 October 1853, 170; Bowring to Caine, 7 December 1854, CO 129/49, p. 148.

18. *Hongkong Register*, 10 April 1849, p. 58.
19. *China Mail*, 19 February 1852, p. 30.
20. Quoted in Hulme to Grey, 8 July 1852, CO 129/41, p. 206.
21. Christopher Munn, 'The Transportation of Chinese Convicts from Hong Kong, 1844-1858', *Journal of the Canadian Historical Association*, 1997, Vol. 8, pp. 113–45.
22. Bridges to Bowring, 20 November 1857, CO 129/65, p. 76.
23. Report of the Gaol Committee, *Hongkong Government Gaxette*, 10 March 1877, p. 123; Colonial Surgeon's Report for 1877, ibid., 6 July 1878, p. 324.
24. MacDonnell to Carnarvon, 14 January 1867, CO 129/120, p. 122.
25. Colonial Office to Davis, 18 February 1847, CO 129/17, p. 165.
26. Gaol Report, *Hongkong Government Gazette*, 9 February 1901, p. 338.
27. Mitchell to Mercer, 8 May 1856, CO 129/55, p. 351.
28. Carnarvon to Hennessy, 3 January 1878, *British Parliamentary Papers: China 25: Correspondence, Dispatches, Reports, Returns, Memorials and Other Papers relating to the Affairs of Hong Kong 1862–81* (Shannon: Irish University Press, 1971), p. 493.
29. Ibid.
30. Peter Wesley-Smith, 'Anti-Chinese Legislation in Hong Kong', in Ming K. Chan (ed.), *Precarious Balance: Hong Kong Between China and Britain, 1842–1992* (Armonk, New York: M.E. Sharpe, 1994).
31. Ordinance no. 3 of 1881. The offences were robbery with violence; attempted choking, strangling or suffocation; and larceny by a male offender under the age of 16.
32. Ordinance no. 16 of 1887.
33. Police report for 1868, *Hongkong Government Gazette*, 17 April 1869, p. 210.
34. *China Mail*, 7 February 1856, 22; *Friend of China*, 9 February 1856, p. 46.
35. Chinese supplement to the *China Mail*, 22 April 1871, p. 3.
36. Foreign Office to Colonial Office, 20 November 1868, CO 129/134, 564-6; Police Report for 1872, *Hongkong Government Gazette*, 8 February 1873, p. 39.
37. Addington, Foreign Office, to Hawes, Colonial Office, 11 August 1849, CO 129/31, p. 46.
38. Davis to Aberdeen, 20 December 1844, CO 129/7, pp. 302–3.
39. *China Mail*, 8 November 1849, p. 178.
40. Shelley to Caine, 27 March 1846, PRO HK/HKRS 100, p. 243; Caine to Hillier, 8 September 1846, ibid., p. 310; *Friend of China*, 18 November 1846, p. 1404; Sir John Francis Davis, *China During the War and Since the Peace* (2 vols, London 1852, repr. Scholarly Resources, 1972), II, p. 187. This seems to have been the standard policy until the enactment of the new Triad Ordinance (no. 8 of 1887).
41. *Friend of China*, 25 February 1857, p. 62; Bowring to Labouchere, 28 February and 22 July 1857, CO 129/62, pp. 338–40, CO 129/63, p. 476.
42. Bowring to Labouchere, 22 July 1857, pp. 474–5.
43. *Friend of China*, 25 February 1857, p. 62.
44. Labouchere to Bowring, 8 June 1857, CO 129/62, p. 344; pencilled marginal note on Bowring's despatch, 22 July 1857, CO 129/63, p. 475.
45. Norton-Kyshe, *History*, II, pp. 424–9; Police Report for 1890, 29 January 1891, *Hong Kong Sessional Papers*, 91/3.

46. Murrow to Granville, 26 November 1869, CO 129/142, pp. 233–4; Police Report for 1869, *Hongkong Government Gazette*, 16 April 1870; report by T. Fitz Roy Rice, 5 October 1871, CO 129/152, pp. 267–8.
47. Legislative Council minutes, 3 July 1891, bound in the *Hong Kong Sessional Papers* (1891).
48. *Hongkong Government Gazette*, 14 March 1868, p. 115.
49. Report by T. Fitz Roy Rice, 5 October 1871, CO 129/152, pp. 264–7.
50. Elizabeth Sinn, *Power and Charity: The Early History of the Tung Wah Hospital, Hong Kong* (Hong Kong: Oxford University Press, 1989), pp. 96–8.
51. 'Correspondence Respecting the Alleged Existence of Chinese Slavery in Hong Kong', *British Parliamentary Papers: China 26: Correspondence, Annual Reports, Returns, Conventions and Other Papers relating to the Affairs of Hong Kong 1882–99* (Shannon: Irish University Press, 1971), p. 212.
52. Ibid., pp. 191, 210; Petition from the Directors of the Po Leung Kuk, 1 February 1892, *Hong Kong Sessional Papers*, 92/11, p. 184.
53. Elizabeth Sinn, 'Chinese Patriarchy and the Protection of Women in 19th-century Hong Kong', in Maria Jaschok and Suzanne Miers, (eds), *Women and Chinese Patriarchy: Submission, Servitude and Escape* (Hong Kong University Press, 1994).
54. Report of the Special Committee to investigate into the Po Leung Kuk, *Hong Kong Sessional Papers*, 1893, p. 133.
55. Registrar General's Report for 1891, ibid., 92/19.
56. See, for example, the criticisms by 'Certain Chinese Justices of the Peace' of the proposal in 1886 to reintroduce the punishment of queue cutting. *Hong Kong Sessional Papers*, 87/16, p. 298.
57. *Hongkong Daily Press*, 26 February 1866.
58. Executive Council minutes, 2 March 1866, CO 131/5, pp. 187–9.
59. Ibid., 13 November 1866, CO 131/5, pp. 260–1; MacDonnell to Carnarvon, 23 November 1866 and 14 January 1867, CO 129/116, pp. 113–14, CO 129/120, pp. 126–7.
60. May to Austin, 11 May 1870, CO 129/149, pp. 146–50.
61. Deportation and the penalty of whipping on return were, however, continued under Ordinance no. 7 of 1870. Opinion by Pauncefote, 23 May 1870 and Austin to Douglas, 25 May 1870, CO 129/149, 151, pp. 152–6.
62. Ordinance no. 4 of 1872.
63. *Hongkong Government Gazette*, 23 November 1878, p. 571.
64. Hennessy to Hicks-Beach, 16 October 1878, ibid., 17 September 1879, pp. 537–8.
65. Ibid., 16 November 1878, p. 540.
66. MacDonnell to Buckingham, 29 April 1867, CO 129/121, p. 386.
67. MacDonnell to Carnarvon, 23 November 1866, CO 129/116, pp. 107–15. Recorded deaths among prisoners did indeed begin to decline slowly from the high points of 92 in 1863 and 108 in 1865, although the deaths of as many as 79 prisoners in 1866, when MacDonnell made this claim, hardly seem to justify such complacency.
68. MacDonnell to Carnarvon, 23 November 1866, CO 129/116, pp. 114–15; gaol returns, Hong Kong Colonial Blue Books, CO 133; Hennessy to Carnarvon, 23 and 30 August 1877, *Hongkong Government Gazette*, 22 September 1877, pp. 420–1.

69. MacDonnell to Buckingham, 29 May 1868, CO 129/130, p. 558.
70. N.G. Mitchell-Innes to Frederick Stewart, 11 October 1887, *Hong Kong Sessional Papers*, 88/6.
71. Norman Miners, *Hong Kong under Imperial Rule, 1912–1941* (Hong Kong: Oxford University Press, 1987), p. 4.
72. For a discussion of this case see Peter Wesley-Smith, 'Kwok A-Sing, Sir John Smale, and the Macao Coolie Trade,' in Shane Nozzal (ed.), *Law Lectures for Practitioners 1993* (Hong Kong Law Journal Ltd, 1993).

3
Judicial Independence under the Basic Law

Byron S.J. Weng

The rule of law is not only a pivot to the effective protection of individual freedoms and rights, but also a key to the stability and prosperity of a society. Judicial independence is essential for sustaining the rule of law. In the case of Hong Kong, the Basic Law defines the basic legal infrastructure of the SAR with effect from 1 July 1997. It also provides the framework for an independent judiciary charged with the role of safeguarding the SAR's rule of law. An analytical examination of the Basic Law is therefore necessary and important.[1]

The Basic Law was drafted by a committee appointed by the National People's Congress (NPC) composed of both mainland and Hong Kong members. As is now well known, its legislative process involved extensive consultation in Hong Kong but was under constant and effective control from Beijing. Since it is based on the authorization of the NPC, the latter can, by another piece of legislation, nullify the whole document. Nonetheless, the Basic Law is, while in effect, the 'constitution'[2] of the SAR. It is a law of the PRC, with a status just below the Constitution.

In this chapter a systematic examination of the Basic Law is made under a number of headings relating to judicial independence. The implementation of the Basic Law in the first two years of the SAR will also be investigated in order to relate the analysis to reality. The limits on length precludes any systematic comparison between the Basic Law and the 1984 Sino-British Joint Declaration.[3] Two hypotheses are offered from the outset. Readers are requested to keep them in mind. Their validity or otherwise will become reasonably clear by the end of this chapter.

Hypothesis One. Hong Kong's government is entrenched in the tradition of the rule of law and the principle of judicial independence. It can function effectively only on the basis of that tradition. The principle of judicial independence is and will be upheld in the SAR as it was upheld in the pre-reversion period whether the political system is democratic or not.

Hypothesis Two. The SAR is not likely to maintain a strong and independent judiciary because (1) the Basic Law has provided a weak basis for judicial independence; and (2) the SAR government and its supporting élite community have doubts and apprehensions about a western liberal democratic system based on individualism.

In my view, the topic involves at least the following analytical points or questions.
1. the judicial autonomy of the SAR
2. the principle of judicial independence
   • potential executive interference
   • potential legislative interference
   • interference from within the judiciary
3. the protection of the judges of the courts
   • appointment of judges (assurance of standards)
   • removal of judges (safety of tenure)
   • immunity of the members of the judiciary (spiritual protection)
   • conditions of service and retirement (material protection)
4. the application of laws
   • the laws applicable in the SAR
   • the national laws
   • precedents of other common law jurisdictions
5. the interpretation of law and judicial review
   • powers of the NPC Standing Committee
   • SAR courts' power of judicial review
   • the right of abode case
6. the SAR courts' jurisdictions
7. the pertinent international factors
In a sense, this list is a kind of research agenda for the topic; the first answers to the core questions are described and some of the peripheral problems are dealt with briefly. More definitive conclusions will have to wait until further research has been completed.

Judicial autonomy of the SAR

According to Article 2 of the Basic Law, the NPC authorizes the SAR 'to exercise a high degree of autonomy and enjoy executive, legislative and independent judicial power, including that of final adjudication, in accordance with the provisions of the Basic Law.' Article 19, paragraph 1 says that the SAR 'shall be vested with independent judicial power'. The face value of these provisions is clear enough. Hong Kong shall have its own autonomous government with three branches, of which the judiciary shall include a Court of Final Appeal (CFA). In other words, there shall be no appeal to the Supreme People's Court (SPC) of the PRC, which shall not interfere with the SAR's judicial proceedings. It is also safe to assume that, unlike the United States where federal courts function in the component states alongside the states' own courts, no Chinese national courts will be set up in the SAR. The courts of China shall not have jurisdiction over the SAR.

Does that mean the SPC shall not even supervise the work of the CFA of the SAR? The answer is not immediately clear. As long as there is no problem that the SAR itself cannot solve, perhaps there will be no supervision, formal or informal. Should there be complaints of the kind that Beijing finds difficult to ignore, it will probably be a different story. As the following analyses will reveal, there are many mechanisms already put in place through which the NPC and the Central People's Government (CPG), if not the SPC, may interfere in the SAR's affairs, including those of the judiciary.

The principle of judicial independence

Judicial independence presupposes a separation of power. Peter Wesley-Smith says that, in Hong Kong, in only one respect is the separation of power taken seriously and that is the independence of the judiciary.[4] This is true. Article 2 of the Basic Law also implies that the judiciary shall be independent from the other two branches of government, the executive and the legislative. More directly, Article 85 stipulates that 'the courts of the SAR shall exercise judicial power independently, free from any interference.' Exercising judicial power independently should be both a right and an obligation of the judges (courts). Interference should refer to both institutions and individuals, public or private, from inside or outside the judicial system, except where called for by law. This doctrine is well established in Hong Kong. In passing, one may note that the Basic Law has also provided for the independence of the Department of Justice (Article 63), the Commission of Audit (Article 58) and the Independent Commission Against Corruption (Article 57). These are bodies of the SAR government that perform some quasi-judicial functions.

Be that as it may, potential interference from each of the three branches of government can still be discerned in the provisions of the Basic Law.

Potential executive interference

By Article 48, the Chief Executive of the SAR may exercise considerable power and functions. Among other things, he decides, 'in the light of security and vital public interests, whether government officials or other personnel in charge of government affairs should testify or give evidence before the Legislative Council or its committees.' Since executive–legislative relations are often political in nature, that provision is not unreasonable. Fortunately, he/she does not have similar powers where the judiciary is concerned. There appears to be no provision in the Basic Law that stipulates a power of executive interference in the work of the judiciary. As a matter of routine, the executive authorities make subsidiary legislation, operate quasi-judicial tribunals and grant remissions or pardons according to law. Such functions generally do not threaten judicial independence. By paragraph (6) of the same article, the Chief Executive can appoint or remove judges of the courts at all levels in accordance with legal procedures. This power is conditioned, as discussed below, and there is no reason to believe that the exercise of this power may constitute a threat to judicial independence under normal circumstances.

The Chief Executive has clear obligations to the central authorities 'to implement the directives issued by the CPG in respect of the relevant matters provided for in this Law' (Paragraph 8) and 'to conduct, on behalf of the government of the SAR, external affairs and other affairs as authorized by the Central Authorities' (Paragraph 9). If and when, for reasons of national concern or of a power struggle, central directives were issued which required a certain amount of pressure to be put on the SAR judiciary in connection with a specific case, a weak Chief Executive might not be able to resist it. After all, the Chief Executive is accountable first to the CPG. (Article 43). Under such extraordinary circumstances, it is conceivable that the vast powers of the position, especially those with regard to personnel (Article 48, Paragraph 6) and budget (Paragraph 10), might become instruments of interference.

Furthermore, in an executive-led system of government, a powerful Chief Executive may choose to challenge the power of the judiciary when the latter is judged to be standing in its way. In fact, there has already been a serious case of executive interference in the January

1999 CFA ruling on the right of abode. In this case, the SAR government not only made an unprecedented request for a 'clarification' from the CFA but also asked for an official interpretation of certain Basic Law provisions from the NPC Standing Committee, with an aim to overturn the CFA ruling. Such executive acts were judged by the legal community to be severely damaging to judicial independence and the rule of law (see below).

Potential legislative interference

Certain power vested in the Legislative Council (Legco) of the SAR may also lead to potential interference in the judiciary's work. According to Article 73, Legco has the power 'to enact, amend or repeal laws in accordance with the provisions of this Law and legal procedures' (Paragraph 1), implying it can pass laws and ordinances to alter or limit the power of the courts. It is 'to endorse the appointment and removal' of the judges of the CFA and the Chief Judge of the High Court (Paragraph 7) and therefore has the opportunity to block the way of a particular judge from being appointed or removed. It can 'debate any issue concerning public interests' (Paragraph 6), 'receive and handle complaints from Hong Kong residents' (Paragraph 8) and, by so doing, put the judiciary under public pressure. Such power need not be taken in only a negative way. They are also necessary for checks and balances among the three branches of government. There is always a possibility of imbalance but, in practice, Legco is restrained by design in the Basic Law and has so far played a relatively minor role in government.

In a limited way, Legco has some quasi-judicial power of its own. Article 73 (10) stipulates that it may summon, as required when exercising the above-mentioned power and functions, persons concerned to testify or give evidence. The procedures involved are quasi-judicial in nature. Furthermore, Paragraph 9 of the same article gives Legco a role in the impeachment of the Chief Executive wherein the Chief Justice is to form and chair an independent investigation committee. There is a possibility here that all three branches of government will become entangled in a semi-judicial, political affair. Judicial independence would be the more important should such a procedure ever be invoked.

Interference from within the judiciary

Questions also arise as to the possibility of interference by a higher court in a lower court's exercise of its judicial power; or interference by the court administrator, or a superior judge of a court in the exercise of judicial power by a member of that court.

Here, the choice of the word 'courts' instead of 'judges' in Article 85 is a matter of special concern. As quoted above, Article 85 stipulates most directly that 'the courts of the SAR shall exercise judicial power independently, free from any interference'. Independence of the courts and independence of the judges mean very different things. The former is collective and the latter individual. In a closed system where power is highly concentrated, the collective can hardly defy instructions from the ruling party. The individual may exercise more discretion but may also sadly be pressured into submission rather than relying on the judge's own conscience. However, in an open and free society, one is tempted to suggest that, the judge actually presiding over a trial is usually more reliable in arriving at the just verdict for a case than a committee of senior court members sitting in a back room.

The fact is that Hong Kong has always subscribed to the independence of the individual judge, not of the court as a collective unit. This is realized through doctrines expounded by scholars and jurists and through the mechanisms of protecting the judges from external influence, including the administrative superior.

In contrast, in the PRC all trial courts have a *shenpan weiyuanhui* (judicial committee) made up of senior members, which is responsible for the verdict.[5] There is a practical reason for it. For a time because of a shortage of qualified judicial personnel particularly in rural areas and outlying provinces it was thought prudent to have such a committee to supervise the less than competent judges. But it is more than a matter of pragmatic needs. This practice is bedded in the Chinese socialist ideology and built into the system. The courts must serve the revolution like other party and state organs. No one is supposed to be free from collective responsibility and party control, not even a judge.

Evidence suggests that from the very first draft, Article 85 (then Article 84) of the Basic Law used the words 'courts' instead of 'judges'. Hence, the use of the word 'courts' was most probably deliberate and made for systematic as well as practical reasons. Was there an attempt to bring the SAR system closer to that of the PRC? Was it force of habit or mere negligence or a case of ignorance? There are good reasons to believe that the drafters were aware of the difference for it had long been in the constitutional law literature.[6] It would seem that the drafters consciously and deliberately chose the word, but it is not possible to ascertain their motives. Curiously, there is no evidence that anyone objected to the choice of the word during the five-year-long drafting and consulting process. At any rate, therein lies a seed of potential trouble, a point of contention in the future.

Through historical experience, liberal democracies have learned to respect the rule of law. To safeguard it they have learned to uphold the principle of judicial independence. And to uphold judicial independence they have discovered that judges of the courts should be made to feel secure so that they can exercise their authority and functions without being subjected to interference or the temptation of corruption. The means of protecting judges are both procedural and substantive. The former attends to the assurance of standards and safety of tenure. The latter involves both the spiritual and the relevant provisions. They cover appointment, removal, immunity, terms of service and retirement. Generally they are sufficient to assure the quality of judges, provide them with safety of tenure and spiritual as well as material protection on retirement. The issues involved are numerous and merit careful analyses (see Chapter 5 by Wesley-Smith).

Two items pertaining to Articles 82 and 85 deserve attention. A controversy erupted in connection with the interpretation of Article 82 in 1991. Article 82 says: 'The power of final adjudication of the SAR shall be vested in the CFA of the Region, which may as required invite judges from other common law jurisdictions to sit on the CFA.' Notice that the word 'judges' is plural. However, in 1991, Beijing managed, through a Sino-British Joint Liaison Group agreement, to change the composition of the CFA to a 1:3:1 formula, that is, a Chief Justice, three permanent judges and one visiting overseas jurist. The Bar Association and Legco both opposed the agreement but to no avail. It is quite clear that 'judges' does not mean 'only one'. But China apparently preferred to have no more than one foreign jurist. Cynics opined that Beijing cared less about the health of the SAR judicial system where China's sovereign 'face' was involved. Chinese patriots praised the move as a far-sighted one that will prove to be wise in due course.

In practice, the record so far has been satisfactory. According to the Department of Justice, there is no nationality restriction for SAR judges save only for two positions, the Chief Justice and the Chief Judge of High Court. These offices must be filled by Hong Kong Chinese nationals who enjoy no right of abode elsewhere. As of early June 1998, over half of the SAR judges were non-Chinese and all three permanent judges were foreign nationals. The appointment of Andrew Kwok-nang Li as Chief Justice and Henry Litton, Kemal Bokhary and Charles Ching as the local, permanent CFA justices has been highly praised. The first overseas panel of jurists[7] has also been highly regarded by the public.

Article 85 deals with judicial independence and provides that 'Members of the judiciary shall be immune from legal action in the performance of their judicial functions.' This provision is certainly necessary but not adequate, for challenges come also from non-governmental sources. In the case of *Secretary for Justice vs. Oriental Press Ltd. & Others*,[8] which Cullen examines in detail in Chapter 7, the chief editor and controller of the *Oriental Daily* was held guilty of contempt of court for publishing a series of articles vilifying the judiciary and for subjecting a judge to paparazzi harassment. The Court of First Instance ruled that the defendant's conduct jeopardized the rule of law by 'scandalizing the court' and 'interfering with the administration of justice as a continuing process'. Such conduct 'could not be said to be an exercise of the right of freedom of expression at all.'

The *Oriental Daily* is one of the two most powerful local printed media. Together with its sister newspaper, the *Sun Daily* and its rival, *The Apple Daily*, they account for about three-quarters of the daily newspaper sales in the SAR as of mid-1999. To uphold judicial independence, the court must stand up to challenges from such powerful public media as well.

Application of the laws of the SAR

One tenet of the principle of judicial independence is that the judiciary obeys only the law. What constitutes the law must be of interest to students of judicial independence.

The laws applicable in the Region

According to Article 84, 'The courts of the SAR shall adjudicate cases in accordance with the laws applicable in the Region as prescribed in Article 18 of this Law and may refer to precedents of other common law jurisdictions.' Article 18 says, 'The laws in force in the SAR shall be this Law, the laws previously in force in Hong Kong as provided for in Article 8 of this Law, and the laws enacted by the legislature of the Region.' But the Article goes on to provide for the application of certain national laws in the SAR. There are then five categories of laws applicable in the SAR, namely the Basic Law; the laws previously in force in Hong Kong; the laws enacted by the SAR legislature; certain national laws; and precedents of other common law jurisdictions. As to the laws previously in force in Hong Kong, Article 8 lists the common law, rules of equity, ordinances, subordinate legislation and customary law, 'except for any that contravene this law, and subject to any amendment by the legislature of the SAR.' The validity of these provisions has since been confirmed by the Court of Appeal in the *SAR v Ma Wai Kwan* case.[9]

Application of national laws

Although the SAR is supposed to be a separate region from the mainland, there are certain PRC laws that must apply also to the SAR. According to Article 18:

> National laws shall not be applied in the SAR except for those listed in Annex III to this Law. The laws listed therein shall be applied locally by way of promulgation or legislation by the Region. The Standing Committee of the NPC may add to or delete from the list of laws in Annex III after consulting its Committee for the Basic Law of the SAR and the government of the Region. Laws listed in Annex III to this Law shall be confined to those relating to defence and foreign affairs as well as other matters outside the limits of the autonomy of the Region as specified by this Law.

In Annex III, six national laws appears on the list, covering such subjects as the capital, calendar, national anthem, national flag, national day, national emblem, the territorial sea, nationality, and diplomatic privileges and immunities. The list will probably get longer as time passes and the need to add to it is acted upon.

Some questions remain. Does the PRC Constitution apply to the SAR in part under the 'one country, two systems' arrangement? If not, can it be interpreted at a later stage so that it does? If so, under what circumstances? Can the NPC indirectly interfere in the work of the SAR judiciary by means of legislation? Can the practice of the PRC regarding the exercise of judicial power be imposed on the SAR by means of such a piece of legislation? These questions require careful analysis. For the time being, the answers might well be in the negative or, if in the positive, treated benignly. In the future it is more difficult to say.

What deserves particular attention is the following provision in Article 18:

> In the event that the Standing Committee of the NPC decides to declare a state of war or, by reason of turmoil within the SAR which endangers national unity or security and is beyond the control of

the government of the Region, decides that the Region is in a state of emergency, the CPG may issue an order applying the relevant national laws in the Region.

Can the principle of judicial independence survive the declaration of a state of war or a state of emergency? Since the judgement about what endangers national unity or security is quite subjective, and whether any turmoil is beyond the control of the SAR government is entirely in the purview of the CPG, this provision effectively gives the CPG a blank cheque to apply national laws to the SAR by declaring emergency. Once that is done, the SAR's autonomy will no doubt be suspended. The independence of the judiciary might well become irrelevant.

Precedents of other common law jurisdictions

Precedents are essential to common law. It is almost impossible to make the common law system work without resort to precedents. Hong Kong courts have all along habitually cited precedents of other common law jurisdictions. It is not surprising that Article 84 of the Basic Law stipulates that SAR courts 'may refer to precedents of other common law jurisdictions' in adjudicating cases. In an April 1999 ruling of *HKSAR v Ng Kung-sui & Another*, for instance, the Court of Appeal cited the opinion of Justice Brennan in two US Supreme Court cases, *Texas v Johnson* 491 US 397 (1989) and *United States v Eichman* 496 US 310 (1990).[10]

The *HKSAR v Ng Kung-sui & Another* is a flag desecration case. In its ruling, the Court of Appeal declared that certain provisions of two flag ordinances on national and SAR flags enacted by the Provisional Legislative Council (PLC)[11] were 'inconsistent with Article 19 of the International Covenant on Civil and Political Rights (ICCPR) and therefore contravened Article 39 of the Basic Law.' Article 19 of the ICCPR protects freedom of expression and Article 39 of the Basic Law validates the ICCPR in Hong Kong courts. The conviction was overturned. Not surprisingly, it became a test case. Community reactions to the Court of Appeal verdict were clearly divided. The pro-Beijing voices seem to be nearly unanimous that any question about national flag 'is a matter of one country'. They caution the CFA not to commit yet another 'mistake' as it did in the right of abode case. Their critics, in contrast, insist that the whole question of flag ordinances belongs to the realm of autonomy and should not be confused with matters of national defence or foreign policy. Furthermore, the freedom of expression guaranteed by the ICCPR should be upheld. At the time of writing the case rests on an application for leave to appeal to the CFA by the Department of Justice on 21 April 1999.

The interpretation of law and judicial review

The interpretation of law is a function closely connected to the rule of law and judicial interpretation of law is a core feature of the separation of power. As A.V. Dicey put it, 'Powers, ... conferred or sanctioned by statute are never unlimited, for they are confined by the words of the Act itself, and ... by the interpretation put upon the statute by the judges.'[12]

The power of interpretation of the constitutional instrument usually implies a power to review the constitutionality of lesser laws and regulations, and is generally referred to as judicial review. This power is normally vested in the judicial organs in most, if not all, common law jurisdictions. But the SAR has a system that is markedly different. According to Article 158, the power of interpretation of the Basic Law is vested in the NPC Standing Committee. The SAR courts may interpret provisions of the Basic Law but only in adjudicating cases and only with limited jurisdictions. People who are familiar with the common law system and the rule of law find this arrangement difficult to understand.

The Basic Law confers several kinds of power in this regard. They include the power to return a law enacted by Legco without amendment, to declare the laws previously in force in Hong Kong contravenes the Basic Law, to interpret the Basic Law, and to interpret Basic Law provisions in adjudicating cases. Of these, the first three come under the NPC Standing Committee. Only the last belongs to the SAR courts.

Powers of the NPC Standing Committee

By Article 17, paragraph 3 of the Basic Law, the NPC Standing Committee might, after consulting its Committee for the Basic Law, return without amendment any law enacted by Legco. The conditions are that the law in question regulates affairs within the responsibility of the central authorities or the relationship between the CPG and the SAR and is not in conformity with the Basic Law. Any law so returned is immediately, though not retroactively, invalidated. This power to return SAR legislation virtually gives the NPC Standing Committee the power of supervision that may affect the scope of laws applicable to the SAR. For what is or is not conforming to the provisions of the Basic

Law can be subjectively interpreted either broadly or narrowly by the body holding such power of interpretation.

According to Article 160:

> Upon the establishment of the SAR, the laws previously in force in Hong Kong shall be adopted as laws of the Region except for those which the Standing Committee of the NPC declares to be in contravention of this Law. If any laws are later discovered to be in contravention of this Law, they shall be amended or cease to have force in accordance with the procedure as prescribed by this Law.

By implication, the NPC Standing Committee has the power to declare certain laws previously in force in Hong Kong to be in contravention of the Basic Law. On the basis of Article 160 and proposals made by the Preparatory Committee of the SAR, the NPC Standing Committee adopted in February 1997 a decision which spelled out certain principles and listed different categories of ordinances and regulations not to be adopted or to be subject to modification, adaptation, limitation or exception.[13]

That the general power of interpretation of the NPC Standing Committee granted by Article 158(1) is the primary and ultimate power to review the constitutionality of SAR legislation is beyond question. Notwithstanding the autonomy of the SAR, and that the Basic Law is the 'constitution' of the region, the final say on the meaning of the Basic Law is not to be made by anybody in Hong Kong. Paragraph 2 of Article 158 says, 'The Standing Committee of the NPC shall authorize the courts of the SAR to interpret on their own, in adjudicating cases, the provisions of the Basic Law which are within the limits of the autonomy of the Region.' This is a compromise. Effectively, two ways of authoritative interpretations, the legislative and the judicial, are permitted in the realm of the autonomy of the region. If left at this, the system might work well, for the judicial interpretation might be the norm and the legislative interpretation needs not be invoked except in extraordinary situations. However, that is not a safe statement. Judging by the action of the SAR government in relation to the right-of-abode case, what amounts to extraordinary can be controversial. The executive branch is likely to invoke what suits its political or policy needs.

Paragraph 4 of Article 158 says, 'The Standing Committee of the NPC shall consult its Committee for the Basic Law of the SAR before giving an interpretation of the Basic Law.' This, some suggest, makes the Committee for the Basic Law a mini-constitutional court. Perhaps not so. But, such talk aside, the role of that Committee can still be quite significant.

SAR courts' power of judicial review

By virtue of Article 81 and Articles 158 (2) and (3), the SAR courts enjoy some power of judicial review in adjudicating cases. Article 81 provides for the establishment of the court system and upholds the judicial system previously practised in Hong Kong. Article 158(2) grants the SAR courts the power of judicial review in adjudicating cases in the realm of SAR autonomy, as explained earlier. This power the courts may exercise 'on their own'. By Paragraph 3 of the same article, the SAR courts may also interpret 'other provisions of the Basic Law' but special restrictions apply. They are required to seek, through the CFA, an interpretation from the NPC Standing Committee of provisions in two excluded categories, namely those concerning affairs which are the responsibilities of the CPG and the relationship between the central authorities and the region. The Standing Committee's interpretation shall be binding, although 'judgements previously rendered shall not be affected.'

In the process of drafting the Basic Law, a debate took place between mainland and Hong Kong members of the Drafting Committee. Hong Kong members wanted to retain the existing system of judicial interpretation. But mainland members had to work under the PRC Constitution which vests the power of interpretation in the NPC Standing Committee. In a consultation report of the Basic Law Consultative Committee (a Hong Kong body) dated October 1988, it was pointed out that procedures such as those stipulated in Article 158 'will make the courts of the SAR unable to handle cases independently, which may jeopardize judicial independence.'[14] Specifically, objections were raised with regard to the power of the NPC Standing Committee, 'a non-judicial organ of a non-common law country', to interpret the Basic Law on its own initiative. The report said such a power could 'undermine the judicial independence of the SAR and interfere with the adjudication of'[15] or 'allow the CPG to interfere in the operation of'[16] the courts of the SAR.

This is complicated and troublesome. Even former Justice Li Fook Sin, known for his readiness to co-operate with Beijing, said so in a May 1988 interview.[17] Instead of requiring a prior interpretation from the NPC Standing Committee that necessitates the suspension of a case, Li would have preferred that such power of interpretation be delegated to the SAR courts. Should any court make a mistake, the NPC Standing Committee could always render its own more authoritative interpretation, he said. However, pro-Beijing sources argued that 'the Basic Law will form part of the Chinese legal system' and, under the premise of '"one country, two systems", it is unrealistic to propose solutions from a single standpoint'. Therefore, in order to make two different legal systems work in concert, the arrangement as stipulated in the Article was acceptable.[18] Hence, Article 158 stands as is.

The right-of-abode case

In this connection, it is useful to take another close look at the rulings of CFA issued in January 1999 in the right-of-abode cases discussed in Chapter 1.[19] The rulings involved two issues with important bearings on judicial independence: the constitutional jurisdiction of the SAR courts, especially with regard to the legislative acts of the NPC and its Standing Committee, and the right of abode of the SAR permanent residents' mainland-born children, especially with regard to those born out of wedlock or born before a parent qualified as a permanent resident. The constitutional jurisdiction issue involves Hong Kong courts' power of judicial review as provided for in Articles 158(2) and 158(3). The right-of-abode issue pertains to the meaning of certain provisions in two Basic Law articles, Articles 24(2) and (3) and Article 22(4). Both issues gave rise to an incidence of executive interference in judicial independence.

By Article 24(2), 'persons of Chinese nationality born outside Hong Kong' of Hong Kong's permanent residents are listed as permanent residents themselves. Their parents must be Chinese citizens born in Hong Kong or having 'ordinarily resided in Hong Kong for a continuous period of not less than seven years' before or after the establishment of the SAR. However, Article 22(4) says that people from other parts of China must apply for approval in order to enter the SAR. Furthermore, those who 'enter the Region for the purpose of settlement' shall be subject to a quota to be determined by the competent authorities of the CPG after consulting the SAR government. This provision in Article 22(4), in turn, raises two questions: whether the right of abode provided for in Article 24(2) is conditioned by Article 22(4); and whether the CFA is obliged to refer this matter for interpretation to the Standing Committee of the NPC in accordance with Article 158(3).

Two ordinances are germane to the cases. Based on Article 22(4), the PLC enacted on 1 July 1997 the Hong Kong Immigration (Amendment) (No 2) Ordinance excluding mainland children born to parents who did not have right of abode at the time of birth and those born out of wedlock (in cases where the parent is a father) from the right of abode entitlement under Article 24(2) of the Basic Law. Moreover, on 10 July 1997, the PLC further enacted the Immigration (Amendment) (No.3) Ordinance and made its effect retroactive to 1 July 1997. By its Section 2AA(2), even those with the right of abode may exercise that right only if they have a 'certificate of entitlement' issued by the SAR government affixed to a 'travel document' issued by a competent mainland government unit.

The judgements of the CFA surprised many people. The SAR government was caught unprepared.[20] In two unanimous judgments on four cases before it and signed by all five justices, the CFA said the following:

- *The courts of the region have the jurisdiction to 'examine whether any legislative acts of the NPC or its Standing Committee are consistent with the Basic Law and to declare them to be invalid if found to be inconsistent'* (emphasis added).
- The court does not have to make a reference to the NPC Standing Committee for an interpretation of Article 24(2) even though Article 22(4) is 'arguably relevant'.
- Article 24(2) confers the right of abode in unqualified terms on permanent residents, including children born out of wedlock or born before a parent qualified as a permanent resident.
- Provisions in the Immigration (Amendment) (No. 2) and (No. 3) Ordinances contravening the Basic Law are null and void.
- Persons seeking recognition in the cases have been as from 1 July 1997 and are permanent residents within the third category in Article 24(2) of the Basic Law.
- The decisions of the Director of Immigration denying persons in the litigation the right of abode, detaining them in custody or requiring them to enter into a recognizance, or demanding a 'certificate of entitlement' affixed to a 'travel document' to establish or exercise the right to abode are quashed.

To say the CFA rulings were immediately controversial is an understatement. It threatened the SAR with a constitutional crisis. First, within the Hong Kong community, the Bar Association spokesman, leading lawyers and constitutional law scholars hailed the judgments as a landmark that will go a long way in upholding Hong Kong's rule of law. The pro-Beijing commentators charged that the CFA had committed a serious mistake that could not go uncorrected. Basic Law Committee members Raymond Wu, Maria Tam and Albert Chen criticized the CFA saying, among other things, that its failure to refer the interpretation of Article 22(4) to the Standing Committee would cause the SAR to lose the CPG's trust.[21] At the same time, individuals and families directly affected by CFA rulings came out of hiding and petitioned the government *en masse* for permission to stay in Hong Kong. Meanwhile, the Chief Executive and other government officials were saying that the judgments were unfortunate and would put a heavy burden on Hong Kong's already strained social services.

On 5 February 1999 Beijing expressed its displeasure through four prominent mainland legal scholars, Xiao Weiyun, Shao Tianren, Wu Jianfan, and Xu Congde.[22] In their view, the CFA had put itself above the national government when it asserted its power to review legislation by the NPC and its Standing Committee. They went as far as to argue that the SAR is not a sovereign entity and the CFA enjoys no power of judicial review. They stressed that it is important that Hong Kong people understand that 'one country' is the premise for 'two systems'. They did not believe granting the right of abode to mainland children born out of wedlock was a wise decision and remonstrated that the CFA would have to carry its historical responsibility when it makes such erroneous judgments. Needless to say, the impact was phenomenal.

On 12 February the government dispatched Elsie Leung, the Secretary for Justice, to Beijing with a mission to 'further communicate'. Leung returned with some kind of understanding with officials of the Hong Kong and Macao Affairs Office and of the NPC Standing Committee. On 24 February Leung made a formal application to the CFA, requesting a clarification of that part of its ruling in which it asserted a power of judicial review over legislative acts of the NPC and its Standing Committee. The shocked legal community was in an uproar. For the procedure was seen as unprecedented and highly questionable as it inevitably put the CFA in a questioned and precarious position. The SAR's judicial independence was said to be in jeopardy for reasons of politics. The court was urged strongly to reject the government's application.

It should be pointed out that the constitutional system of the PRC is based on the idea of a people's congress system, not a separation of power. Constitutionally the NPC assumes all political power in the name of the people and the executive and judicial branches are required to make reports to the NPC. Power relations are vertical. The NPC constitution provides that the superior organ has the power to review and can nullify the legislation or decisions of the subordinate organ. In this system, it is not conceivable that the court of a lower level government can have the power of judicial review by which the legislative act of a higher level government is declared unconstitutional.

The constitutional system of the SAR is closer to the separation of power model where power relations are horizontal. The judiciary is independent, not only from the executive but also from the legislature. The court's constitutional jurisdiction is traditional and considered innate. However, under the 'one country, two systems' formula, Hong Kong's 'constitution', the Basic Law, was enacted by the NPC and is subject to interpretation by the NPC Standing Committee. A host of important constitutional questions are necessarily new and unanswered, for example, which provisions of the PRC Constitution apply to the SAR and which do not? The contest for power as reflected in the January 1999 judgments of the CFA represents but one logical manifestation of problems inherent in this unique arrangement.

On 26 February the five justices complied with a short statement of clarification[23] in the face of 'an exceptional situation'. It said that the court's judicial power is derived from the Basic Law; and its power of judicial interpretation of the Basic Law is derived from the authorization from the Standing Committee under Articles 158(2) and 158(3). The court's judgment in January 'did not question the authority of the Standing Committee' to make an interpretation binding on the SAR courts. 'The court accepts that it cannot question that authority.' The final sentence of this short statement reads:

> Nor did the court's judgement question, and the court accepts that it cannot question, the authority of the NPC or the Standing Committee to do any act which is in accordance with the provisions of the Basic Law and the procedure therein.

Strictly interpreted, the CFA has held on to its position that it can question an act of the NPC or the Standing Committee that is *not* in accordance with the provisions of the Basic Law. However, the tone of this sentence is very different from that section of the original judgment that discussed the reference issue. In that discussion, the CFA had asserted that 'it is for the CFA and for it alone to decide' whether a reference was within purview and necessary. It asserted that the provision that had to be interpreted was 'predominantly' not an excluded provision and to make the reference, 'would be a substantial derogation from the Region's autonomy and cannot be right.'

It was reported that Chief Justice Li was given a forewarning by Secretary Leung that a government application for clarification was forthcoming. Most likely, Li was made to understand the reality that the CFA and Hong Kong faced. Reasonable people would surmise that politics did indeed play a role as the justices pondered over the implications of the CFA's answer to the government's application. At any rate, the problem raised by the CFA's assertion of power was considered settled after the 'clarification'.

Yet, the matter did not end there. In May the Legco was informed officially that the Chief Executive had decided to request the NPC Standing Committee to interpret Articles 22(4) and 24(2(3)) of the Basic Law in accordance with its 'true legislative intent'. This was presented in a paper entitled *Right of Abode: the Solution*.[24] The solution to what problem? The government said the interim findings of a survey conducted by the Census and Statistics Department indicated that, given a broad interpretation, the number of persons who may enjoy the right of abode in accordance with category 3 of Article 24(2) after the CFA's January rulings might be as large as 1 675 000. Such an influx would adversely affect Hong Kong's housing, education, employment, transport, other social services and public order.[25]

The request for interpretation spawned another uproar from the Hong Kong legal community. Just the same, Legco endorsed the Chief Executive's request. A report was submitted to the State Council which was duly put to the NPC Standing Committee in mid-June 1999.[26] The NPC Standing Committee consulted its Committee for the Basic Law during the week of 14 June. It is poised to make its first interpretation of the Basic Law by the end of June.

Further complications came in when the Court of Appeal delivered its judgment on the two-way permit holders case on 11 June 1999.[27] The Court quashed the existing removal orders issued by the Director of Immigration against the 17 overstaying two-way permit holders. It held that in the absence of a specified scheme for applications for certificates of entitlement by mainland residents, the Director is obliged to consider materials submitted by an applicant in Hong Kong before making a removal order. However, the applicants still may be subject to another removal order after the Director has considered such material. The Court also refused to grant an order of mandamus to the applicants requiring the Director to specify the manner in which applications can be made since it requires time to come up with a workable scheme. The government said it would apply for leave to appeal to the CFA.

The saga continues as this chapter is submitted for final editing in late June 1999. A paid statement from the tertiary academic sector published in a local newspaper on 22 June severely criticized the SAR government for 'putting itself above the law' and being 'disrespectful of the judicial system and the legislature', among other things. It says, 'using urgency as an excuse, the government has forced the legislature to debate and vote on the government's proposal within 24 hours, despite the fact that it has far-reaching impact for Hong Kong.'

Jurisdictions of the SAR courts

One important message of Article 158, Paragraph 3 is that the SAR courts shall have restricted jurisdictions over 'affairs that are the responsibility of the CPG, or concerning the relationship between the Central Authorities and the Region'. Generally, jurisdictions of the SAR courts are more clearly delineated in Article 19. It says:

> The courts of the SAR shall have jurisdiction over all cases in the Region, except that the restrictions of their jurisdiction imposed by the legal system and principles previously in force in Hong Kong shall be maintained. The courts of the SAR shall have no jurisdiction over acts of state such as defence and foreign affairs. The courts of the Region shall obtain a certificate from the Chief Executive on questions of fact concerning acts of state such as defence and foreign affairs whenever such questions arise in the adjudication of cases. This certificate shall be binding on the courts. Before issuing such a certificate, the Chief Executive shall obtain a certifying document from the Central People's Government.

'Acts of state such as defence and foreign affairs' Are they the same as 'affairs which are the responsibility of the CPG, or concerning the relationship between the Central Authorities and the Region'? Are they the same as 'affairs which are the responsibility of the CPG, or concerning the relationship between the Central Authorities and the Region'? Not quite. 'Acts of state' is certainly 'affairs which are the responsibility of the CPG.' But 'affairs concerning the relationship between the Central Authorities and the Region' are not exactly that. One is compelled to ask: will the courts' jurisdiction, and consequently, judicial independence, be affected by the interpretation of what constitute 'acts of state' or 'the relationship between the central authorities and the region'?

In one post-reversion case, *HKSAR v Ma Wai Kwan*, a three-judge panel of the Court of Appeal ruled on 29 July 1997 that SAR courts have no jurisdiction to question the legality of an act of the sovereign, such as a decision of the NPC. The case was actually a challenge to the legitimacy of the PLC. As a result of that ruling, the PLC was accepted as legitimate, even though the Basic Law provided for no provisional or appointed legislature.

The question of jurisdiction need not relate to defence and foreign affairs. Where the courts of both the mainland and the SAR claim jurisdiction over a case, Hong Kong is also likely to be a loser. We already have two cases in this category as discussed by Tsang in Chapter 1: Cheung Tse-keung, 'the Big Spender', who kidnapped two Hong Kong tycoons, and Lee Yuk Fai, the *feng shui* master, who committed five murders in Hong Kong's Telford Gardens. In these cases, many in Hong Kong's legal profession argued that the two defendants should have been tried in the SAR under SAR law since their criminal deeds were committed primarily in Hong Kong. However, the Secretary for Justice chose to respect the PRC claim that the cases were rightly tried on the mainland in accordance with its law. As things turned out, both defendants were tried in mainland courts, sentenced to death and promptly executed. Had they refrained from travelling to the mainland or had they been tried in Hong Kong, they would still be alive.

The method of determining the SAR courts' jurisdiction and the method of obtaining the NPC Standing Committee's interpretation of Basic Law also make an interesting comparison. In the former, the SAR courts are to 'obtain a certificate from the Chief Executive on questions of fact concerning acts of state' which in turn requires 'a certifying document from the CPG.' In the latter, the SAR courts must 'seek an interpretation of the relevant provisions from the Standing Committee of the NPC through the CFA of the Region. Meticulous indeed. But the matter of jurisdiction is to be handled by the executive bodies, that is, the CPG and the Chief Executive. The matter of interpretation is in the domain of the legislative–judicial bodies, that is, the NPC Standing Committee and the CFA. What is the rationale for this division of labour? Why is the certificate issued by the Chief Executive rather than by the CPG directly? As yet, the answers to these questions are not clear.

Pertinent international factors

When the SAR is put side-by-side with other legal jurisdictions upholding the principle of judicial independence, the likelihood of Hong

Kong overcoming the difficulties discussed above, present and potential, appears greater. However, this need not prevent the SAR from engaging in international judicial assistance or seeking international support. In this connection, the following articles of the Basic Law are pertinent:

- Article 39   The provisions of the International Covenant on Civil and Political Rights, the International Covenant on Economic, Social and Cultural Rights, and international labour conventions as applied to Hong Kong shall remain in force and shall be implemented through the laws of the SAR. The rights and freedoms enjoyed by Hong Kong residents shall not be restricted unless as prescribed by law. Such restrictions shall not contravene the provisions of the preceding paragraph of this Article.
- Article 94   On the basis of the system previously operating in Hong Kong, the Government of the SAR may make provisions for local lawyers and lawyers from outside Hong Kong to work and practise in the Region.
- Article 96   With the assistance or authorization of the CPG, the Government of the SAR may make appropriate arrangements with foreign states for reciprocal juridical assistance.

Since the principle of judicial independence is enshrined in the ICCPR, the incorporation of that document in the Basic Law is indeed very significant. The arrangements for foreign lawyers to work in Hong Kong and international reciprocal juridical assistance are likewise conducive to mutual support for the purpose of upholding judicial independence.

The opposite may be true with regard to Article 23. It says:

> The SAR shall enact laws on its own to prohibit any act of treason, secession, sedition, subversion against the CPG, or theft of state secrets, to prohibit foreign political organizations or bodies from conducting political activities in the Region, and to prohibit political organizations or bodies of the Region from establishing ties with foreign political organizations or bodies.

As Fu explains in Chapter 4 this article was amended from the draft version in the aftermath of the 1989 Tiananmen incident. Clearly, Beijing wanted to limit foreign political involvement in the SAR because Hong Kong was seen as a potential subversion base. Though the article only bans political linkages, the shadow it casts may be a long one.

The hypotheses

Now return to the hypotheses set out at the beginning of this chapter. If my assessment so far is correct, it would seem reasonable to say that Hypothesis One is less tenable than Hypothesis Two. It may be true that Hong Kong's government system is entrenched in the tradition of the rule of law and the principle of judicial independence (Hypothesis One). But there is little ground to assert that judicial independence will be upheld in the SAR as it was in the British period whether the political system is democratic or not (Hypothesis Two).

Reflect further on this. According to Article 63 of the Basic Law, the Department of Justice controls criminal prosecutions, 'free from any interference'. But the discretionary power is not and should not be inunune from public scrutiny. During the past two years, the Department of Justice has twice been taken to task by the legal professions and the public media for alleged 'selective non-prosecution'. The questioned beneficiaries were the Xinhua News Agency in Emily Lau's personal data disclosure request case (as examined in Chapter 7) and Sally Aw in the *Hong Kong Standard* fraud case (analyzed in Chapters 1 and 6). Both cases left the public with the impression that the law treats the powerful and rich differently than the common people. To that, we have to add the 'Big Spender' case and the Telford Gardens murder case referred to above. The SAR government clearly has shown itself to be unable if not unwilling to fight for the SAR in jurisdiction disputes. It seems resigned to the view that, in this contest, the SAR can hardly win whenever the NPC has a clear position.

Readers should have also noticed by now that the performance of the executive differs significantly from that of the judiciary during the first two years of the SAR. The former has been too keen to court Beijing's approval or favour while the latter has time and again been speaking for Hong Kong without fear of offending Beijing. Like it or not, we have to conclude at this stage that the Basic Law provides a weak basis for judicial independence. The SAR might not be able to maintain a strong and independent judiciary. However, a strong and independent judiciary is critical to the protection of human rights and the development of a democratic political system. Unfortunately, the Chief Executive and his supporting élite seem to have doubts and apprehensions about establishing a western liberal democratic system based on individualism at this juncture.

In a nutshell, perhaps one can say that the contradiction between 'one country', and 'two systems' is inherent and will surface now and then. There is a clash of two cultures, in this case, two legal cultures and it is likely to continue.

Notes

1. For comprehensive treatises on the Basic Law of the HKSAR, see Yash Ghai, *Hong Kong's New Constitutional Order: the Resumption of Chinese Sovereignty and the Basic Law* (Hong Kong: Hong Kong University Press, 2nd edn, 1999); Renmin Ribao Haiwaiban, (ed.), *Jibenfa–Chuangzhaoxing de Jiezuo* (The Basic Law – A Creative Masterpiece) (Beijing: Renmin Ribao Chubanshe, 1991); Wang Shuwen (ed.), *Xianggang Tebie Xingzhengqu Jibenfa Daolun* (Introduction to the Basic Law of the HKSAR) (Beijing: Zhonggong Zhongyang Dangxiao Chubanshe, 1990); Xiao Weiyun (ed.), *Yiguo Liangzhi yu Xianggang Jibenfalu Zhidu* (One Country, Two Systems and the Hong Kong Legal System) (Beijing: Beijing Daxue Chubanshe, 1990); Yun Guanping, *et al.* (eds), *Jibenfa Gailun* (Introduction to the Basic Law) (Guangzhou: Daxue Chubanshe, 1993).
2. Beijing maintains that the Basic Law may be a constitutional document but it is not a 'constitution'. It insists that every sovereignty power can have only one constitution and China has the Constitution of the PRC; Hong Kong is not a sovereign entity and therefore cannot have a constitution.
3. Many of the provisions of the Basic Law are based on Section III of Annex I to the Joint Declaration which outlines the CPG's basic policies regarding Hong Kong. The Basic Law elaborates them and in a legal form.
4. Peter Wesley-Smith, *Constitutional and Administrative Law in Hong Kong*, Vol. II (Hong Kong: China & Hong Kong Law Studies, Ltd., 1988) p. 479.
5. See Xiong Xianjue, *Zhongguo Sifa Zhidu* (China's Judicial System) (Beijing: Zhongguo Zhengfa Daxue Chubanshe, 1986), pp. 159–60; Wu Lei (ed.), *Zhongguo Sifa Zhidu* (China's Judicial System) (Beijing: Zhongguo Renmin Daxue Chubanshe, 1988), p. 193; and Chang Hsin, *Zhongguo Falu: Jieshuo yu Shiwu* (Chinese Law: Interpretations and Practices) (Hong Kong: Chinese University Press, 1994), p. 264.
6. See K.S. Liao, 'Judicial Independence and the Legal System', in Weng Song-jan (Byron S.J. Weng) (ed.) *Zhonghua Renmin Gongheguo Xianfa Lunwenji* (Essays on the Constitution of the People's Republic of China) (Hong Kong: Chinese University Press, 1984, 1990), pp. 223–45.
7. The first overseas panel of CFA jurists is composed of Lord Hoffmann and Lord Nicholls, both of the House of Lords; Sir Anthony Mason, former Chief Justice of Australia; Sir Daryl Dawson, former High Court judge of Australia; Lord Cooke of Thorndon, former President of the New Zealand Court of Appeal; and Sir Edward Somers, New Zealand Court of Appeal judge.
8. Court of First Instance, Misc. Proceedings No. 408 of 1998. Full report in *Hong Kong Law Reports & Digest* 1998, 2, pp. 123–78.
9. [1997] HKLRD 761. See also Daniel Fung, 'Paradoxes of Hong Kong's Reversion to China: the First Year (An Abstract)' June 1998 (unpublished).

The court cited the Privy Council's decisions of *AG of the Gambia v Jobe* [1984] AC 689 and *Minister of Home Affairs v Fisher* [1980] AC 319.

10. *HKSAR v Ng Kung Siu & Another* Court of Appeal, Magistracy Appeal No. 563 of 1998. *Hong Kong Law Reports & Digest* 1999, 2, pp. 783–92.

11. The two ordinances in question are the National Flag and National Emblem Ordinance (no. 16 of 1997) (now Cap. 1557) and the Regional Flag and Regional Emblem Ordinance (no. 17 of 1997) (now Cap. 1558).

12. A.V. Dicey, *An Introduction to the Study of the Law of the Constitution* (London: Macmillan, 10th edn, 1979) p. 413.

13. *Decision of the Standing Committee of the NPC on Treatment of the Laws Previously in Force in Hong Kong in Accordance with Article 160 of the Basic Law of the HKSAR of the PRC*. Full unofficial English text in Ghai, op.cit., Appendix 6.

14. The Consultative Committee for the Basic Law of the HKSAR of the PRC, *Draft Basic Law of the HKSAR of the PRC (For Solicitation of Opinions): Consultation Report* (hereafter, *Consultation Report*), Volume 2, October 1988, p. 42, para. 6.4.1.

15. Ibid., para. 6.4.2.

16. Ibid., p. 43, para. 7.3.1–2.

17. *Renmin Ribao* (overseas edition), 5 May 1988.

18. *Consultation Report*, p. 47, para. 9.1.

19. The major decision was issued for three cases together, namely *Ng Ka Ling, et al. v Director of Immigration* (FACV No. 14 of 1998), *Tsui Kuen Nang v Director of Immigration* (FACV No. 15 of 1998), and *Cheung Lai-wah, et al. v Director of Immigration* (FACV 16 of 1998). See also *Chan Kam Nga et al v Director of Immigration* (FACV 13 of 1998).

20. Having won the case at the Court of Appeal level, the government was quite sure, too sure, of a victory at the CFA. Here, one can see how the CFA and the Chief Executive differ in their priorities and values.

21. Albert Chen's views are spelled out at length in his paper, 'The Court of Final Appeal's Ruling in the "Illegal Migrant" Children Case: Congressional Supremacy and Judicial Review', Faculty of Law, The University of Hong Kong, *Law Working Paper Series*, Paper no.24, March 1999.

22. See *Mingbao Daily*, 6 February 1999.

23. The 'clarification' was rendered in the form of another judgment on FACV No. 14–16 of 1998, that is, *Ng Ka Ling, et al. v Director of Immigration* (FACV No. 14 of 1998), *Tsui Kuen Nang v Director of Immigration* (FACV No. 15 of 1998), and *Cheung Lai-wah, et al. v Director of Immigration* (FACV No. 16 of 1998).

24 'Right of Abode: The Solution', a paper tabled at the Legco House Committee special meeting of 18 May 1999. See also, 'Interpretation of Hong Kong's Basic Law', May 1999.

25. Two documents entitled 'Estimates of the number of Mainlanders with Right of Abode in Hong Kong', and 'Judgements of the CFA on the Right of Abode: Estimates of Impact on Services' were circulated and given to the public media. Top level officials gave speeches on the topic, emphasizing the potential negative impact of the CFA judgments. See, for example, Acting Chief Secretary Michael Suen's speech at the Legco House Committee on 6 May 1999.

26. See 'Chief Executive's Report to State Council' 20 May 1999 and 'Chief Executive's Report to State Council put to NPCSC', press release, 10 June 1999.
27. See HKSAR government press release, 11 June 1999 and Statement by Department of Justice, 12 June 1999.

4

The National Security Factor: Putting Article 23 of the Basic Law in Perspective

Hualing Fu*

Introduction

Article 23 is one of the most sensitive articles in the Basic Law. It states:

> The Hong Kong Special Administrative Region shall enact laws on its own to prohibit any act of treason, secession, sedition, subversion against the Central People's Government, or theft of state secrets, to prohibit foreign political organizations or bodies from conducting political activities in the Region, and to prohibit political organizations or bodies of the Region from establishing ties with foreign political organizations or bodies.[1]

Article 23 is fundamental and political as it relates to offences and activities endangering China's national security. This is particularly so when it is imposed by a Communist party state on a liberal and free society. Its remit is potentially wide. As Yash Ghai argues, it is tempting for the government to cast a wide net in implementing it as to limit protections of individual rights provided by other articles in the Basic Law.[2] To a degree, Article 23 is, on the face of it, inconsistent with certain rights and freedoms protected by the Basic Law. Whether Article 23 legislation is consistent with the protection of individual rights depends on how activities listed in Article 23 are defined in enacted legislation and what their parameters are. How the Legislative Council (Legco) in the Special Administrative Region (SAR) enacts laws to comply with it, how courts will interpret such laws and, in general, how the government will respond to this responsibility will help determine the direction which the SAR's political life will take. How Article 23 plays out in practice can be seen as an index of civil liberties enjoyed in Hong Kong. It is a 'battle field' not only between the Hong Kong government (before and after the transition) and the Chinese government, but also among different interest groups, including political parties as they attempt to define Hong Kong's political future according to their own political persuasions and institutional interests.

National security and criminal law

Article 23 offences have variously been referred to as political offences, national security offences or even counter-revolutionary offences. Regardless of the description, they include threats that challenge the fundamental structure of a particular society. These threats can arise from both foreign hostile forces and domestic subversion. In Canada, national security interests include territorial integrity and the democratic process of government; and threats to national security can arise from foreign intelligence activities, domestic subversion and terrorism. In Australia, national security concerns include espionage, active measures by a foreign power through agents of influence, misinformation and deceptive action, domestic subversion and sabotage.[3]

Several points should be made about national security offences. First, each country has different priorities with regard to national security concerns owing to 'its own character, interests, and vulnerability'.[4] Peter Hanks argues that the precise meaning of a national security threat 'lie[s] in the broad geopolitical and strategic factors on which the version ... of the concept have been based.'[5] National character abounds in identifying the elements of national security.

Second, the term 'national security' is elastic, vague, controversial and is incapable of precise definition. The courts have given it different interpretations at different times. It concerns matters relating to sedition, subversion or treason, which are probably the most controversial offences in common law. Yet it is so important that in both domestic constitutions and in international law, rights and freedom have been suspended in its interest, and the abuse of power by government has been justified in its name. The invocation of national security has clearly outweighed other considerations. And a national government is generally entitled to determine when a national security concern arises.[6]

Third, a state reacts strongly when it perceives a threat to its national security. Many political crimes are created at such moments of crisis and then remain permanently on the statute book. The British Official Secrets Act (OSA) 1911, for instance, primarily targeted German spies who flagrantly engaged in espionage in the United Kingdom (UK) before the First World War, but it remained after the war.[7] When Canada became involved in the Korean War, the offence of treason was amended to include aiding any armed forces against which Canadian forces were engaged in hostilities.[8] China's National Security Law was passed to counter the perceived threats posed by 'hostile foreign forces' after the 1989 Tiananmen movement. Article 23 of the Basic Law as it is was added to the draft Basic Law by the Chinese government to prevent Hong Kong from becoming a base for over-throwing Communist rule on the mainland.

Fourth, these offences, specific in their origins, have little application in contemporary societies. With the exception of the OSA in the UK,[9] they have rarely been used since the Second World War. Political trials of different kinds have virtually disappeared in western democracies; vehement political dissidence is simply tolerated.[10] The suspension of political prosecutions, however, does not mean that activities threatening a state's fundamental interests have not been punished. There has been a depoliticization process in which political activities are increasingly punished by ordinary criminal legislation. Public order offences, such as unlawful assembly, become an important alternative to more political charges, such as seditious libel.[11] In British Hong Kong, immigration offences and deportation used to constitute the primary measures against Communists.[12] The enemies are no longer traitors, spies, counter-revolutionaries or subversives, they are now terrorists, rioters, fundamentalists and so on. This de-politicization process has also taken place in China recently when the amended Criminal Law replaces counter-revolutionary offences with national security offences. However, the reform might represent no more than a switch to a less offensive name in the sense that all the previous counter-revolutionary offences can still be punished by different provisions of the new criminal law.[13]

Finally, subsequent punishment through political trials and perse-cution in public is replaced by more covert political surveillance by each national security establishment. Covert political surveillance has been intensified in the major common law jurisdictions. Western democracies became, as the cold war progressed, national security states and surveillance societies. Political control became more preven-tive and proactive. It also became more expansive and assertive. Well equipped national security agencies enable each state to respond to potential threats to national security before they mature. For western democracies today the immediate threats to civil liberties are not the

classical political trials, but the abuse of power by their national security agencies and, consequently, the 'normalization' of the use of
emergence powers.[14]

The political context of Article 23

The 1989 Tiananmen movement and its subsequent political suppression generated unprecedented fear in Hong Kong for the future erosion
of civil liberties after the transition. It accelerated and deepened Hong
Kong's democratization process. Article 23 was a direct consequence of
the suppression and presented a direct threat to liberties in Hong Kong.
Because the offences in it were not defined, there were concerns that
the Chinese government may impose its definitions in Hong Kong
after the transfer of sovereignty.

Look at the PRC criminal law for indications on how Article 23 may
be complied with, one finds counter-revolutionary offences, recently
renamed as national security offences, which are not clearly defined.
The 'counter-revolutionary purpose' was normally imputed objec-
tively. It was determined by the nature of the act. Once the act was
determined, the subjective aspect of the act was almost irrelevant.
There is little legislative guidance for the court in its application of the
law. The court is able to sweep various forms of harmless political
behaviour into the sedition and subversion category. There is *a priori*
justification for penalising speech against the government. No force or
the threat of force is required.

The prosecution and conviction of Xi Yang, a Hong Kong based jour-
nalist, for stealing state secrets in China in 1994, and the prosecution
and conviction of Wang Dan and Wei Jingsheng for subversion in
1996 highlighted the vagueness of China's criminal law.[15] They caused
widespread fear and concern in Hong Kong that the political prosecution may be brought to Hong Kong because Article 23 contains the
equivalent offences. These political trials on the mainland triggered
legislative efforts in Hong Kong to limit the remit of Article 23.

Hong Kong's concern about applying mainland criminal law within
the SAR is also pragmatic. Theoretically, the jurisdiction of mainland
criminal law cannot be exercised in the SAR against SAR residents.[16]
Hong Kong and the mainland are two equal and mutually exclusive
criminal jurisdictions. The SAR's high degree of autonomy is protected
by the Basic Law. Under the 'one country, two systems' doctrine, its
legal system will remain unchanged after the transition.[17] It will have
a separate and independent criminal law regime. Hong Kong courts

will have exclusive jurisdiction over crimes committed within its boundary by its residents, who will have no duty to abide by PRC criminal law.

The high degree of autonomy of Hong Kong's criminal law may be qualified in two aspects, however. First, all SAR legislation must be consistent with the Basic Law. The National People's Congress (NPC) Standing Committee retains extensive power under Articles 17 and 160 of the Basic Law to review and repeal Hong Kong legislation that is deemed to contravene the Basic Law. The veto power may not need to be actually used, the threat itself may be sufficient to achieve compliance. Second, less visible or invisible political influence could be easily deployed by the Chinese government to affect SAR laws. Beijing's influence over the Chief Executive (CE), other officials and law makers is substantial. The unholy alliance between Beijing's top Communists and Hong Kong's richest capitalists provides the most effective channel for Beijing to influence Hong Kong's political and legal development.

In response to the Tiananmen crackdown the British government adopted several measures to speed up Hong Kong's democratic process. Two events are especially important. The first is the enactment of the Hong Kong Bill of Rights Ordinance (BORO) in 1991 which incorporated the International Covenant on Civil and Political Rights (ICCPR). Section 3(2) of the BORO provides that: 'All pre-existing legislation that does not admit of a construction consistent with this Ordinance is, to the extent of the inconsistency, repealed.' The Letters Patent (a constitutional instrument) was amended to put this into effect.

The incorporation of the ICCPR into Hong Kong's domestic law has had the most profound impact on criminal law and added a constitutional dimension to it. BORO challenges were frequently raised in criminal litigation and the courts have struck down several legislative provisions for BORO inconsistency. At the same time, the government reviewed certain legislative provisions, including the controversial provisions in the Public Order Ordinance (POO) and Societies Ordinance (SO), which were likely to be inconsistent with the BORO, and proposed their repeal. In doing so, the government was able to satisfy those arguing for the wide application of the BORO and at the same time, pre-emptively limit the remit of Article 23.

The second event was Legco electoral reforms. In 1991, the first popularly elected members took their seats, who constituted 30 per cent of Legco. The 1991 electoral reform was sanctioned by both the Chinese and British governments. After Christopher Patten became the last governor he introduced further democratization despite China's strong objection, which eventually led to the 1995 elections. These elections were unique in Hong Kong's history. They were the most democratic ever held in Hong Kong and returned a large group of liberal-oriented legislators (many from the Democratic Party). Popularly elected, they had a stronger sense of representation and tended to be highly critical of both the colonial and the Chinese governments. They were instrumental in compelling the former to legislate on Article 23 according to democratic values and international human rights standards.

It is within this context that the colonial government amended and enacted laws to comply with Article 23, to prevent Article 23 from becoming Beijing's instrument for political suppression and to alleviate widespread fear. These moves were designed also to prevent the post-colonial legislature from casting too wide a net against political dissidents in Hong Kong.

Crimes (Amendment) (No.2) Bill 1996

In anticipation that the Provisional Legislative Council (PLC) would take action after the handover to implement Article 23 by specific legislation to control sedition, subversion, treason and secession, the Hong Kong government, with the support of the Democratic Party, tabled a Crimes (Amendment) (No.2) Bill in November 1996. By which two new offences, secession and subversion were introduced, and certain changes were made to the existing offences of treason and sedition.[18]

The Chinese government had repeatedly refused to discuss issues relating to subversion and secession and, in principle, refused to discuss matters relating to Article 23 offences. It deemed the issue a matter for the SAR legislature. Its response to the tabling of the Bill was swift and firm. The Hong Kong and Macao Affairs Office under the State Council promptly announced that any attempt by the colonial government to legislate any Article 23 offences would infringe upon the authority of the SAR legislature and consequently violate the Basic Law. The Chinese foreign ministry echoed the same view. In December 1996, the Preparatory Committee (PC) for the SAR recommended to the NPC Standing Committee that the Bill, if passed, should not be adopted.[19]

The issue was fiercely debated in Hong Kong, and the concern was aggravated by the high profile prosecutions of Wei Jingsheng and

Wang Dan on the mainland in 1996 for the offence of subverting the government under a loosely defined criminal law provision. According to the Secretary for Security the government tabled the bill because the community was deeply concerned about the remit of Article 23 offences. It hoped that by legislating to prohibit subversion prior to the handover the SAR government would be prevented from enacting an anti-subversion law which would be harsher.[20] The assumption was that a consensus in Hong Kong would make the Chinese government more hesitant to scrap the law and replace it with a more restrictive one.[21]

This was precisely the reason why the Chinese government opposed the proposal. On the surface, the central issue appeared to be a legal one: whether the colonial government had the authority to legislate as it proposed to do, and whether the SAR legislature would be pre-empted. But the political motive was very clear. Hong Kong Affairs Adviser, Elsie Leung, who later became the first Secretary for Justice in the SAR, said that the amendment 'gave a clearer definition of what constituted sedition and treason, something which was not usually clearly spelled out in Chinese Law'.[22] Some PC members, including Lau Siu-kai, indicated that Beijing wanted a tougher law passed by the post-handover legislature. For this reason, it was thought that the amendment could only add to the uncertainty in the community if it were passed because the law would definitely be interpreted as contrary to the Basic Law and be nullified.[23]

When the Bill went to the committee stage,[24] the focus soon shifted from the new offences of subversion and secession to the existing offences of treason and sedition. It became evident after the consultation process that, despite the liberal nature of the draft subversion definition, the legal profession and other deputations did not support the creation of the offences of subversion and secession, for three reasons. First, although the Basic Law did obligate the Hong Kong government to prohibit subversion and secession, it did not necessarily demand that the government create new statutory offences. Second, public order was sufficiently safeguarded by other measures and offences. Finally, the two new offences could be covered by the existing offence of treason.[25]

When the bill emerged from the Bills Committee, it had a very different content. The two new controversial offences were removed. Provisions on treason were not amended because of the constraints of time and resources. The issue was left to the Law Reform Commission. The substantial change proposed by the administration and accepted by the Bills Committee was the amendment in relation to sedition. Under the bill, no offence of sedition would be committed unless the accused had the intention to cause violence or create public disorder or a public disturbance.

At the second reading further amendments were proposed. The Democratic Party proposed to incorporate the concepts of subversion and secession into the provisions of treasonable offences.[26] Emily Lau, an independent, proposed to repeal the offence of sedition.[27] Neither proposal was accepted. But a proposal to water down the offences of treason was adopted, and as a result, section 3 of the Crimes Ordinance on treasonable offences was repealed.

The bill was passed, 23 to 20, on 24 June 1997 after long debates. Governor Patten signed it on 26 June 1997, four days before the hand-over.[28] He said that although he preferred the original government draft, the law as passed was fine. He hoped that the government Bill could provide a very helpful benchmark and the future SAR would find it a useful base for any subsequent on subversion and secession.[29] A spokesman for the Office of the Chief Executive-designate reiterated the Chinese position that the SAR government should enact laws to comply with Article 23, and 'we will not accept these amendments which are themselves confusing, and we will take necessary action to rectify the situation.'[30] But the Ordinance has not become effective. Section 1 of the Ordinance provides that the 'Ordinance shall come into operation on a day to be appointed by the Secretary for Security by notice in the Gazette.' No such notice has been given.

Official secrets ordinance

The UK OSA 1911 was part of Hong Kong law and OSA 1989 was extended to Hong Kong in 1992. By early 1994, local legislators began to criticize the colonial government for failing to address the issue of localizing the UK official secrets legislation. The government was afraid of consulting the Chinese government on this sensitive issue.[31] As the UK laws would lapse on 1 July 1997 there would be a legal vacuum if the law were not localized by then. While it was not ideal to have a legal vacuum, localizing the UK law also ran the risk that China might suspect a British conspiracy and simply scrap any reform in 1997.[32]

The Xi Yang case, the detention of other Hong Kong journalists on the mainland and the strong reactions to them in Hong Kong finally induced the colonial government to localize the OSA.[33] It started secret negotiations with the Chinese government through the Joint Liaison Group (JLG) and an agreement was quickly reached. In September 1994, the Preliminary Working Committee (PWC)[34] recommended localization before 1997 and stated that it would not contravene the Basic Law. Clearly, the Chinese government also had an interest in showing that the Chinese secrets law, which is largely an executive prerogative would not be replicated in Hong Kong. The unexpected Chinese decision was welcomed by civil libertarian legislators, including James To and Christine Loh.[35] By the middle of 1995 an agreement was formally reached in the JLG and the colonial government was ready to take a bill to Legco.[36] In December 1996, the government tabled the Official Secrets Bill in Legco to localize the OSAs. With certain revisions on espionage because of possible ICCPR inconsistency and other minor technical changes, the bill contained the UK OSA 1911, 1920, 1939 and 1989. The Chinese government consented.[37]

Once the bill was tabled, the legislators and other interest groups, including the Bar Association and the Hong Kong Journalists' Association, (re)discovered its draconian aspect and called for its liberalization. The main concern was that the part on espionage, which was enacted in 1911 in the UK was outdated, that it did not provide for a proper defence and that it did not provide the harm test for the unlawful disclosure of certain official secrets. If the bill were passed as it was, it would suppress press freedom and the free flow of information after the transition.[38] The liberal legislators were determined to dilute the law by adding the defence of public interest and prior publications to the bill. They succeeded at the committee stage.

China's consent was however conditional. The condition was that the UK legislation would be localized in its totality, subject to minor technical changes. Through a deputy Director of the Xinhua News Agency Beijing asserted that the secrets law was localized according to a Sino-British agreement, which was binding on the colonial government and its Legco.[39] The colonial government also firmly rejected any proposed change, stressing the fact that the bill was to localize, not to conduct, a comprehensive review of the official secrets legislation.[40]

The alliance between the Chinese and the colonial governments angered many democratic legislators. As Christine Loh said at the resumption of the second reading:

We are told that Britain and China had agreed to the Bill, and as such, any amendment to it runs the risk of the post-1997 government throwing it out. If we were to adopt this attitude, then we might as well not have formed a Bills Committee at all.[41]

The Democrats urged members to accept their amendment. Otherwise, 'the enactment of this Bill will be an unmitigated disaster for the people of Hong Kong',[42] and 'we will live in the dark age'.[43] Despite the efforts, the bill was passed on 4 June 1997 without amendment.[44]

Connection with foreign political organizations

The power to veto Hong Kong legislation by the NPC Standing Committee under Article 160 of the Basic Law can be forcefully deployed. In February 1997, it passed a decision[45] to repeal laws which it said were in contravention of the Basic Law, including major amendments to the Society Ordinance since 1992 and Public Order Ordinance since 1995.

Even in a case in which a dramatic decision is taken, there is room for negotiation and compromise, because the NPC decision, to a large extent, reflected the antagonism between Governor Patten and Beijing. Records have to be corrected if only for the sake of honour and face. But how the repealed laws are to be redrafted after the transition is a totally different matter.

The Societies Ordinance has a long history in Hong Kong. It was liberalised in 1992 to comply with the BORO.[46] Previously a society had to apply within 14 days of its establishment to the Registrar (the Commissioner of Police) for registration or for exemption. The Registrar may accept or refuse registration according to the enumerated grounds. The operation of a society became unlawful if its application was rejected or registration not exempted. One of the grounds for rejection was where the society was a branch of, or was affiliated to, or was connected with any organization or group of a political nature, established outside Hong Kong.[47]

The registration requirement was replaced by a notification requirement after the 1992 amendment, and accordingly, a society only needed to notify the Societies Officer. His discretion was limited. He could prohibit a society only if he 'reasonably believes that the operation or continued operation of a society may be prejudicial to the security of Hong Kong or to public safety or public order.'[48] Foreign political connections *per se* were no longer a ground for prohibition.

The Chinese government claimed that the post-1992 SO was

inconsistent with the Basic Law and should be repealed after the transition, on the grounds, among others, that the deletion of the foreign political connection test violated Article 23 of the Basic Law. In April 1997 the Office of the Chief Executive designate proposed the amendment of the POO and SO.[49] It was to revert to the situation before 1992. It argued that the proposals were based on three principles: to strike a proper balance between civil liberties and social order; to uphold the Basic Law and the parts of the ICCPR applicable to Hong Kong; and to guard against interference by foreign political forces in local political activities.[50] It was adamant that the proposed restrictions were necessary. It stressed that '... we must also take steps to prevent Hong Kong from being used for political activities against China. This has been a long-standing policy of the Hong Kong Government. This policy should be maintained after the establishment of the HKSAR.'[51] In addition, it believed the restrictions were acceptable by international standards and required by Article 23.

The proposed amendments were commonly known as the reinstatement of the draconian/evil laws. The colonial government criticized them as being 'sadly predictable and a retrograde step which will deal a body blow to human rights protection in Hong Kong.' It was also pointed out that they could hardly be reconciled with the Basic Law.[52] The international community led by the US called upon China to re-examine them.[53] Most local political and community organizations were firmly against the amendments.

What were the draconian aspects of the proposed amendments? They restored a registration system abolished in 1992. The Societies Officer was authorized to refuse to register a society if he reasonably believed that such refusal was in the interest of, among others, national security. The final and the most problematic aspect was the prohibition of a society which engaged in political activities in Hong Kong from soliciting or accepting any forms of financial support from an alien or from a foreign organization and from establishing a connection with a foreign political organization.[54]

The main criticism of the amendments was that they were more than necessary and they went far beyond the pre-1992 version of the SO. The Chairman of the Hong Kong Bar Association, Audrey Eu, argued that '... the proposed amendments go much further than Article 23 in seeking to catch foreign influence, and not just foreign political ties, and in seeking to catch aliens and foreign organizations. The entire focus of Article 23 is shifted.'[55] Even some members of the PLC thought terms like 'political body', 'connection' or 'alien' too vague.[56] The colonial government doubted whether mere acceptance of assistance from an alien or foreign political organization, or affiliation with a foreign political organization could be valid grounds under the ICCPR for refusing registration.

The net of prohibition was cast too wide in prohibiting foreign political contributions and influence. As Audrey Eu pointed out, 'In this day and age, in a cosmopolitan, modern democratic society like Hong Kong, it is absurd, if not suicidal, to exclude foreign influence.'[57] Many of the non-government organizations also raised similar concerns, for their major financial sources are often from foreign donations.[58] The Democratic Party and the Hong Kong Alliance in Support of the Patriotic Democratic Movement in China, two leading political bodies disliked by the Chinese government, claimed that they were the true victims of the proposed amendments.[59]

Another issue taken up by the critics was whether donations from Taiwan and mainland China would be prohibited. It was clear that either connection with or donation from Taiwan would be prohibited, the reason, as explained by the post-handover Executive Councillor, Henry Tang, being that Taiwan has a history of influencing foreign governments through political funding.[60] But the Chief Executive designate strongly insisted that donations from mainland China would not be prohibited, as Hong Kong and China are one country and Hong Kong is part of China. In response to the concern that the proposed amendments would encourage the mainland government to influence Hong Kong politics, Tung said that since China is the sovereign entity to which Hong Kong belongs, if China wants to influence Hong Kong, it has many other channels, apart from political donations.[61]

The term political activities was also criticized as being potentially too broad, as human rights groups, environmental groups and labour unions engage in political activities in the broadest sense.[62] Human rights advocacy would be hampered if the amendments were adopted. Religious groups were also concerned. They wondered whether they, too, would be regarded as political. The Secretary for Justice designate responded firmly that they would not be so regarded. She agreed with religious groups that a separate law should be enacted to regulate the political activities of the political parties.[63]

When the Societies (Amendment) Bill 1997 was tabled, it was revised in response to some of the criticisms raised above. The revisions were substantial. The Bill was passed by the PLC and came into effective on 1 July 1997.[64] The prohibition of foreign donations are restricted to

direct or indirect financial contributions from foreign political organizations. The references to 'alien' and 'foreign organizations' were
removed. 'Political body' replaced 'society engaging in political activities', and was defined as 'an organization whose principal function or
main object is to promote or prepare a candidate for an election'.[65]
Non-government organizations existing in Hong Kong would not be
subject to this restriction. 'Foreign political organization', 'political
organization of Taiwan' and 'connection' are also defined with relative
clarity.[66] The prohibition on foreign donations only restricts direct or
indirect financial contributions from foreign political organizations or
political organizations from Taiwan.[67] The 'draconian law' was re-
enacted but its remit was limited and clearly defined.

National security

Considerable restrictions have been imposed in Hong Kong on public
assembly and demonstration, partly due to its nature as a crowded and
bustling place and partly due to the political need to contain, control
and preferably pre-empt riots and disturbances. Control of public
order was achieved through a licensing system, according to which
the holding of a public procession required a licence from the
Commissioner of Police.[68]

Following the enactment of the BORO, the licensing system was
regarded by the colonial administration as inconsistent to it. In 1995
Legco amended the POO in order to comply with the BORO. The most
important change was to replace the original licensing system with a
'notification system'.[69]

After the NPC Standing Committee decided to repeal the 1995
amendment after the handover, the Office of the Chief Executive-
designate undertook to prepare the necessary law in order to fill the
legal vacuum. In April 1997, it published a consultation document
proposing the amendment of the POO. In addition to resurrecting the
licensing system, new grounds were provided for the Commissioner of
Police to reject an application for a procession. In particular, it introduced national security as a ground for rejection. According to this
document, an application for procession should be rejected if the
Commissioner considers it not in the interests of national security or
public safety, public order, the protection of public health or morals or
the protection of the rights and freedom of others.[70]

This provoked a widespread outcry even though the term national
security has been adopted in BORO and the ICCPR as a possible

ground for restricting rights. It was seen as part of the effort of the Chinese government to curtail human rights in Hong Kong principally to protect its interests as a Communist regime on the mainland. Political dissidents are punished on the mainland based on an ill-defined ground of endangering 'national security'.[71] There was a possibility, as noted by a pro-China member in the PC, Kenneth Chow, that the term may be interpreted according to Chinese law.[72]

The bill was severely criticized. The colonial government pointed out that the term national security was used in the ICCPR in a different context. It needs further definition in any domestic legislation.[73] The then Attorney General Jeremy Mathews pointed out that here was no comprehensive and authoritative common law definition of 'national security'. He emphasized, and he was supported by local legal academics, that national security should be limited to the situation when territorial integrity was threatened by force.[74] As such, the proposed amendment in the public order context would be inconsistent with the Basic Law and international human rights covenants.[75] The spokesperson for the Hong Kong branch of Amnesty International, Robyn Kilpatrick, reminded the Chief Executive-designate that 'national security should not become a reason to restrict freedom'.[76] The spokesman for the Alliance in Support of the Patriotic Democratic Movement in China said: 'National security is like a knife hanging over the head of the Alliance. The order of execution lies with Mr Tung.'[77] To alleviate public fear, the Chief Executive-designate responded that 'national security' would be defined in accordance with the common law and within the international covenant,[78] and its use confined to upholding the territorial integrity, national independence and sovereignty of China. He also conceded its interpretation to the courts.[79]

As a result, although the term was retained in the amended POO, its definition was changed and limited to 'the safeguarding of the territorial integrity and the independence of the People's Republic of China'. In addition, the SAR government publicized the Administrative Guidelines on National Security in July 1997 (the Guidelines). According to its spokesman, the Commissioner of Police was given the authority to apply the concept of national security according to the ICCPR, and the ground of national security would be invoked only if the Commissioner believes it reasonable and necessary to do so.[80] More specifically, the Guidelines state that

> in coming to his decision, the Commissioner of Police will take into consideration, among other things, whether or not the declared

purpose of the notified public meeting or procession is to advocate separation from the People's Republic of China including advocacy of the independence of Taiwan or Tibet. [81]

This is a very narrow concept of national security in the sense that it includes only the territorial integrity of China. But the Guidelines are too broad in the sense that they ban any such advocacy even if no violence or no use of force is advocated. In addition, they require the Police Commissioner to determine what constitutes a national security threat to China – an act that politicize the Police. It is not certain whether or not and how the SAR courts may review such police decisions. As former Attorney General Mathews rightly stated, it would be for the executive to decide primarily what constitutes a national security concern, and the scope of judicial review 'would be extremely limited'.[82]

Keeping the common law tradition[83]

The Basic Law requires the SAR government to enact laws to prohibit those activities listed in Article 23. The Basic Law does not require it to create the respective offences in a manner unknown to Hong Kong's common law tradition. The government could comply with the demands in Article 23 without disturbing the existing criminal offences. The sensitive offences of secession and subversion are not formally part of Hong Kong's criminal law. They are part of the mainland criminal law but are vaguely defined and frequently abused. It would help maintain Hong Kong's autonomy if these offences were not added to its criminal law.

One commonly expressed concern is that as subversion is a peculiar Chinese concept and, as a result, the Chinese definition might be imposed upon Hong Kong criminal law. This raised in some people's mind the unacceptable prospect of having to rely on the PRC criminal law for guidance in order to comply with Article 23. But this view is wrong because it takes extremist views about subversion in both common law jurisdictions and in the PRC. It is possible to comply with the common law tradition and satisfy the requirements of Article 23 of the Basic Law.

Although the precise offence of subversion is not an offence in common law, it is misleading to say that subversive activities are not criminal is common law. This is because sedition, blasphemy and treason (all common law offences) provide crucial sanctions for subversive activities. Not every subversive activity is criminalized, but many are and all serious subversive activities are criminalized. While subversion is not an offence in itself in common law, subversive activities can readily be punished by invoking the existing criminal law. Legislatures and the courts have used the term subversion in the course of describing certain criminal offences. Blasphemy has been described as subversive language against Christianity, seditious libel as subversive language against the government, and treason might be committed as a result of a subversive act against the state.[84]

The interesting question is: when the state tries to pre-empt subversive activities by using the criminal law, what criminal offence can be alleged to have occurred, given that subversion is an offence unknown to the common law? In the US, the criminal charge frequently used is conspiring to advocate or teach the forcible overthrow of the US government.[85] In the UK, the most recent prosecutions included the use of the Disaffection Act 1934 in *Arrowsmith*[86] and the OSA 1911 in *Chandler v DPP*.[87] Subversive activities are criminalized if they are genuine threats to national security. In sharp contrast in China subversion is a criminal offence.

It follows that Hong Kong does not need to create a new offence of subversion. Subversive activities can be punished by the existing laws where those activities pass the necessary threshold of criminal liability. The effort made by the colonial administration to create the offence of subversion might have been unnecessary. Hong Kong has an impressive or frightening, depending on your standpoint, array of laws and processes designed to monitor and control subversive activities, which readily satisfy the requirements spelled out in Article 23. The same is true of the offence of secession, which, while not a criminal offence known to common law, is easily punishable under the offence of treason.

Democratic conception of Article 23

National security and respect for human rights are compatible. The promotion of one does not necessarily mean the derogation of the other. As Lustgarten and Leigh point out 'political and civil rights are major constituents of national security *itself*'.[88] They call for 'a democratic conception of national security', which purports to 'strip the concept down to its irreducible minimum': political violence, foreign political influence, invasion and unlawful disclosure of narrowly defined official secrets.[89] Under this minimalist approach, the government should be required to present a comprehensive elaboration of the character of the danger, its degree of seriousness and immediacy, the interests and range of persons affected, the reasonable anticipated duration of the proposed measure, and a credible explanation of why it is likely to achieve results beyond the capacity of existing repressive powers.[90]

By limiting the scope of national security, this approach draws a clear distinction between legitimate dissent and a national security threat. It is a distinction which recognizes the difference 'between, on the one hand, those who wish to overthrow the democratic system or use violence or threats of violence to violate democratic procedures and, on the other hand, those who seek radical change in the social, economic or political arrangements within the democratic system'.[91] A principal milestone of any real democracy is the recognition of the right to dissent, to criticize the government and to uphold and disseminate unpopular opinions. Friedman argues that the problem of distinguishing subversion from legitimate dissent is unique to democratic states.[92] A dictatorial or authoritarian state allows no political dissent: difference means deviance and is suppressed.

A democratic concept means that laws passed in compliance with Article 23 should be consistent with the ICCPR. Article 39 of the Basic Law states that the ICCPR and other specified international instruments as applied to Hong Kong shall remain in force and shall be implemented through the laws of Hong Kong. Ghai has argued that, because of Article 39, 'the ICCPR enjoys a special constitutional status, governing other laws'.[93] Such a view was also adopted by the SAR court in a recent decision. In *Secretary for Justice v. Oriental Press Group Ltd*, Chan CJHC and Keith J held that:

> The effect of art 39 is to permit restrictions on the rights protected in Ch III [of the Basic Law], provided that those restrictions are provided by law (for example, art 16(3) of the Bill of Rights) and are compatible with various international instruments, including the International Covenant on Civil and Political Rights.[94]

As laws passed to implement Article 23 should be consistent with the ICCPR, and restrictions on rights and freedom have to be necessary in a democratic society, the parameters of Article 23 are restricted.

Finally, a democratic concept of Article 23 mandates a vigorous judicial review of any executive power exercised in relation to legislation made in complying with Article 23, including the classification of official secrets and the definition of national security. The judiciary in Hong Kong is burdened with a difficult task of protecting civil liberties. In an executive led political system where the authority of the legislature is restrained and the legislature is only partly directly elected, the judiciary needs to be more creative and innovative to balance executive power. The court should have the right to decide whether a matter is a genuine national security concern, whether a document is properly classified as containing official secrets and above all, whether a law enacted by the SAR legislature is consistent with the Basic Law. It is not certain how the courts will respond to this legal challenge.

The limits of Article 23

The role of law in protecting civil liberties is limited. A well-defined legal test cannot guarantee freedom. Many existing political offences, however vaguely defined, may be buried in the statute books and be rarely, if ever, used. However, a better drafted law did not produce a fair system. As Lobban argues, in the context of political persecution in South Africa in apartheid: 'what appeared to be an ancient offence well honed by authority could be vague in its application, very much depending on a judge's interpretation of intention and facts. In this uneasy space between legitimate protest and sedition, colour would obviously play a major part.'[95]

It would be misleading to think that a 'well honed' law could only be abused in a regime such as South Africa under apartheid. The 'clear and present danger' test invented by the US Supreme Court has been considered to be the most rigid test for sedition. However, according to its critics, as strict as it is, the test protected only 'puny anonymities',[96] and the 'incredible fatuities of the lunatic fringe'.[97] It depends on the judge's subjective interpretation.[98]

Political tradition is more important in protecting civil liberties. Mere penal provisions can never be effective in creating and sustaining an oppressive national security regime. A repressive political culture is essential. When the Rosenburgs were convicted and executed, the courts in the US simply joined in the witch-hunting against communists. The trial paralleled both McCarthyism and the Korean War.[99] Political trials were shaped by political panic and in turn reinforced it. Liberal law cannot protect civil liberties in a repressive age, when previously innocuous activities were regarded as ominous.

Repressive laws are difficult to pass if there is a free and rigorous press, a multi-party system, genuine political participation, and above all, a political culture supportive of civil liberties. Repressive laws, even if passed, cannot be easily enforceable where there is a restrained government and a truly independent judiciary. The courts may inter-pret the law in favour of civil liberties. The application of the OSA in Canada illustrates the point. Judges might give repressive laws a liberal interpretation to such an extent that they defeat the original purpose of the law. A purposive and innovative interpretation of law can expand the scope of political freedom.[100] Even when a judge faithfully applies the repressive law, arguing that it is for Parliament to make the law, a jury may still nullify it.[101]

Hong Kong has had many repressive laws on its statute book, but political prosecution has been rare. Hong Kong's political and legal tradition has determined the extent to which civil liberties are enjoyed. Today, a number of 'draconian' provisions remain in the laws of Hong Kong. But the prophecy of political prosecution and the erosion of civil liberties have yet to be fulfilled. Political activism continues and political protest becomes even louder. A developing political culture on the mainland, which is less conducive to political suppression, allows space for this process to persist.

Conclusion

Hong Kong is now part of the PRC. Under the Basic Law it is meant to enjoy a high degree of autonomy. With regard to its criminal law it is an independent jurisdiction seeking a new identity. The challenge for the SAR is to maintain its self-identity and, at the same time, positions itself within the broad political context of the new sovereign.

The Chinese government has already made an impact on the devel-opment of Hong Kong criminal law. Some of the influences are direct and express, such as the NPC's pronouncement on the illegality of various sections of POO and SO. Others are more subtle and indirect, such as the threat of using the NPC Standing Committee's veto power in relation to the proposed Crimes (Amendment) Bill and the Official Secrets Ordinance.

The Chinese government is most concerned about Article 23 laws in the SAR. Hong Kong has exerted profound economic and cultural influences on the mainland. One can anticipate that its political influ-ence will grow in the future. Hong Kong's democratic process could serve as a catalyst for political reform on the mainland.[102] Beijing has a vested interest in watching closely how the sensitive political activities listed in Article 23 of the Basic Law are regulated in Hong Kong, and in ensuring that political activism there will not be directed at it on the mainland.

But Beijing's political concerns are bound to be vague, extensive and broad. It is inconceivable that they could be entertained in Hong Kong to their full extent (assuming it can be known). Many of their concerns were nationalistic and formalistic and related to issues arising from the Sino-British antagonism in the final years of transition. Even in these circumstances, Beijing showed that it could compromise and was prepared to accommodate local interests in certain cases. As Steve Tsang notes: 'a more assertive population, particularly if ably represented and organized by an adept political leadership, could have secured for themselves a greater say in local politics and perhaps even in the pace or extent of political reform.'[103]

Article 23 as it is would not have existed without the Tiananmen incident of 1989. The basis for its enactment was Beijing's fear of Hong Kong being used as a base for the overthrow of the Communist rule on the mainland. Now the fear seems to have been diminished to a great extent and the new generation of Communist leadership is much more confident in the SAR's self-governance,[104] the political circumstances that produced Article 23 no longer exist. The Basic Law (not to mention Hong Kong's tradition and material and human resources) provides firm ground for active assertiveness of Hong Kong's interests in enacting laws to comply with Article 23 of the Basic Law. Article 23 is only an enabling provision. Any power exercized by the executive in Hong Kong cannot come from Article 23 but from legislation enacted in pursuance of Article 23. They will be made by the Legislative Council, applied by the independent judiciary, and operated in the existing legal system in Hong Kong.

Notes

*   The author wishes to thank Johannes Chan, Albert Chen, Pinky Choy, Richard Cullen, Yash Ghai, Peter Wesley-Smith and Steve Tsang for their comments on earlier drafts of this paper.

1. *The Basic Law of the Hong Kong Special Administrative Region of the People's Republic of China* (Hong Kong: One Country Two Systems Economic Research Institute Ltd., 1992).
2. Yash Ghai, *Hong Kong's New Constitutional Order: The Resumption of Chinese Sovereignty and the Basic Law* (Hong Kong: Hong Kong University Press, 1997).

3. H.P. Lee, P.J. Hanks, and V. Morabito, *In the Name of National Security: The Legal Dimension* (NSW: LBC Information Services, 1995); and Laurence Lustgarten and Ian Leigh, *In from the Cold: National Security and Parliamentary Democracy* (Oxford: Clarendon Press, 1994).

4. Lustgarten and Leigh, ibid., p. 3.

5. Peter Hanks, 'National Security – A Political Concept,' *Monash University Law Review*, Vol. 14 (1988), p. 117.

6. It is likely that many national security claims 'turn out on closer examination to be no more than disguised attempts by a favored class, ethnic group, or political–military élite to seize some advantage for itself.' Lustgarten and Leigh, *In from the Cold*, p. 8.

7. James Michael, *The Politics of Secrecy* (London: Penguin, 1982).

8. Law Reform Commission of Canada, *Crimes against the State* (Canada: Law Reform Commission of Canada, 1986), p. 10.

9. Michael, *The Politics of Secrecy*.

10. Eric Barendt, *Freedom of Speech* (Oxford: Clarendon Press, 1985).

11. Michael Lobban, 'From Seditious Libel to Unlawful Assembly: Peterloo and Changing Face of Political Crime c1770–1820', *Oxford Journal of Legal Studies*, Vol. 10 (1990), p. 306.

12. Lo Ah, *Zhengzhibu Huiyilu* (Memories of Special Branch, RHKP) (Hong Kong: Hong Kong Institute of Asia-Pacific Studies, The Chinese University of Hong Kong, 1997).

13. The key offences, including treason, secession, espionage, subversion, sedition have been renamed state security offences. Many counter-revolutionary offences were abolished only when the same activities were covered by other criminal offenses. Others are regrouped into state security offences and ordinary offences. For a critical analysis see *Whose Security? 'State Security' in China's New Criminal Code* (New York: Human Rights in China and Human Rights Watch/Asia, 1997).

14. Lustgarten and Leigh, *In from the Cold*.

15. H.L. Fu and Richard Cullen, *Media Law in the PRC* (Hong Kong: Asia Law and Practice, 1997).

16. H.L. Fu, 'The Relevance of Chinese Criminal Law to Hong Kong and its Residents' *Hong Kong Law Journal*, Vol. 27 (1997), p. 229.

17. Ghai, *Hong Kong's New Constitutional Order*.

18. Subversion was defined as: 'A person who (a) does any unlawful act with the intention of overthrowing the Government of the United Kingdom by force; (b) incites or conspires with any other person to overthrow the Government of the United Kingdom by force; or (c) attempts to overthrow the Government of the United Kingdom by force, is guilty of subversion and liable on conviction on indictment to imprisonment for 10 years.'

Secession was defined as: 'A person who incites or conspires with any other person or who attempt to supplant by force the lawful authority of the Government of the United Kingdom in respect of any part of the United Kingdom or in respect of any British dependent territory is guilty of secession and liable on conviction on indictment to imprisonment for 10 years.'

19. 'Decision of the Preparatory Committee of the Hong Kong Special Administrative Region of the National People's Congress on Problems

relating to the Legislation on Article 23 of the Basic Law,' *People's Daily*, 13 December 1996.

20. Chris Yeung, 'Patten move sure to anger China', *South China Morning Post (SCMP)*, 27 November 1996.

21. Ibid.

22. Linda Choy, 'Beijing will want to take tougher line', *SCMP*, 27 November 1996.

23. Ronald Arculli, 'Subversion bill just political posturing', *SCMP*, 5 December 1996. According to a NPC 1990 decision, the PC was to be set up by the NPC in 1996 for the purpose of preparing the establishment of the SAR. See *Decision of the National People's Congress on the Method for the Formation of the First Government and the First Legislative Council of the Hong Kong Special Administrative Region* (4 April 1990).

24. At the Bills Committee, some boycotted the deliberations because they thought the matter should be reserved for the post-handover legislature. As a result, the pro-democracy members dominated the discussions.

25. Legco, *Report of the Bills Committee on the Crimes (Amendment) (No. 2) Bill 1996* (Paper for the House Committee meeting on 13 June 1997), Ref.: CB2/BC/6/96.

26. The Democratic Party did not agree to create the two offences. Its ideal solution was to amend Article 23 and to take out subversion and secession.

27. *Hong Kong Hansard*, 23 June 1997, pp. 270–3.

28. Crimes (Amendment) (No. 2) Ordinance 1997.

29. *SCMP*, 25 June 1997, p. 1.

30. Ibid.

31. Michael Smith, 'Post-1997 secrets law still up in the air', *Hong Kong Standard*, 1 March 1994.

32. Mary Blinks, 'State Secrecy Dilemma', *Eastern Express*, 4 August 1994.

33. Article 19 and the Hong Kong Journalists Association, *Freedom of Expression in Hong Kong: 1994 Annual Report* (30 June 1994) and *Broken Promises: Freedom of Expression in Hong Kong, 1995 Annual Report* (30 June 1995); and Chris Yeung, 'Proposal "threat" to China', *SCMP*, 11 June 1996.

34. The PWC was set up in 1993 by the NPC Standing Committee to do preparatory work before the establishment of the PC in 1996. See Albert Chen, 'Legal Preparation for the Establishment of the HKSAR: Chronology and Selected Documents', *Hong Kong Law Journal*, Vol. 27 (1997), p. 405.

35. M.Y. Sung and Moria Holden, 'PWC call to adopt Britain's secrets act', *Hong Kong Standard*, 7 September 1994.

36. Wing Kay Po, 'Localization of secrets act planned', *Eastern Express*, 25 July 1995.

37. Secretary for Security, *Hong Kong Hansard*, 4 June 1997, pp. 101–2.

38. The OSA was also criticized for wider in scope than required by Article 23, which only prohibits the 'theft of State secrets'.

39. *Ta Kung Pao*, 14 December 1996.

40. *Hong Kong Hansard*, 4 June 1997, p. 103.

41. *Hong Kong Hansard*, 4 June 1997, p. 92.

42. *Hong Kong Hansard*, 4 June 1997, p. 204.

43 *Hong Kong Hansard*, 4 June 1997, p. 205.

44. On the day of voting, several key supporters of the amendment from the

Democratic Party had left the Council early to attend the anniversary of the 1989 democracy movement in China and missed the voting. See *Hong Kong Journalists Association Annual Report 1997*, p. 5.

45. *Decision of the Standing Committee of the National People's Congress on the Treatment of the Laws Previously in Force in Hong Kong in accordance with Article 160 of the Basic Law of the Hong Kong Special Administrative Region of the People's Republic of China* (Adopted by the Standing Committee of the Eighth National People's Congress at its 24th session on 23 February 1997).
46. Societies (Amendment) Ordinance No. 75 of 1992.
47. For a thoughtful analysis, see Johannes Chan, 'Human Rights: From One Era to Another', in Joseph Cheng (ed.) *The Other Hong Kong Report 1997* (Hong Kong: Chinese University Press, 1997).
48. Section 2, Societies (Amendment) Ordinance No. 75 of 1992.
49. Chief Executive's Office, *Civil Liberties and Social Order: Consultation Document* (Hong Kong: Chief Executive's Office, Hong Kong Special Administrative Region, People's Republic of China, 1997).
50. Ibid.
51. Ibid., p. 11.
52. Hong Kong Government, *Commentary on Civil Liberties and Social Order Consultation Document* (Hong Kong Government, April 1997). 'Government's response to human rights recommendations', 19 January 1997.
53. 'Britain will express its discontent about the repeal of laws by Preparatory Committee through diplomatic means', *Ming Pao*, 21 January 1997; Lin Xiujuan, 'US urges China to consider the proposal for repealing laws seriously', *Ming Pao*, 23 January 1997; Simon Beck and Agencies, 'Freedom key to prosperity: US', *SCMP*, 30 January 1997 and Simon Beck, 'China, US row over rights law changes', *SCMP*, 12 April 1997.
54. Chief Executive's Office, *Civil Liberties and Social Order*.
55. Audrey Eu, 'The flaws in this exercise', *SCMP*, 30 April 1997.
56. Sharon Cheung, 'Rule on overseas links "too vague"', *SCMP*, 9 April 1997.
57. Eu, 'Flaws in this exercise'.
58. 'Genuine Fears', *SCMP*, 21 April 1997.
59. No Kwai-yan and Sharon Cheung, 'Patten lashes out at "bid to tighten screw"', *SCMP*, 10 April 1997. In explaining the amendments, Tung emphasized that the proposal was not targeted at a particular individual or organization, he informed the public that almost every country in the world has their own legislation prohibiting foreign political interference in local politics, which is often more restrictive.
60. Genevieve Ku, 'Curbs on Taiwan donations defended', *SCMP*, 16 April 1997.
61. 'Tung considered to relax political donation', *Apple Daily*, 18 April 1997. When Tung was challenged on the basis that he had donated to the Conservative Party in the UK, Elsie Leung defended him by explaining that at the time when Tung made the donation Hong Kong was still a British colony and the donation was, thus, lawful.
62. 'Genuine fears', *SCMP*, 21 April 1997.
63. 'NGOs object to the introduction of the concept of political organization

into the consultation document, Elsie Leung agrees to have separate law for political parties', *Apple Daily*, 21 April 1997. Linda Choy, 'Christian groups call for documents withdrawal', *SCMP*, 22 April 1997.
64. Societies (Amendment) Ordinance 1997.
65. Section 3(1), Societies (Amendment) Ordinance 1997.
66. Ibid.
67. Ibid.
68. A license would not be granted on the grounds that 'the applicant or any person associated with the application has, in relation to any past public gathering, acted contrary to the Public Order Ordinance or any other law or any condition of a license issued under the Public Order Ordinance or any other law'. Section 13(6)(a), Public Order (Amendment) Ordinance 1980.
69. Under section 13(1) of the Public Order (Amendment) Ordinance 1995, 'a public procession may take place if (a) the Commissioner of Police is notified of the intention to hold a public procession; (b) the holding of the procession is not prohibited by the Commissioner of Police; and (c) the statutory conditions are complied with …'.
70. Chief Executive's Office, *Civil Liberties and Social Order*, B4. National security is also a ground to prohibit the establishment of a society in Hong Kong. Section 5A(3)(a), Societies (Amendment) Ordinance 1997.
71. H.L. Fu and Richard Cullen, 'National Security Law in China,' *Columbia Journal of Transnational Law*, Vol. 34 (1996), p. 449.
72. May Sin-mi Hon, 'Proposals seen as more restrictive', *SCMP* 11 April 1997.
73. Ibid.
74. Sharon Cheung, 'Move to pin down "national security"', *SCMP*, 20 April 1997.
75. Political desk, 'National security notion must go, say legal experts', *SCMP*, 2 May 1997.
76. Quoted in ibid.
77. J. Pang, 'National security "knife hanging over us"', *SCMP*, 16 May 1997.
78. Hon, 'Proposals seen as more restrictive', op. cit.
79. Chris Yeung and Kwai-yan No, 'National security terms attacked by A-G', *SCMP*, 19 April 1997.
80. Government Information Centre, 'Administrative Guidelines on national security issued', *Daily Information Bulletin*, 18 July 1997.
81. Ibid.
82. Mr Mathews quoted Lord Diplock's well known passage in *Council of Civil Service Unions v Minister of Civil Service* [1985] A.C. 374 at 412: 'National security is the responsibility of the executive government; what action is needed to protect its interests is … a matter on which those on whom the responsibility rests, and not the courts of justice, must have the last word. It is par excellence a non-justiciable question. The judicial process is totally inept to deal with the sort of problems which it involves.'
83. This section is based upon H.L. Fu and Richard Cullen, 'Subversion and Article 23 of the Basic Law', unpublished paper.
84. Under s. 24AA of the Australian Crimes Act 1914 (as amended)(Cm), it is treachery to 'do any act or thing with intent: (i) to overthrow the constitution of the Commonwealth by revolution or sabotage; or (ii) to

overthrow by force or violence the established Government of the Commonwealth of a state or of a proclaimed country.'

85. Athan Theocharis, 'FBI Surveillance: Past and Present', *Cornell Law Review*, Vol. 69 (1984), p. 883; see also Paul Chevigny, 'Politics and the Law in the Control of Local Surveillance', *Cornell Law Review*, Vol. 69 (1984), p. 786.
86. *R v Arrowsmith* [1975] QB 678.
87. [1962] 3 All ER 142.
88. Lustgarten and Leigh, *In from the Cold*, p. 5.
89. Ibid., p. 35.
90. Ibid., pp. 14–15.
91. Lee, Hanks and Morabito, *In the Name of National Security*, op. cit., p. 17.
92. Martin L. Friedland, *A Century of Criminal Justice: Perspectives on the Development of Canadian Law* (Toronto: Carswell, 1984).
93. Ghai, *Hong Kong's New Constitutional Order*, p. 420.
94. [1998] 2 HKC 627, p. 672.
95. Michael Lobban, *White Man's Justice: South African Political Trials in the Black Consciousness Era* (Oxford: Clarendon Press, 1996), pp. 228–9.
96. *Abrams v US* 250 US 624 (1919).
97. David A.J. Richards, 'Free Speech as Toleration' in W. J. Waluchow (ed.) *Free Expression: Essays in Law and Philosophy* (Oxford: Clarendon Press, 1994).
98. Judith Schenck Koffer and Bennett L. Gershman, 'The New Seditious Libel', *Cornell Law Review*, Vol. 69 (1984), p. 816.
99. Marjorie Carber and Rebecca L. Walkowitz (eds), *Secret Agents: The Rosenberg Case, McCarthyism, and Fifties American* (New York: Rouledge, 1995); Mary S. McAulife, 'Liberals and the Communist Control Act of 1954', *Journal of American History*, Vol. 63 (1976), p. 351; Michael E. Parrish, 'Cold War Justice: The Supreme Court and the Rosenbergs', *The American Historical Review*, Vol. 82 (1977), p. 805; and Allen Weinstein, 'The Symbolism of Subversion: Notes on Some Cold War Icons', *Journal of American Studies*, Vol. 6 (1972), p. 165.
100. See *R v Boyer* (1946), 94 C.C.C. 195 (Que. C.A.), *R v Biernacki* (1962) 37 C.R. 226, and *R v Toronto Sun Publishing Limited et al* (1979) 98 D.L.R. (3d) 524.
101. Jury revolted in the case of *Ponting* [1985] *Crim LR* 318.
102. Michael Yahuda, 'A Catalyst for Change? The Hong Kong Special Administrative Region and Chinese Politics' in Beatrice Leung and Joseph Cheng (eds), *Hong Kong SAR: In pursuit of domestic and international order* (Hong Kong: Chinese University Press, 1997).
103. Steve Tsang, 'Realignment of Power: The Politics of Transition and Reform in Hong Kong', in Pang-kwong Li (ed.) *Political Order and Power Transition in Hong Kong* (Hong Kong: Chinese University Press, 1997).
104. In the 1998 annual meeting of the NPC held in Beijing in March 1998, the Assistant to the Director of the New China News Agency (Hong Kong), Li Weiting, said that anti-China forces continued to carry out anti-China activities in Hong Kong after reunification. 'Li Weiting: Hong Kong has anti-China forces', *Kuai Bao*, 7 March 1998. But Li's view was not shared by the senior state and party leaders in China. In his speech made at the one year anniversary celebration of Hong Kong's reunification held in Hong Kong on 1 July 1998, President Jiang Zemin said that Hong Kong's

reunification was a dramatic historical event and it is normal that some people could not get used to the new environment quickly. He was confident that those people would sooner or later get used to the change if they loved China and Hong Kong. 'Jiang Zemin: The Central Government Support Hong Kong', *Hong Kong Commercial Daily*, 2 July 1998.

5
Individual and Institutional Independence of the Judiciary

*Peter Wesley-Smith**

Introduction

The most frequently discussed issues in relation to judicial independence are the appointment and removal of judges. But the topic is more fecund than that and covers a much broader range of questions, such as judicial administration, training, financial security, promotion, appraisal and accountability, immunity, public commentary by and about judges, administration of the courts, and the theoretical role of judges *vis-à-vis* the law they apply. It is also commonly overlooked that the terms of service of persons performing judicial functions are not necessarily equivalent. This chapter examines some of the detailed arrangements affecting judges in the Hong Kong SAR and draws attention to the position of those playing an important role in the judicial system whom I call 'non-regular' judges.

Theory[1]

The question arose in *Valente v The Queen*[2] whether a particular court was an independent tribunal within the meaning of s 11(d), Canadian Charter of Rights and Freedoms. This has Hong Kong relevance in relation to both the Basic Law and Art 10 of the Bill of Rights, the latter requiring in civil and criminal cases a fair hearing by an independent (and competent and impartial) tribunal established by law. The Supreme Court of Canada held that

1. independence 'connotes not merely a state of mind or attitude in the actual exercise of judicial functions, but a status or relationship to others, particularly to the executive branch of government, that rest on objective conditions or guarantees';[3]

2. independence involves 'both individual and institutional relationships: the individual independence of a judge, as reflected in such matters as security of tenure, and the institutional independence of the court or tribunal over which he or she presides, as reflected in its institutional or administrative relationships to the executive and legislative branches of government' (p. 687);

3. the primary meaning is 'the objective status or relationship to judicial independence' (p. 688);

4. the test for independence includes whether the tribunal may be reasonably perceived as independent in the sense of enjoying 'the essential objective conditions or guarantees of judicial independence', not in terms of how the tribunal will in fact act;[4]

5. where there is a variety of tribunals and provisions relating to their independence it is not feasible 'to apply the most rigorous and elaborate conditions of judicial independence';[5] 'it is the essence of the security afforded by the essential conditions of judicial independence that is appropriate for application under s 11(d) and not any particular legislative or constitutional formula by which it may be provided or guaranteed';[6]

6. there are three essential conditions of judicial independence: security of tenure, financial security, and institutional independence relating to administration;

7. security of tenure requires 'that judges be removable only for cause, and that cause be subject to independent review and determination by a process at which the judge affected is afforded a full opportunity to be heard';[7]

8. financial security means in essence 'that the right to salary and pension should be established by law and not be subject to arbitrary interference by the Executive in a manner that could affect judicial independence';[8]

9. institutional independence does not necessarily require a large degree of independence in preparation and presentation of the budget, allocation of expenditure, and control of supporting personnel; what is essential is 'judicial control over the administrative decisions that bear directly and immediately on the exercise of the judicial function';[9]

10. judicial control of discretionary benefits is not an essential condition of judicial independence.[10]

In *The Queen v Beauregard*[11] the Supreme Court of Canada emphasized that, although the core of the principle remains the complete liberty of judges to decide cases without interference from any outsider, the theory of judicial independence recognizes that courts do not merely adjudicate individual cases: they are also 'protector of the Constitution and the fundamental values embodied in it – rule of law, fundamental justice, equality, preservation of the democratic process, to name perhaps the most important.'[12] 'The role of the courts as resolver of disputes, interpreter of the law and defender of the Constitution requires that they be completely separate in authority and function from *all* other participants in the justice system';[13] and 'the essence of judicial independence for superior court judges is complete freedom from arbitrary interference by *both* the executive and the legislature.'[14]

The views expressed in *Valente* and *Beauregard* may be supplemented by the Beijing Statement of Principles of the Independence of the Judiciary in the LAWASIA Region adopted in 1995 at a conference of Chief Justices of Asia and the Pacific.[15] This was unanimously adopted, assented to even by Chief Justices from countries where judicial independence does not substantially exist; the Chief Justice of Hong Kong, then Sir T.L. Yang who is presently a member of Tung Chee-hwa's first Executive Council, supported the Statement. The principles set out in this document ('BSP') will also be referred to as criteria of measurement in the analysis below.

Judicial officers in Hong Kong

A comprehensive examination of judicial independence requires distinctions between types of judicial officer. A judicial officer is defined in the Judicial Officers Recommendation Commission Ordinance (JORCO) as the holder of a judicial office specified in the first schedule and embraces those listed below. Some belong to 'courts', others to 'tribunals'; some are 'judges', some are 'members of the judiciary other than judges'. How these terms may be defined is discussed subsequently. One major distinction is between 'regular' judges, who are appointed until retirement age, and 'non-regular' judges who are not so appointed: some 'non-regular' judges may be sitting during extension of office post-retirement, others may be appointed for a specific term, and there are recorders, acting judges and deputy judges as well. The term 'non-regular' does not mean 'irregular', nor does it imply that non-regular judges have less power or jurisdiction than their regular brethren; the important question is whether the difference in the terms of service of regular and non-regular judges results in variable standards of independence.

The regular and non-regular judges are as follows:

1. Regular judges in the Court of Final Appeal (CFA) –
   (a) the Chief Justice (CJ) and the permanent judges (appointed by the Chief Executive (CE) acting in accordance with the recommendation of the Judicial Officers Recommendation Commission (JORC). Unless extended in office they must vacate their positions on attaining the retirement age of 65 years);
2. Non-regular judges in the CFA –
   (b) Non-permanent judges, either Hong Kong judges or judges from other common law jurisdictions, when sitting on the court (selected from lists consisting of judges appointed by the CE acting in accordance with the recommendation of JORC. There is no retirement age for a non-permanent judge, who holds office for a term of three years, which term can be extended for one or more periods of three years by the CE acting in accordance with the recommendation of the CJ);
   (c) 'extended' judges (the terms of office of the CJ and of permanent judges may be extended for not more than two periods of three years by the CE, acting in accordance with the recommendation of JORC in the case of the CJ and in accordance with the recommendation of the CJ in the case of permanent judges);
   (d) 'post-retirement' judges (a person who has attained the retirement age of 65 years may be appointed CJ or permanent judge for a term of three years, with one three-year extension, by the CE acting in accordance with the recommendation of JORC in the case of the CJ and in accordance with the recommendation of the CJ in the case of a permanent judge).
3. Regular judges in the High Court (Court of First Instance (CFI) and Court of Appeal) –
   (e) the Chief Judge, Justices of Appeal, and judges of the CFI (appointed on the recommendation of JORC until retirement age of 65 years);
4. Non-regular judges in the High Court –
   (f) recorders (persons eligible to be appointed judge of the CFI may be appointed as recorders of the CFI by the CE on the recommendation of JORC, for such period as may be specified);
   (g) acting judges (on the vacancy of the office of Chief Judge or Justice of Appeal, or if the Chief Judge or a Justice of Appeal is temporarily ill or absent, the CE may appoint another person, eligible to be appointed as a judge of the High Court, to act until the vacancy is filled or the substantive judge resumes duties. It

seems that JORC is not necessarily involved in the appointment process);

(h) deputy judges of the CFI (appointed by the CJ if the office of any judge of the CFI becomes vacant or if the CJ considers that the interests of the administration of justice require that a deputy judge should be appointed temporarily. Appointment may be for a specified case or class of cases or for a specified period only. The CJ may terminate the appointment of a deputy judge at any time);

(i) 'extended' judges (the term of office of a High Court judge may be extended for a specified period or periods not exceeding five years in the aggregate by the CE in accordance with the recommendation of JORC);

(j) 'fixed-term' judges (a person may be appointed as a High Court judge whatever his age for a specified period or periods not exceeding five years in the aggregate by the CE in accordance with the recommendation of JORC).

5. Regular judges in the District Court –
    (k) District Judges (appointed by the CE on the recommendation of JORC until retirement age of 65 years (60 years for those appointed before 1 January 1987));

6. Non-regular judges in the District Court –
    (l) deputy District Judges (the CJ may appoint a fit and proper person as a deputy District Judge, either to fill a vacant office or otherwise if the CJ considers it desirable to do so, until the vacant office has been filled or for such period as the CJ may think fit; the appointment may be terminated by the CJ at any time);

    (m)'extended' District Judges (the term of office of a judge appointed before 1 January 1987 may be extended for a specified period or periods by the CE acting in accordance with the recommendation of JORC. An extended judge attains retirement age at the expiration of the specified period; the ordinance makes no provision for prior termination of the appointment).

7. Other judicial officers (judicial personnel who come within the jurisdiction of JORC (which advises on appointment and terms of service and so on) include also coroners, magistrates, High Court registrars (though not, strangely, CFA registrars), members of the Lands, Labour, and Small Claims Tribunals, and adjudicating officers of the Minor Employment Claims Adjudication Board (MECAB)).

The Basic Law

Judicial independence enshrined

BSP(4) states: 'It is essential that [judicial] independence be guaranteed by the State and enshrined in the Constitution or the law.' The Basic Law has a number of provisions which can be said to enshrine the principle: the Region shall be vested with independent judicial power (BL19), courts shall have jurisdiction over all cases (BL19), and they shall exercise judicial power independently, free from any interference (BL85). The appointment of 'judges of the courts' must be made on the recommendation of an independent commission (BL88) and 'a judge of a court' may be removed only for cause and only on the recommendation of a special tribunal composed of local judges (BL89); the previous system of appointment and removal shall be maintained for 'members of the judiciary other than judges' (BL91). 'Judges and other members of the judiciary' shall be chosen on the basis of their judicial and professional qualities (BL92) and their emoluments are given a degree of protection (BL93).

The meaning of terms

The provisions in the Basic Law enshrining judicial independence depend on the three crucial terms 'courts', 'judiciary', and 'judges'. These expressions are not defined, however, and their meaning is unclear.[16]

'Courts': BL80 provides, unhelpfully, that the courts of the HKSAR shall be the judiciary. This equates institutions with their personnel, which is somewhat curious. Since it is the courts/judiciary which are to exercise the judicial power of the Region (BL80), and therefore under the separation of powers doctrine bodies which are not courts and persons who are not judiciary may not exercise judicial power,[17] it is essential to know precisely what is meant by these terms.

According to BL81, the Court of Final Appeal (CFA), the High Court, district courts, magistrates' courts, 'and other special courts' shall be established in the HKSAR. 'Other special courts' are not defined, which gives rise to uncertainty in two respects: (a) are the well-known 'tribunals' (Labour, Small Claims and Lands) to be regarded as 'special courts'? If so, are they to be distinguished from the numerous other bodies in Hong Kong which are also called 'tribunals' and which appear to exercise at least quasi-judicial power and functions? If a distinction exists, what is it? Does it depend on whether true judicial power is exercized, or can the HKSAR legislature specify which tribunals are courts and which are not?; (b) does BL81 authorize the establishment of 'special courts' to deal with particular problems? Would it be legitimate, for example, to create a special court to adjudicate upon claims to right of abode, with such claims withdrawn from the jurisdiction of the 'ordinary' courts? The institution of *ad hoc* courts offends judicial independence,[18] though the addition of permanent bodies to the structure of HKSAR courts would not.

The other references in the Basic Law to courts are:

a) The structure, powers, and functions of the courts at all levels shall be prescribed by law (BL83). It is inconceivable that anything which could be called a court could be established, and its structure etc. prescribed, by anything other than law. Even if a statute is not employed for the purpose, the Chief Executive (CE) possesses prerogative or common law powers[19] which would probably be regarded as available.[20]

b) The courts shall adjudicate cases in accordance with the Region's laws and may refer to precedents of other common law jurisdictions (BL84). It is difficult to imagine non-courts which may adjudicate in accordance with principles outside the expression 'laws applicable in the Region' or which are not entitled to refer to common law precedents from elsewhere.

c) The courts shall exercize judicial power independently, free from any interference (BL85). This seems to restrict judicial independence to courts, but it is of no moment if bodies which are not courts may not exercize judicial power at all (BL80).

d) Judges of the courts shall be appointed and removed in accordance with a prescribed procedure (BL88, 89). Thus 'judges' of non-courts may presumably be appointed and removed in accordance with other procedures.

'*Judiciary*': BL85 grants immunity from legal action in the performance of their judicial function to members of the judiciary. The term thus, of course, includes judges, but in two other articles reference is made to 'judges and other members of the judiciary' (BL92, 93) and BL91 uses the expression 'members of the judiciary other than judges'.

The distinction between 'judges' and 'other members of the judiciary' doubtless depends on who or what is a judge, though it will still be unclear who or what is a member of the judiciary other than a judge. From BL80 we can perhaps say that the judiciary are members of courts – but courts are usually composed of judges; who therefore are members of the judiciary other than judges? If however certain 'tribunals' are courts, their adjudicating personnel, not normally regarded as judges, would seem to fit the description of 'other members of the judiciary.'

'Judge': in BL88 and 89 the expression used is 'A judge [or Judges] of a court [or the courts] of the HKSAR.' This excludes a judge, if such can exist, of a body which is not a court, but it is otherwise of no assistance since we do not know what a 'court' is. If certain 'ordinary' tribunals are courts whose members are not judges, the jurisdiction of 'regular' courts is exercised by 'judges' – and perhaps the 'regular' courts are those mentioned in BL81 (the CFA, the High Court, district courts, magistrates' courts, and 'other special courts'). Even so, there remains uncertainty whether 'non-regular' judges of the regular courts – extended judges, recorders, deputy judges, fixed-term judges and so on – are 'judges' in this respect.

The common law

There are two strategies one might use to decide whether a body is a court. The first relies on the common law, which employs the elusive concept of judicial power. No hard-and-fast test is available: various factors may be taken into account but none is determinative,[21] thus reposing considerable discretion in judges.

HKSAR legislation

The second strategy is to look to the Hong Kong legislature to clarify and augment the Basic Law. Thus we can consult the statute governing each court or tribunal. Does it specify that the body, whatever its name or title, is a court of law? If yes, it is a court so far as the Basic Law is concerned. Its adjudicatory personnel are members of the judiciary, but they are not necessarily judges. No clear test to distinguish between judges and other members of the judiciary emerges, and perhaps mere subjective impression is ultimately the only guideline we have, which is a scarcely satisfactory procedure when determining crucial terms in the constitution.

The only tribunals which are expressly termed 'courts of record' by the legislature are the Lands Tribunal, the Labour Tribunal, and the Small Claims Tribunal ('the principal tribunals'), all of which exercize judicial power. The Obscene Articles Tribunal, the Inland Revenue Board of Review, and MECAB are not termed courts of record. Magistracies are not so designated either, though by common law criteria they clearly *are* courts, and magistrates are listed in BL81. The Lands Tribunal consists of a president (a High Court judge), presiding officers (district judges and deputy district judges), and 'other members' (such other persons appointed by the CE). The Labour Tribunal is constituted by presiding officers, the Small Claims Tribunal by adjudicators. It may be suggested that, in relation to the Basic Law, (a) magistrates, though they constitute 'courts', are not 'judges'; (b) the principal tribunals are 'courts'; (c) 'other members' of the Lands Tribunal, presiding officers of the Labour Tribunal, and adjudicators of the Small Claims Tribunal are not 'judges', though all are 'members of the judiciary'; and (d) members of tribunals not specified as courts of record are not 'members of the judiciary'. If this is so, it follows that (a) magistrates, 'other members' of the Lands Tribunal, presiding officers of the Labour Tribunal, and adjudicators of the Small Claims Tribunal, not being judges, do not come within BL88 and 89 *vis-à-vis* appointment and dismissal; (b) being members of the judiciary other than judges, however, such personnel must be chosen on the basis of their judicial and professional qualities and so on (BL92), they enjoy immunity (BL85) and the limited security of tenure and financial security afforded under BL93, and the previous system regulating their appointment and removal shall be maintained (BL91); (c) the officers of tribunals which are not courts, not being 'members of the judiciary', do not enjoy immunity and do not come within BL92 and 93, and previous arrangements for their appointment and removal may be altered (BL91); and (d) magistrates and the principal tribunals are required by the Basic Law to exercize judicial power independently (BL85) but other tribunals are not.

The provisions for appointment and dismissal of regular judicial officers seem generally to accord with this scheme. JORC, the body referred to in BL88 and which succeeded the Judicial Service Commission, advises on the appointment of judges of the CFA, the High Court, and the District Court, coroners, magistrates, High Court registrars, members of the principal tribunals, and the Adjudication Officers of MECAB. All these officers are appointed by the CE (except the last, who are appointed by the Commissioner for Labour); only those who are judges of the courts, however, must be appointed on the advice of JORC.[22] The discipline, including removal from office, of judicial officers other than a judge of the CFA, Justice of Appeal, a judge of the Court of First Instance (CFI), or a District Judge is governed by the Judicial Officers (Tenure of Office) Ordinance. Thus magistrates, members of the principal tribunals, and the Adjudication Officers of MECAB are subject to removal procedures which do not comply with BL89.

The legislation dealing with courts does not seem, however, to have adopted a consistent scheme in relation to the 'non-regular' judges of the CFA, the High Court, and the District Court. No non-regular judicial office is expressly listed in the first schedule to the Judicial Officers Recommendation Ordinance except that of recorder. JORC has no role regarding dismissal from judicial offices, whereas the dismissal of officers – all those appointed to offices in the JORCO schedule other than those filling the offices of CFA judge, Justice of Appeal, CFI judge, or District Judge – is governed by the Judicial Officers (Tenure of Office) Ordinance (abbreviated here to TO). Are non-regular judges subject to the TO? This depends on whether they occupy the offices last mentioned, requiring analysis of who is a judge of the CFA,[23] a Justice of Appeal, a CFI judge,[24] or a District Judge.

The result of such analysis (appearing in the preceding footnotes) seems to be that (a) post-retirement judges and non-sitting non-permanent judges of the CFA are not judges of a court and for the purposes of removal do not come within BL89 or the TO; (b) in the CFI the Chief Judge, regular judges, recorders, and deputy judges, being judges of a court, are subject to the appointment and removal provisions of the Basic Law, yet the legislature treats deputy judges and recorders otherwise and acting judges are not regarded as judges of a court at all; and (c) deputy District Judges, though judges of a court, are not afforded the protection of BL89 in relation to dismissal.

The legislation affecting judges, therefore, suffers from a general lack of consistency in relation to non-regular judges, and its compatibility with the Basic Law is problematic.

Appointment and removal of judges

The Basic Law provides that the CE's powers and functions include '[t]o appoint or remove judges of the courts at all levels in accordance with legal procedures' (BL48(6)). In regard to appointment, judges shall be appointed by the CE 'on the recommendation of an independent commission composed of local judges, persons from the legal profession and eminent persons from other sectors' (BL88), and the pre-existing Judicial Service Commission was renamed the Judicial Officers Recommendation Commission accordingly. JORC has jurisdiction over all judicial officers, from the CJ of the CFA to assistant registrars of the High Court and adjudicators in the Small Claims Tribunal,[25] though not, as we have seen, to all non-regular judges. Its remit is set out in s 6 of its ordinance: 'The Commission shall advise or make recommendations to the Chief Executive regarding – (a) the filling of vacancies in judicial offices …'. In carrying out this task it is constrained by BL92: 'Judges and other members of the judiciary of the HKSAR shall be chosen on the basis of their judicial and professional qualities ...' (compare BSP(11): 'To enable the Judiciary to achieve its objectives and perform its functions, it is essential that judges be chosen on the basis of proven competence, integrity and independence'). JORC is supposed to be an independent body, though it is appointed by the CE, but its current composition – which complies with both the Basic Law and BSP(15) – is unfortunately tainted not only by inclusion of the Secretary for Justice but also by what can only be seen as the political appointment of two of its members.[26] Nevertheless, if it takes BL92 seriously one can expect that political and nepotistic appointments to the Bench will not be made.[27] This depends also on whether the CE is *obliged* under BL88 to accept the Commission's recommendations. The view apparently taken within the judicial branch, and not disputed by the present CE, is that appointment is a purely formal process following in effect selection by the Commission. Indeed, a number of appointments must by statute be made by the CE 'in accordance with' JORC's recommendations.[28] This is important to our assessment of judicial independence in relation to other matters. If the executive branch of government is constitutionally prohibited from exercising discretion in the appointment of judges, the case for judicial independence is considerably enhanced.

The same point is relevant to dismissal: judges of the courts (though not 'members of the judiciary other than judges' (BL91)) may be removed by the CE, but only 'on the recommendation of' a tribunal (appointed by the Chief Justice, unless the Chief Justice himself is to be investigated (BL89)). It is unthinkable that the CE should be free to prefer his own decision in favour of any recommendation by a tribunal.

Regular judges of the CFA, High Court, and District Court are appointed until retirement age. Magistrates, however, are initially appointed for three years and the contract usually renewed once, after which the officer can choose whether to move to permanent and pensionable terms or to take further three-year contracts. This is a probationary system and therefore in theory objectionable, but on first appointment candidates may have very little experience and it is thought desirable to check their suitability before offering them security of tenure.[29] As probationers their interest is of course to satisfy JORC rather than the executive branch, and it might be thought excessively purist to demand that they be given tenure from the beginning.

In only one case in recent years was a magistrate's contract not renewed (on the ground of incompetence); disciplinary matters would be routinely dealt with under the TO. One magistrate resigned when the appointment of a TO tribunal was imminent.

Provisions for removal depend on the status of the judicial officer concerned. Members of the judiciary other than judges are guaranteed that the 'previous system' of removal will be maintained (BL91). The previous system is set out in the Judicial Officers (Tenure of Office) Ordinance, which provides in s 3(1) that, if it is represented to the CJ 'that an officer is unable to discharge his duties or has misbehaved, the Chief Justice may notify the officer of the particulars of the representations received and where he does so he shall call on the officer to state in writing ... any grounds on which he relies to justify himself.' The CJ shall appoint a tribunal, consisting of two High Court judges and a public officer, to investigate the matter if the judicial officer fails to justify himself to the CJ's satisfaction. After investigation, which requires that an opportunity to be heard be afforded the officer, the tribunal shall submit a report to JORC containing *inter alia* its opinion whether the officer is unable to discharge his duties or has misbehaved, and JORC shall recommend to the CE either that no action be taken or that a sanction ranging from reprimand to dismissal be imposed. On receipt of a report the CE may take the recommended action, any other action referred to in s 8, or no action.[30]

These provisions can be compared with BSP(6): 'In the decision-making process, any hierarchical organisation of the Judiciary and any difference in grade or rank shall in no way interfere with the duty of the judge exercising jurisdiction individually or judges acting collectively to pronounce judgment in accordance with Art 3(a)': that is, 'the Judiciary shall decide matters before it in accordance with its impartial assessment of the facts and its understanding of the law without improper influences, direct or indirect, from any source.' I take this to mean that differences in conditions for judicial officers do not necessarily infringe judicial independence provided an impartial decision can at all times be made (and see *Valente*, ruling (5) above); the Judicial Officers (Tenure of Office) Ordinance would seem to pass this test. BSP(22) ('Judges should be subject to removal from office only for proved incapacity, conviction of a crime, or conduct which makes the judge unfit to be a judge') is satisfied, as are BSP(26) ('... the judge who is sought to be removed must have the right to a fair hearing') and *Valente*, ruling (7). But BSP(24), 'procedures for the removal of judges must be under the control of the judiciary', is not, since the final decision belongs to the CE. The ordinance does not require, as BSP(28) requires, that judgments in disciplinary proceedings, whether held in camera or in public, be published.

In Australia in recent times members of courts have been effectively dismissed through the device of replacing the courts in which they operate and failing to reappoint them to the new bodies.[31] This is contrary to BSP(29). It has not happened in Hong Kong and was expressly forbidden by BL93 in relation to the transition. The Basic Law does not otherwise deal with the question. Nor does it deal with the discipline of judges of the courts short of dismissal, and no formal procedure exists for delivering, say, a reprimand. A former Chief Justice admitted that some judges during his term of office had resigned because they had been pushed rather than because they wanted to go. One commentator wrote:

> To 'push' a judge out of office, even when the pressure is exerted by his peers, does not appear to be consonant with the dignity of the court. Nor does it seem compatible with the independence that is guaranteed by the Constitution and which is indispensable if justice is to be administered, in terms of the judicial oath, without fear or favour, affection, or ill will.[32]

Financial security

The Beijing Statement says that 'Judges must receive adequate remuneration and be given appropriate terms and conditions of service.'[33] The essence of financial security is that it should be 'established by law and not be subject to arbitrary interference by the Executive in a manner that could affect judicial independence.'[34] 'Neither the executive nor the legislature can interfere with the financial security of superior court judges. That security is crucial to the very existence and preservation of judicial independence as we know it.'[35]

Salaries

The Basic Law protects the salaries of judges and other members of the judiciary serving in Hong Kong before 1997 on terms no less favorable than before (BL93). There is no express requirement of adequate remuneration for judges appointed after establishment of the SAR, but such could be regarded as a necessary implication.

In Hong Kong there is a Standing Committee on Judicial Salaries and Conditions of Service, which is a non-statutory body required to 'keep under review the structure, i.e. the number of levels, and the pay rates appropriate to each rank of judicial officer together with the other conditions of service of judicial officers.'[36] The Standing Committee, of which no representative from the judiciary is a member, is housed in and is administered by, the Civil Service Branch of the Government Secretariat and makes recommendations to the Chief Executive who determines its composition. The functions of the Judicial Officers Recommendation Commission include advising the CE on 'such representations from a judicial officer concerning conditions of service' and any other matter as may be referred to it by the CE;[37] it seems unlikely that complaints about pay would be so referred.

The latest revision (1 April 1998) of the Judicial Officers' Salary Scale pegs judicial salaries to the Directorate Pay Scale (DPS) and the Master Pay Scale (MPS) (not to the Directorate (Legal) Pay Scale, which extends only to point 7, whereas the DPS goes up to point 10 (though Directorate (Legal) salaries are higher than at corresponding points on the DPS)). The CJ of the CFA is on the same level (D10) as the Administrative Secretary; judges of the CFA and the Chief Judge of the High Court are paid a salary between D9 and D10, Justices of Appeal between D8 and D9, and CFI judges D8. These salaries may be compared with the Financial Secretary (D9) and the Secretary for Justice (DL7, between D8 and D9 and between the salaries for Justices of Appeal and CFA judges). Registrars of the High Court and the CFA, District Judges, the Chief and Principal Magistrates, Lands Tribunal members, the Principal Presiding Officer and the Presiding Officer of the Labour Tribunal, the Principal Adjudicator and Adjudicators of the Small Claims Tribunal, and the Coroner all receive pay equivalent to points on the DPS, and magistrates begin at MPS49 and reach D1 within four years. Non-regular judges, who receive no fringe benefits, are paid pro rata in accordance with the salary of the substantive office.

Judicial salaries certainly amount to 'adequate remuneration', whether in relative terms (relative to the civil service or professors of law, though not necessarily to the upper ranks of the legal profession) or in absolute terms. Nearly 40 judges are at D8 or above, compared with only eight civil servants. The effective decisionmaker is however the CE, who could in theory break the peg at any time and predetermine all judicial pay scales. There appears to be no consolidated fund in Hong Kong and thus provision for judicial salaries ultimately depends on annual vote in the Legislative Council, which in turn relies on decisions by the Establishment Committee of the Finance

Committee. Rates of pay are 'established by law' but only in the annual Appropriation Ordinance.

> Making judicial salaries a charge on the Consolidated Revenue Fund instead of having to include them in annual appropriations is, I suppose, theoretically a measure of greater security, but practically it is impossible that the legislature would refuse to vote the annual appropriation in order to attempt to exercise some control or influence over a class of judges as a whole.[38]

In practice judicial salaries appear to be secure – though there are recent suggestions that they will be reduced in line with pay cuts affecting the public service generally[39] – and in theory the arrangements are probably as favourable as most in the common law world.

Pensions

In *Valente* it was said that the right to a pension should be established by law and not be dependent upon 'the grace or favour of the Executive.'[40] BL93 requires the government to pay to judges and other members of the judiciary who retire or leave the service 'all pensions, gratuities, allowances and benefits due to them on terms no less favourable than before ...'. The Pensions Benefits (Judicial Officers) Ordinance provides for judicial pensions generally, and according to s 4 'Except as otherwise provided in this Ordinance, the entitlement to pension benefits is a right.'

The ordinance applies only to judicial officers appointed on or after 1 July 1987 – those appointed before that date receive pensions in accordance with the ordinances relating to the civil service generally – and on terms which attract pension benefits.[41] The latter refers to appointment on 'local PE terms'; officers appointed on 'local agreement terms' receive instead a gratuity of 25 per cent of gross salary. It would be very dull to analyze the terms of the ordinance in detail, but the following points, most of them subject to qualifications and exceptions, may be noted: (1) a pension shall be granted in respect of pensionable service on retirement on or after attaining normal retirement age and after completion of qualifying service (ten years if appointed before the age of 50, otherwise five years); (2) similarly a pension shall be granted to an officer taking voluntary early retirement; (3) officers who leave the service on the abolition of or removal from office, compulsory retirement for the purpose of facilitating improvement in the organization of the judiciary, retirement on

medical grounds, and resignation after completion of ten years qualifying service are also entitled to a pension; (4) the CE in Council may
approve a compensation scheme which differs from the terms of the
ordinance; (5) in certain circumstances a death gratuity shall be and an
ex gratia award may be paid; (6) for judges appointed on or after 1 July
1987, 100 per cent of salary and personal allowance shall be taken as
pensionable emoluments and a pension shall not exceed two-thirds of
the highest pensionable emoluments enjoyed or drawn by him; (7)
after taking into consideration the advice of JORC a designated officer,
appointed by the CE, may refuse to grant a pension or cancel or reduce
a pension already granted to a judicial officer who wilfully suppressed
material facts or who retired during, or resigned to avoid, disciplinary
proceedings brought against him when in the opinion of JORC they
would have led to dismissal; (8) a pension ceases on bankruptcy or
insolvency and resumes on discharge; (9) pension benefits may be
cancelled, suspended, or reduced on conviction of certain offences;
(10) a pension may be suspended if the officer undertakes certain post-
retirement employment; and (11) a short service gratuity shall be
granted to an officer whose service is less than the qualifying service.

In *Beauregard* the introduction by the federal Judges Act of a scheme
for contributory pensions was upheld. Chief Justice Dickson saw no
connection between the essential conditions of judicial independence
(the free rendering of decisions and 'preservation of the separateness
and integrity of the judicial branch and a guarantee of its freedom
from unwarranted intrusions by, or even intertwining with, the
legislative and executive branches') and establishment of a contributory pension scheme. All that the Act did was to 'treat judges in
accordance with standard, widely used and generally accepted pension
schemes in Canada. From that factual reality it is far too long a stretch,
in my opinion, to the conclusion that s 29.1 of the Judges Act violates
judicial independence.'[42]

Other benefits

The conditions of service for all regular judges and judicial officers
include pension or gratuity, housing benefits (non-accountable cash
allowance, departmental quarter, or home financing scheme
payments, depending on level of appointment), leave (annual or vaca-
tion leave in many cases with passage, sick leave), free medical and
dental treatment for the officer and his family, and education
allowance for children. The CJ has a non-accountable entertainment
allowance of $366 400, and there are judicial dress allowances, special

allowances, and extraneous duties allowances in certain circumstances. In the draft Estimates 1998–99 these amount to 3.8 per cent of the salaries bill (the total for all personal emoluments, including salaries, is $728.01m). Like salaries, all benefits are subject to annual vote by the legislature.

In *Valente* it was argued (though unsuccessfully) that exercize by the executive government of control over discretionary benefits, such as post-retirement reappointment, leave of absence with or without pay, and the right to engage in extra-judicial employment, prevented reasonable perception of the courts as independent.[43] Such an argument could not in any event be sustained in Hong Kong, since decisions on such matters are made either by the CE on the recommendation of JORC or by the CJ.

The independence of non-regular judges

It is proposed in this section to consider two recent decisions of the Canadian courts which provide standards by which we can assess the position of Hong Kong's non-regular judges.

Recorders

Judges of certain municipal courts in Quebec operated part-time and were permitted by statute to continue practice as lawyers, and the issue before the Supreme Court of Canada in *R v Lippé*[44] was whether such judges constituted an independent and impartial tribunal. The court, measuring the statute against the standard of s 11(d) of the Charter, held that (1) judicial independence is but a means to the end of a reasonable perception of impartiality, though it is a necessary prerequisite; (2) a lack of independence is only one factor which could cause impartiality: institutional impartiality may be jeopardized despite the existence of independence. '[I]f the system is structured in such a way as to create a reasonable apprehension of bias on an institutional level, the requirement of impartiality is not met';[45] (3) a system allowing part-time judges is not ideal, but the ideal is not required; (4) the test for institutional impartiality is 'what would an informed person, viewing the matter realistically and practically – and having thought the matter through – conclude.'[46] It is not a question of how the tribunal will in fact act, but of 'whether the tribunal enjoys the essential objective conditions or guarantees of judicial independence';[47] (5) the fact that a judge is part-time does not in and of itself raise a reasonable apprehension of bias, but the Charter guarantees that a part-time judge will not engage in activities incompatible with his duty as a judge; (6) in determining whether an occupation is so incompatible, the test is whether there would be a reasonable apprehension of bias in the mind of a fully informed person in a substantial number of cases, thus avoiding institutional impartiality; (7) applying the test, the occupation of practising law gives rise to a reasonable apprehension of bias in a substantial number of cases and is therefore *per se* incompatible with the functions of a judge; (8) in this case, however, various safeguards existed which took the system outside the category of institutional impartiality. These were the swearing of a judicial oath, judicial immunity and subjection to a code of ethics with enforceable duties imposed on the judges.

The provisions affecting recorders in Hong Kong are very sparse. The High Court Ordinance merely states that the CE may appoint a person who is eligible to be appointed a CFI judge to be a recorder 'for such period as may be specified in the instrument by which the appointment is made',[48] and a recorder 'shall have and may exercise all the jurisdiction, powers and privileges and shall have and perform all the duties of a judge of the CFI, and any reference in any law to such a judge shall be construed accordingly.'[49] Recorders are usually, though not necessarily, barristers who sit full-time for regular periods, for example one month per year; no permission is granted by the legislature for them to continue to engage in legal practice during the term of appointment. Thus they do not come directly within the *Lippé* ruling, but the general propositions of that case can be considered in relation to them. Indeed a recorder may have returned to his practice at the Bar while continuing to act in a judicial capacity: if proceedings are adjourned or judgment reserved, a recorder 'shall have power to resume the hearing and determine the proceedings or deliver judgment, notwithstanding that his appointment as a recorder … has expired or has been terminated.'[50] In that situation he is acting in a part-time capacity while practising law. Lamer CJC in *Lippé*[51] explained why a part-time judge practising law is *per se* incompatible with the functions of a judge:

> A judge is expected to remain somewhat detached and objectively adjudicate each case on its merits. A lawyer, on the other hand, plays a more active, aggressive role, one which appears incompatible with the impartial state of mind required of a judge. To illustrate this general incompatibility, the respondents give a number of examples of conflicts of interest which could arise:

a) Part-time judges who are also practising law could be pressured by clients to make a particular decision on an issue.
b) An appearance of a conflict of interest could arise if a lawyer of the judge's firm or a lawyer involved in a deal with the judge's firm appeared before the judge.
c) If the judge's firm was pursuing a particular government contract, the judge may feel pressured to favour the government position in a decision.
d) Clients of the judge could be called to testify in a case before the judge.

These examples of conflicts of interest are not so compelling when applied to barristers in a fused profession, as in Hong Kong,[52] but they apply with full force to solicitors, and solicitors in Hong Kong are eligible to be appointed to the CFI and thus are eligible to become recorders. The fact that recorders take leave from their practices for the duration of their appointments does not significantly alleviate the institutional partiality which their occupation as lawyers before and after appointment creates;[53] nor does the lack of express legislative permission to engage in legal practice, since recorders must be lawyers to be eligible and it is not conceivable that they should be employed in some other (compatible) profession. It thus seems that solicitors, at least, and barristers completing judicial work after their term of office has expired, cannot as recorders constitute an independent and impartial tribunal, unless there are safeguards which prevent a reasonable apprehension of bias in the mind of an informed person.

Recorders must swear an oath[54] and they enjoy judicial immunity.[55] There is no code of ethics for judges in Hong Kong, however, and no legislation which imposes enforceable duties on recorders to recuse themselves in cases of potential conflicts of interest. If recorders are subject to discipline under the Judicial Officers (Tenure of Office) Ordinance they are so only for inability to discharge duties or misbehaviour, and thus the general obligation on all judges to avoid conflicts of interest cannot be enforced. It is therefore arguable that the safeguards are insufficient to remove the apprehension of institutional bias. Further, the TO permits disciplinary action, including removal, by the CE regardless of the recommendations of the tribunal, and recorders' security of tenure is accordingly insufficient to satisfy the judicial independence doctrine.

Deputy judges and others

In *Reference re Territorial Court Act*[56] the validity of provisions for the appointment of deputy judges was considered. Deputy judges were appointed by the Commissioner (the chief executive officer of the government) and, by s 6(2), an appointment 'shall have effect for a period of two years or for a shorter period as may be specified in the appointment, unless sooner revoked by the Commissioner on the written recommendation of the Chief Judge.' The practice was to appoint as deputy judges persons who held full-time appointments as provincial or superior court judges in other jurisdictions, and they sat when needed, usually for a short term. Vertes J held that, because the Act excluded the appointment of district judges from review by the JORC-like Judicial Council, the power of the Commissioner to appoint and reappoint district judges could be exercized unilaterally and arbitrarily and was incompatible with the principles of judicial independence, leading to the perception of a lack of impartiality. Revocation of appointment 'on the written recommendation of the Chief Judge' was an insufficient safeguard against arbitrary action. The Canadian concept of judicial independence involves freedom from pressure or interference by another judge.[57]

> The fact that the Chief Judge has a role to play in the revocation process, indeed a key role, is in my opinion no answer to this problem [of service at pleasure]. If a Chief Judge recommends the revocation of an unpopular deputy judge, it could be perceived that the Chief Judge was merely an extension of the executive. I fail to see how one arbitrary power could validate another one. Granted one should be able to rely on the integrity of the Chief Judge. But that is not to say that all Chief Judges can be impervious to the demands of the executive, whether they be to control budgets or to influence decisions. This is especially worrisome when it is the Chief Judge who primarily has the role of representing the judiciary in day-to-day administrative matters and negotiating with the executive over financial and other matters. In my view a reasonable objective observer would not regard the involvement of the Chief Judge as a sufficient safeguard to the arbitrary revocation of a deputy judge's appointment.[58]

Vertes J also considered the position of persons appointed as judges for a fixed term. Any such appointment or reappointment must involve the Judicial Council, tenure must be secure for the term of the appointment, revocation or removal must be for cause and subject to the same process as for full judges, and the total remuneration available for district judges and full judges must be the same.[59] If, and only if, these conditions are satisfied, (1) the term appointment of a district judge who is already a sitting judge in another jurisdiction would be constitutionally permissible, and (2) the term appointment of any other qualified person – such as a 'retired' judge, one who has reached retirement age – is valid provided that part-time appointees are prohibited from practising law in the jurisdiction. In addition, the court noted the disapproval of temporary appointments expressed in international codes of standards of judicial independence, warned that they could be abused by the selection of persons likely to be compliant to the government's wishes, and said (in the context of the term appointment of lawyers as district judges, though the words apply more widely):

One of the arguments against temporary or short-term judgeships is that a judicial position should not be seen as merely a stepping stone to some more lucrative position. One should not be able to use the judicial role as a means of material self-aggrandizement. That is exactly what one could be tempted to do by a temporary appointment knowing that it is merely temporary.[60]

The Hong Kong provisions for non-regular judges who are appointed by the CE on the recommendation of JORC are unobjectionable in terms of judicial independence. But, if we apply the Canadian jurisprudence, the appointment of acting High Court judges by the CE without JORC involvement is constitutionally improper, and extensions for permanent CFA judges, the appointment of 'post-retirement' judges in the CFA on the recommendation of the CJ, and the appointment by the CJ alone of deputy CFI judges are all surely dubious. The lack of any requirement in the legislation that removal of post-retirement judges, non-sitting non-permanent judges of the CFA, and acting CFI judges be in accordance with BL89 is quite unsatisfactory. The power of the CJ to terminate the appointment of a deputy judge at any time cannot be allowed, particularly as the ordinance provides for no process or grounds. According to the Hong Kong practice, deputy judges 'act up' from the District Court and therefore termination of appointment merely sends them down again and does not deprive them of employment – but this, if it has any persuasiveness at all, relates only to the personal independence of the judge, not to the court's institutional independence and impartiality.[61] The primary purpose of appointing deputy judges (and perhaps of recorders as well) is in effect to put them on probation, a practice deprecated by the IBA Code of Minimum Standards of Judicial Independence (1982) and the Montreal Declaration (1983).

Institutional independence

Judicial control over the assignment of judges (see BSP(35)), sittings of the courts and court lists is well established in Hong Kong. These are the minimum requirements for institutional independence – but, as pointed out in *Valente*,[62] the claim for greater administrative autonomy extends primarily to a stronger role in the financial and personnel aspects of court administration. The Supreme Court of Canada nevertheless restricted the 'essentials' of institutional independence to 'judicial control over the administrative decisions that bear directly and immediately on the exercise of the judicial function.'[63]

Judiciary administration

'The Chief Justice shall be the head of the Judiciary and shall be charged with the administration of the Judiciary and such other functions as may from time to time be lawfully conferred on him.'[64] He recruited and effectively may dismiss the Judiciary Administrator, who is nevertheless formally appointed by the CE though paid out of the judiciary vote. The Judiciary Administrator is responsible to, and takes instructions from, the CJ. Described in the judiciary's report of 1994–95 as 'the administrative head of the Judiciary, assisting the Chief Justice in its overall administration', the Judiciary Administrator's Office comprises two divisions: the development division (including the press and public relations office and the statistics office) and the administrative division (responsible for such areas as court interpreters, court reporters, bailiffs, accounts, library, management services and project management). In addition there are registries for each court and tribunal; they file and maintain documents and provide general support for judges and tribunal officers. The Clerk of Court's Office fixes dates for hearing of cases in the CFA and the High Court, issues jurors' summonses, administers criminal cases in the CFI, and assists the listing judge. The Probate Registry processes applications for and issues grants of administration and assists the Official Administrator in administering small estates of deceased persons. Like the Judiciary Administrator, the registrars are answerable to the CJ. Since July 1994 court leaders (Chief District Judge, Principal Adjudicator of the Small Claims Tribunal, Principal Presiding Officer of the Labour Tribunal, and Chief Magistrate; since 1997 the list of course includes the Chief Judge of the High Court) have been appointed, whose duties include assistance with court administration. The total judiciary establishment (judges, judicial officers and support staff) at the end of March this year was just over two thousand permanent posts (1832 non-directorate), all of them ultimately responsible to the CJ. Thus BSP(36) ('The principal responsibility for court administration, including appointment, super-vision and disciplinary control of administrative personnel and support staff must vest in the Judiciary, or in a body in which the Judiciary is represented and has an effective role') is satisfied in Hong Kong.

Budget

BSP(37) states: 'The budget of the courts should be prepared by the courts or a competent authority in collaboration with the Judiciary having regard to the needs of the independence of the Judiciary and administration. The amount allocated should be sufficient to enable each court to function without an excessive workload.' The Judiciary Administrator co-ordinates preparation of the judiciary budget and accounts for expenditure under the Estimates, liaises with the court leaders and, with the approval of the CJ, takes the budget to the exec-utive branch and negotiates with the Financial Secretary and staff. The Judiciary Administrator will also appear before the Finance Committee to explain and defend budget proposals. There is no one-line appro-priation: the judiciary must comply with government rules regarding the allocation of expenditure, but these provide for flexibility, and more money outside the budget can be sought. The Judiciary Administrator claims that the judiciary has established good rapport with executive and legislative personnel and no undue difficulties are experienced in the budgetary process.

Performance appraisal and accountability

Court leaders are responsible for monitoring the performance of their judges, with assessment based on professional competence as displayed in written work, judicial temperament (relying largely on feedback from practitioners and fellow judges) and case management. The outcome of proceedings is not a relevant factor. Review is a formal process carried out annually. Appellate judges also give their views, and reports, together with the officer's response, are filed in the confi-dential registry of the judiciary. Summaries are prepared for JORC if needed and the reports themselves will be made available if requested. An unsatisfactory report may lead to an interview with the court leader or the CJ, but there are no direct sanctions for District Judges and above short of proceedings for removal. Other judicial officers may be dealt with for inability to discharge duties or misbehaviour and, as discussed above, after investigation by a tribunal appointed by the CJ and report by JORC an errant officer may be dismissed, compulsorily retired with or without pension, gratuity, or other allowances, reduced in rank, may lose future salary increments, or be reprimanded or severely reprimanded by the CE.[65] There is no standing committee or commission and no code of conduct relating to discipline or judicial ethics. It may be noted that BSP(27) requires that all disciplinary proceedings 'must be determined in accordance with established standards of judicial conduct'.

Training and education

Although judicial officers are not required to attend, the Judicial Studies Board conducts a number of seminars, training courses and visits. The Board is appointed by the CJ and chaired by a judge of the CFI. Its terms of reference are to devise induction programmes for new appointees, run other programmes, and advise the CJ on how he might best use judicial studies in respect of the appointment of judges, the matching of judicial resources to demands, and the creation of opportunities for changes of work. The Board has produced various manuals and guides, held conferences on sentencing and such matters as Chinese law, set up courses on language training, technology, work-related skills and so on, and sent officers to overseas conferences. The Chairman's report for 1994–96 states that the Board 'is committed to providing continuing judicial education and training and will use its best endeavours to meet the rising expectations of judges, judicial officers and the community.'

Andrew Li CJ has stated:

> No modern institution can retain its vigour without good in-service education and training. We will place great emphasis on this in our endeavour to maintain high standards and to improve them. Continuing education and training for judges must be strengthened and sufficient resources must be obtained and devoted to this important task.[66]

While judicial training can be seen to promote independence, the possibility has recently been raised that training, together with performance appraisal and an emphasis on public service, consistency

and standardization, as in the United Kingdom, might lead to a weak-
ened culture of individualism which will jeopardize the independence
of mind judges have hitherto exhibited.[67]

Other aspects

A number of other situations can result in deviations from the principle of judicial independence.

Immunity from suit

BSP(32) says 'judges should enjoy personal immunity from civil suits
for monetary damages for improper acts or omissions in the exercise of
their judicial functions.' 'Members of the judiciary', it is stated in
BL85, 'shall be immune from legal action in the performance of their
judicial functions'. This is the position at common law, reinforced by
statute,[68] and judges are unlikely to acquiesce in any attempt to
weaken the protection it provides them.

Immunity from political attack

In the last presidential election in the USA both Republican and
Democratic candidates strongly criticized named judges who were
perceived as soft on crime.[69] There have been no examples of politically motivated campaigns against judges in Hong Kong, although as
elections to the post of CE and to the Legislative Council become more
democratic, and as judges become more involved in the political deci-
sionmaking the Basic Law requires, the temptation for candidates to
engage in such behaviour will increase. This is not to say that the
public has no right to criticize judicial behaviour. But critical
comments made by quasi-government officials both in Hong Kong
and on the mainland following the CFA's judgment in the Ng Ka-ling
case[70] in January 1999 came perilously close to infringing judicial
independence.[71] The principal cause of complaint from the Central
People's Government was the court's attitude towards decisions of the
National People's Congress (NPC) and its Standing Committee *vis-à-vis*
Hong Kong, and the Secretary for Justice returned from a trip to Beijing
announcing that the authorities there wanted the decision 'rectified'.
She apparently twice contacted the Chief Justice to tell him that a
motion was to be made to the CFA seeking 'clarification' of its views,
and the court acceded. In the original unanimous judgment Andrew Li
CJ stated, unequivocally, that HKSAR courts have the jurisdiction to
examine whether legislative acts by the NPC and its Standing

Committee 'are consistent with the Basic Law and to declare them to be invalid if found to be inconsistent'; in the clarification, termed a 'judgment', the CFA accepted that it cannot question 'the authority of the NPC or the Standing Committee to do any act which is in accordance with the provisions of the Basic Law and the procedure therein.' Undoubtedly not a 'rectification', this reassertion of the original view somehow gave satisfaction to both the Hong Kong government and the Central People's Government. In the process a good deal of damage was done to the dignity and independence of the court.[72]

Reticence[73]

Extra-judicial commentary on political issues can be very damaging to confidence in the judiciary. Statements by the CJ in 1995 concerning the Hong Kong Bill of Rights Ordinance, expressing views in the context of Sino-British controversy which happened to be embarrassingly wrong,[74] did the judiciary no favour. They risked the retrospective appearance of having been calculated to assist Sir T.L. Yang's later attempt to become CE. It is more usual however for judges, if they make public speeches at all, to restrict themselves to platitudinous utterances unlikely to be seen as political. They should not be shy to take whatever action is necessary to promote and protect their independence (compare BSP(9)). There has never been a local equivalent of the Kilmuir Rules which at one time inhibited the British judiciary from extra-judicial comment, and judges in other jurisdictions tend to be more readily available to the media than they were or than judges are in Hong Kong; this, if exercized cautiously, can be beneficial to public understanding of the judiciary.[75]

Judicial method

BSP(10) reads: 'The objectives and functions of the Judiciary include the following: (a) to ensure that all persons are able to live securely under the Rule of Law; (b) to promote, within the proper limits of the judicial function, the observance and the attainment of human rights; and (c) to administer the law impartially among persons and between persons and the State.' Judges who are avowedly activist jeopardize the courts' reputation as impartial umpires in the resolution of disputes.[76] This does not mean that they should not develop and apply policy objectives when appropriate, particularly in relation to interpretation of the Basic Law.[77] The CFA must take seriously its responsibility to develop the law of the Hong Kong SAR and should not be deterred by the unfamiliarity of the techniques they are called upon to employ.

Conclusion

In 1986 a consultant was commissioned to recommend to the CJ how to improve the efficiency and economic administration of the courts, whether business between courts and tribunals should be rearranged, and whether the structure and hierarchy of the courts should be altered. Mr Peter D. Robinson, from the Lord Chancellor's department in the United Kingdom, prepared the report,[78] and many of his recommendations were adopted. These include the appointment of court leaders, creation of the post of Judiciary Administrator, appointment of recorders, improvements in listing and court reporting, and the establishment of the Judicial Studies Board. Robinson's ideas were expressly founded upon the principle of judicial independence. Thus he proposed, for example, that 'in official lists of public servants all judicial officers from Chief Justice to Special Magistrate should be segregated from all other public servants and classified as one homogeneous group',[79] and that 'the pay and other terms and conditions of service of judicial officers be looked at quite separately from those of other public servants.'[80] 'Completely separate classification will also enhance the corporate independence of the Judiciary – the second meaning of judicial independence. That will be further emphasised by the systematic judicial leadership and strengthened administration which I am recommending.'[81]

It is now possible to speak of a 'judicial service' distinct from the civil service. The separation is not complete, but the judiciary is not subject to the Public Service Commission Ordinance, judicial appointments are handled by a commission chaired by the CJ on which judges serve and which allows the CE little or no discretion, discipline and dismissal are dealt with by procedures dominated by judges, remuneration is kept under review by a separate standing committee, the budgetary and expenditure processes are under the direction of the CJ, pensions are governed by special ordinance, and the assignment of cases, judicial training, performance appraisal, and all matters of internal administration are kept in-house. Some of these are constitutionally protected. The judicial branch of government, it might be concluded, enjoys a high degree of autonomy in an arrangement of 'one public service, two systems'. Judicial independence, in both its individual and institutional manifestations, seems largely secure; there are deficiencies, certainly, but regular judges are in general well protected from interference from outside in their exercize of judicial functions.

The ambiguity of the Basic Law, however, creates uncertainty where precision is essential and local legislation is insufficient to specify clearly the detailed position of the non-regular judiciary. Moreover the standards adopted in recent cases in Canada, if applied to Hong Kong, suggest that provisions affecting the conditions of service of non-regular judges are in some respects unsatisfactory. When the position of some non-regular judges is taken into account it seems that the constitutional requirement of judicial independence has not been fully implemented. The practical consequence is that in some cases judicial decisions could be subject to challenge under Art 10 of the Bill of Rights.

This is part, I suspect, of a general problem with the transition from British colony to Chinese special administrative region: pre-1997 arrangements which no one had ever questioned, and which were consistent with British experience, have become subject to more searching standards under the Basic Law, and it is taking the legal profession some time to recognize the need for change and to work through the difficulties.

Notes

* Some preliminary research was conducted by Mr James Ding, and much information was generously provided by the then Judiciary Administrator, Ms Alice Tai; this assistance is gratefully acknowledged. The original paper has been combined with a paper presented in February 1999 to a conference on the judiciary in Asia organized by the World Jurist Association and held in New Delhi.
1. See the brief discussion in Peter Wesley-Smith, *Constitutional and Administrative Law in Hong Kong* (Hong Kong: Longman Asia, 2nd edn 1994), pp. 142–4.
2. [1985] 2 SCR 673.
3. Ibid., p. 685.
4. Ibid., p. 689.
5. Ibid., p. 692.
6. Ibid., p. 693.
7. Ibid., p. 698.
8. Ibid., p. 704.
9. Ibid., p. 712.
10. Ibid., pp. 711–14.
11. [1986] 2 SCR 56.
12. Ibid, p. 70.
13. Ibid, p. 73.
14. Ibid, p. 75. For a critical analysis of these two cases see Ian Green, 'The Doctrine of Judicial Independence Developed by the Supreme Court of Canada' (1988) 26 Osgoode Hall LJ 177. Subsequent Canadian cases rele-

vant to judicial independence are discussed in Martin L. Friedland, *A Place Apart: Judicial Independence and Accountability in Canada* (Ottawa: Canadian Judicial Council, 1995), pp. 12–18. This report contains much useful comparative material on all the issues discussed in the present paper.

15. See (1996) 70 ALJ 299.

16. See also BL87's reference to 'the judicial organs'. Compare BL95: what are the judicial organs of other parts of the country?

17. See Peter Wesley-Smith, 'Executive Orders and the Basic Law' in Alice Lee (ed.) *Law Lectures for Practitioners 1998* (Hong Kong: Hong Kong Law Journal Ltd, 1998), pp. 188–91. The provision in BL81 that 'The judicial system previously practised in Hong Kong shall be maintained except for those changes consequent upon the establishment of the Court of Final Appeal of the HKSAR' arguably sustains the pre-1997 exercize of judicial power by tribunals which are not courts.

18. See the Universal Declaration on the Independence of Justice (Montreal, 1983), para 2.06(a) (in Shimon Shetreet and Jules Deschênes (eds), *Judicial Independence: The Contemporary Debate* (Dordrecht, Boston, Lancaster: Martinus Nijhoff, 1985), p. 450); Shetreet, 'Judicial Independence: New Conceptual Dimensions and Contemporary Challenges' in ibid., p. 615.

19. Hong Kong Reunification Ordinance, s 24(2).

20. See Joseph Chitty, *The Prerogatives of the Crown* (London: Joseph Butterworth & Son, 1820), pp. 75–7.

21. See for example Kristen Walker, 'Disputed Returns and Parliamentary Qualifications: Is the High Court's Jurisdiction Constitutional?' (1997) 20 UNSWLJ 257, 262–3. See also 8 *Halsbury's Laws of Hong Kong* para 125.003.

22. JORCO provides that JORC 'shall advise or make recommendations to the CE regarding (a) the filling of vacancies in judicial offices' (s 6); the obligation of the CE to act on such advice or recommendations arises from the Basic Law, not the ordinance.

23. A judge of the CFA includes the CJ, a permanent judge, and a non-permanent judge when sitting as a member of the court (the Hong Kong Court of Final Appeal Ordinance (HKCFAO), s 5(1) provides that the CJ and the permanent judges shall be the judges of the court, though according to sub-s (4) a judge when sitting as a member of the court shall be deemed to be a member of the court (and thus, presumably, a judge of the CFA)). A permanent judge is a judge appointed under s 7 of the HKCFAO, and a non-permanent judge is appointed under s 8 or s 9, whereas a post-retirement judge appears to be appointed under s 14(2)(b). A post-retirement judge is thus not a judge of the CFA, unless 'includes' somehow brings him in, and therefore, rather oddly, is not, if HKSAR legislation is permitted to supplement the constitution, a judge of a HKSAR court as that expression appears in the Basic Law. Not being a judge of the CFA, he may properly be appointed on the recommendation of the CJ rather than through BL88, and his removal is not subject to BL89. But he does not come under the TO, either, and thus there are no provisions for his dismissal. The same logic applies to non-sitting non-permanent judges who, though required to be appointed by the CE in accordance with the recommendation of JORC, are subject to neither the TO nor BL89. An extended judge is a judge originally appointed under s 7, s 8, or s 9 but whose appointment is extended under

s 14(2)(a). He is therefore a CFA judge if extension is not equivalent to appointment, and this would seem a sensible assumption (though with the unattractive consequence that continuation in office is not achieved through the procedure for appointment, since not JORC but the CJ recommends extension).

24. There is no definition in the HCO of a CFI judge; the CFI, however, consists of the Chief Judge, regular judges, recorders, and deputy judges (but not acting judges), and these would thus seem to come within the expression 'judge of the CFI' in the JORCO schedule (in which case, however, it is redundant to list separately the Chief Judge and recorders). The result is that they should all be appointed through JORC (and, being judges of a court, their dismissal should be in accordance with BL89). But deputy judges are appointed not by the CE on the recommendation of JORC but by the CJ, and their appointments may be terminated not by the CE on the recommendation of a special tribunal but by the CJ apparently on his own advice. Further, recorders appear to be within the purview of the TO for disciplinary purposes, and acting judges of the High Court are not expressly required to be appointed following JORC's recommendation. The appointment of recorders and of extended and fixed-term High Court judges complies with BL88. It is important to notice that the TO provisions for removal do not comply with BL89 (see below); thus either the dismissal of a recorder, for instance, under the ordinance would be invalid or else a recorder is not a judge of a court and is thus presumably a member of the judiciary other than a judge. Yet recorders (and deputy judges) are statutorily granted and may exercise all the jurisdiction, powers, and privileges, and shall perform all the duties, of a judge of the CFI, and it sits uneasily with the Basic Law to regard them (and acting judges) as other than judges of a HKSAR court.

25. JORCO, sched 1.
26. See Peter Wesley-Smith, 'The SAR Constitution: Law or Politics?' (1997) 27 HKLJ 125, 127.
27. See Harry Gibbs, 'The Appointment and Removal of Judges' (1987) 17 FLR 141.
28. See s 11A(3), DCO; s 11A(3)(a) and (b), HCO; ss 7(1) and (2), 8, 9, 14(2)(a) and (b), (4), HKCFAO.
29. 'Permanent and pensionable' terms do not fully comply with independence. 'The "permanent" part of the terms refers not to any guarantee of tenure in a particular office but to tenure in government service generally, that is, in practice, a guarantee against dismissal from the service except for good cause. There is no formal guarantee that a judicial officer appointed on such terms will not be removed from judicial office to some other office in the government service': Eric Barnes, 'The Independence of the Judiciary in Hong Kong' (1976) 6 HKLJ 7, 21. It does not seem that the subsequent enactment of the Judicial Officers (Tenure of Office) Ordinance in 1996 has altered this formal position, though disciplinary transfer to another post must in practice be obsolete.
30. See ss 7–9, TO.
31. See for example Michael Kirby, 'Judicial Independence in Australia Reaches a Moment of Truth' (1990) 13 UNSWLJ 187.

32. Nihal Jayawickrama, 'Public Law' in Raymond Wacks (ed.), *The Law in Hong Kong 1969–1989* (Hong Kong: Oxford University Press, 1989), pp. 70-1.
33. BSP(31).
34. *Valente* (note 2 above), p. 704.
35. *Beauregard* (note 11 above), pp. 75–6.
36. *Civil and Miscellaneous Lists* (Hong Kong: Government Printer, 1996), item 109.
37. s 6(b) and (c), JORCO.
38. *Valente* (note 2 above), p. 706.
39. See Peter Wesley-Smith, 'Injudicious Pay Cuts?' (1999) 29 HKLJ 2.
40. Note 2 above, p. 704.
41. s 3(1), Pensions Benefits (Judicial Officers) Ordinance. The ordinance also applies to officers whose application regarding previous pensionable service is approved (s 9) or who, being already retired, exercise an option (s 10) or who died before exercizing an option (s 11).
42. *Beauregard* (note 11 above), p. 77.
43. *Valente* (note 2 above), pp. 711–14.
44. (1991) 64 CCC (3d) 513.
45. Ibid., p. 531.
46. Per Grandpré J in Committee for Justice and Liberty v Canada (National Energy Board) (1976) 68 DLR (3d) 716, 735.
47. *Valente* (1985) 23 CCC (3d) 193, 204–5.
48. s 6A(1), HCO.
49. s 6A(3), HCO. See also s 6B (appointment of recorders may be retrospective), s 7 (precedence), and s 11 (powers of recorders in cases which are part-heard on termination of appointment).
50. s 11, HCO.
51. Note 44 above, p. 535.
52. See *Reference re Territorial Court Act* (1997) 152 DLR (4th) 132, 175 (Northwest Territories SC) (appointment of deputy judges).
53. Ibid., p. 176.
54. Oaths and Declarations Ordinance, s 17, sched 3, Part II.
55. They are 'members of the judiciary', whether or not they are judges of a court under the Basic Law and, thus, 'shall be immune from legal action in the performance of their judicial functions' (BL85).
56. Note 52 above.
57. See also para 2.03 of the Universal Declaration on the Independence of Justice (Montreal, 1983).
58. See note 52 above, p. 154.
59. See also *Pellerin v Thérien* (1997) 148 DLR (4th) 255 (Quebec CA) (appointment of retired judges): the term appointment of a retired judge was permitted: his term of office was not contingent on government goodwill, he enjoyed financial security, his duties were assigned by the chief judge, and 'He had no cause for fear and no cause for hope' that he would be re-appointed.
60. See note 52 above, p. 173.
61. 'How those provisions may affect any specific deputy judge is irrelevant. It is the objective status that must conform to constitutional standards': ibid, p. 164. See also Shimon Shetreet, 'Judicial Independence: New Conceptual

Dimensions and Contemporary Challenges' in Shetreet and Deschênes (eds), op. cit., p. 627.

62. See Wesley-Smith, Constitutional and Administrative Law in Hong Kong, op. cit., pp. 709–10.

63. Ibid., p. 712.

64. s 6(2), HKCFAO.

65. s 8, Judicial Officers (Tenure of Office) Ordinance.

66. See Andrew Li CJ's address at the opening of the legal year on 12 January 1998 (text on the judiciary's homepage). See T. David Marshall, *Judicial Conduct and Accountability* (Scarborough, Ont: Carswell, 1995), chap. 3 for arguments in favour of extensive judicial education, including the provision of study leave fellowships.

67. Kate Malleson, 'Judicial Training and Performance Appraisal: The Problem of Judicial Independence' (1997) 60 MLR 655.

68. For example s 71, DCO.

69. See John Gibeaut, 'Taking Aim', *ABA Journal*, November 1996, p. 50; Jon O. Newman, 'The Judge Baer Controversy' (1997) 80 Judicature 156; Stephen B. Bright, 'Political Attacks on the Judiciary: Can Justice be Done amid Efforts to Intimidate and Remove Judges from Office for Unpopular Decisions?' (1997) NYULR 308.

70. *Ng Ka-ling v Director of Immigration* (1999) 1 HKC 291.

71. According to BSP(5), it is the duty of non-judicial institutions of government 'to respect and observe the proper objectives and functions of the Judiciary.'

72. See Yash Ghai, 'A Play in Two Acts: Reflections on the Theatre of the Law' (1999) 29 HKLJ 5. For the Secretary for Justice to contact the CJ in the absence of counsel for the parties was arguably improper (see the discussion in *Canada (Minister of Citizenship and Immigration) v Tobiass* (1997) 15 DLR (4th) 119, 141–7 (SCC)); it may be doubted whether the concept of inherent jurisdiction is broad enough to allow the court to accept this unprecedented jurisdiction to explain its decision (see I.H. Jacob, 'The Inherent Jurisdiction of the Court' (1970) 23 Current Legal Problems 23); in any event the Basic Law gives only the power of final adjudication to the CFA, with which its second 'judgment' had nothing to do, and the Hong Kong Court of Final Appeal Ordinance provides no further authority to the court; and by in effect giving an advisory opinion to the executive branch the court was in breach of the doctrine of the separation of powers (see Peter Wesley-Smith, 'The Separation of Powers' in Peter Wesley-Smith (ed.), *Hong Kong's Basic Law: Problems and Prospects* (Hong Kong: Faculty of Law, University of Hong Kong, 1990), p. 80 n33). For a vigorous defence of the government's action and the CFA's response see Albert H.Y. Chen, 'The Court of Final Appeal's Ruling in the "Illegal Migrant" Children Case: Congressional Supremacy and Judicial Review' (Faculty of Law, University of Hong Kong; Law Working Paper Series, Paper no. 24, March 1999).

73. See also the use of judges in the conduct of inquiries: Gavin Drewry, 'Judicial Inquiries and Public Reassurance' (1996) Public Law 368.

74. See Peter Wesley-Smith, 'Judicial Review of Legislation in Hong Kong' (1996) 26 HKLJ 1.

75. See Anthony Mason, 'Judicial Independence and the Separation of Powers

– Some Problems Old and New' (1990) 13 UNSWLJ 173, 180–1; 'The Courts as Community Institutions' (1998) 9 Public LR 83, 86–7.

76. R.D. Nicholson, 'Judicial Independence and Accountablility: Can They Co-exist?' (1993) 67 ALJ 404, 411–13; see also Ken Marks, 'Judicial Independence' (1994) 68 ALJ 173, 182–7.
77. See the discussion in R.D. Nicholson, 'Human Rights Aspects of Constitutionalism' [1993] NZLJ 441, 443–4.
78. Peter D. Robinson, *Study of the Judiciary 1986* (Hong Kong: Government Printer, 1986).
79. Ibid., para 15.
80. Ibid., para 16.
81. Ibid., para 18.

6
Prospect for the Due Process under Chinese Sovereignty
Johannes Chan

A now untraceable commentator was reported to have said that if there is any philosophy in Hong Kong, it is the rule of law. While it is not easy to define precisely what the rule of law means, it embodies, at the very least, the fundamental notions of equality before the law, the right to the due process of law,[1] and non-retrospective application of legislation. Whether the rule of law can be maintained after the PRC resumed sovereignty over Hong Kong has long been a matter of international concern. More than a year after the transition, it appears that law and order has basically been preserved. However, there are signs and indications which suggest that the golden thread of the rule of law may be more fragile than we used to believe.

Equality before the law

'The King is under no man, but under God and the law.' This time honoured principle set out by Bracton has since been quoted time and again over the history of the common law, although it cost both the throne and the head of Charles I to have it reaffirmed. Hence it comes almost as a surprise when the government of the SAR argued that a different set of law should apply to the state. Almost eight months after the handover, the SAR government introduced an amendment to section 66 of the Interpretation and General Clauses Ordinance.[2] The original section 66 reads:

> No Ordinance shall in any manner whatsoever affect the right of or be binding on the Crown unless it is therein expressly provided or unless it appears by necessary implication that the Crown is bound thereby.

The amendment sought to substitute the word 'State' for 'Crown'. 'State' is defined to include any central authorities of the PRC that exercize *executive functions* or functions for which the Central People's Government (CPG) has responsibility under the Basic Law and any of their *subordinate organs* which exercizes any of those functions on behalf of the central authorities and which do not exercize any commercial function. According to the SAR government, the amendment was purely technical: 'Its effect is to reflect the reunification, but otherwise to maintain the legal position as it was immediately before, and after, the reunification ... this is not an exercise of law reform. The Bill does no more than to retain and adapt to the common law principle in section 66.'[3] Therefore, by a stroke of pen, PRC organs exercizing executive functions are now equated with the 'Crown' and inherit, no more and no less, the colonial principle that they are not subject to the ordinary law of the land unless otherwise stated.

The principle that the Crown is not bound by statutes save by express words or necessary implication has its origin as a prerogative immunity.[4] Technically there are two meanings for 'the Crown': the first refers to the monarch in his or her personal capacity and the second refers to the executive government. The monarch can no longer claim a personal immunity from Acts of Parliament these days.[5] Hence the Crown can only refer to the executive government, or more accurately, the Queen in Parliament. The constitutional rationale is that since an Act is made by the Queen in Parliament for regulating her subjects, thus, in the absence of contrary intention, the Act does not bind the Crown itself.[6]

Under this principle, which is no more than a presumption in statutory interpretation, the Crown (but not the Crown servants in their personal capacity) is immune from liability to income tax. Government departments, and in particular the armed forces, do not have to obtain planning permission in order to effect a material change in the use of land occupied by them.[7] Land occupied for Crown purposes is immune from rates,[8] and the Crown is not required to comply with various building requirements.

Prior to the changeover, this colonial principle is preserved under the constitution of Hong Kong. A distinction is drawn between the Crown in the right of the United Kingdom, which is the sovereign, and the Crown in the right of Hong Kong. Under the Letters Patent, the Governor was only authorized, 'by and with the advice and consent of the Legislative Council, to make laws for the peace, order and good government of the Colony'.[9] The colonial legislature had no power to make laws which were binding on the Crown in the right of the United Kingdom.[10] At the same time, the immunity of the Crown in the right of Hong Kong is preserved in the former section 66 of the Interpretation and General Clauses Ordinance. The SAR government, by amending section 66, sought to preserve the colonial principle of immunity of the Crown in the right of the sovereign by extending this principle to the state organs of the PRC and at the same time preserve the presumption of immunity of the Crown in the right of Hong Kong.

It is inappropriate to equate the Crown before the changeover with the state organs of the PRC. The constitutional rationale for the immunity, namely that the Crown made law for its subject, has no application to the 'State' in the constitutional arrangements since 1997. Under the Basic Law, the 'State' has no power to make law for the SAR, save perhaps, the power to remit local legislation for being inconsistent with the Basic Law and the power to amend the Basic Law.[11] Yet even in these situations the power is vested only in the Standing Committee of the National People's Congress, and not in any of its subordinate organs.

There are more fundamental grounds of objection. Article 22 of the Basic Law expressly provides that 'All offices set up in the Hong Kong Special Administrative Region by departments of the Central Government, or by provinces, autonomous regions, or municipalities directly under the Central Government, and the personnel of these offices shall abide by the laws of the Region.' This article was introduced to allay the fear and the worries of the people of Hong Kong that central organs stationed there after the change of sovereignty would be above the law. These state organs shall abide by the law of the SAR. Under Article 11 of the Basic Law, no law enacted by the SAR legislature shall contravene the Basic Law. The new section 66, which creates a presumption of immunity in favour of state organs stationed in Hong Kong, is clearly inconsistent with Article 22 of the Basic Law.

Indeed, the new section 66 expands the scope of the common law. Since the *Case of Proclamations*,[12] the courts have jealously guarded their jurisdiction to define the ambit of the Crown and are reluctant to expand the scope of Crown immunity.[13] *In re M*,[14] Lord Templeman summarized the judicial sentiment in these terms:

> Parliament makes the law, the executive carry the law into effect and the judiciary enforce the law. The expression 'the Crown' has two meanings; namely the monarch and the executive. In the 17th

century Parliament established its supremacy over the Crown as monarch, over the executive and over the judiciary. Parliamentary supremacy over the Crown as monarch stems from the fact that the monarch must accept the advice of a Prime Minister who is supported by a majority of Parliament. Parliamentary supremacy over the Crown as executive stems from the fact that Parliament maintains in office the Prime Minister who appoints the ministers in charge of the executive. Parliamentary supremacy over the judiciary is only exercisable by statute. The judiciary enforces the law against individuals, against institutions and against the executive. The judges cannot enforce the law against the Crown as monarch because the Crown as monarch can do no wrong but judges enforce the law against the Crown as executive and against the individuals who from time to time represent the Crown.

Accordingly, this presumption of immunity of the Crown from the ordinary law is, like all other prerogatives, of a residual if not dying nature. As Lord Diplock remarked in colourful language, 'it is 350 years and a civil war too late for the Queen's courts to broaden the prerogative.'[15] Prerogatives have been abrogated by statute; the Crown Proceedings Ordinance has deprived the Crown of certain immunities in civil litigation. The appearance of a representative legislature in a colony may result in the loss of its plenary legislative powers.[16] Since the celebrated decision in *Council of Civil Service Unions v Minister for the Civil Service*,[17] a Minister's power, be it statutory or prerogative, is now subject to judicial scrutiny. Refusal to issue a passport is now open to review.[18] A Minister, even acting in his official capacity, can be made personally liable for contempt of court.[19]

Contrary to this general trend, the new section 66 extends the immunity by introducing a new and broad concept of 'State'. It covers central authorities and their subordinate organs in the exercize of their 'executive functions', which is undefined. Under the Basic Law, the CPG is responsible for national defence and foreign affairs. These matters are already outside the scope of autonomy of the SAR.[20] The SAR legislature and judiciary have no jurisdiction in these areas.[21] Therefore, to be meaningful, section 66 has to confer immunity outside the areas of foreign affairs and defence. So far the SAR Government has failed to explain what other 'executive functions' outside these areas the central authorities and their subordinate organs should have in the SAR which are not appropriate to be regulated by the law of the SAR.

The constitutional framework set out in the Basic Law also makes it inappropriate to draw an analogy from federal systems, where there are cases to the effect that a state parliament cannot enact law to bind the federal government.[22] Some of these case law rest on a residual power of the federal parliament to make law, especially in the context of foreign affairs, which would be beyond the jurisdiction of the SAR in any event and the new section 66 would not add anything.[23] Some of them rest on the common law presumption of immunity of the Crown in the right of the sovereign,[24] which has been shown above to be inapplicable to the SAR.

The SAR government argued that PRC organs which fell within the definition of 'State' would continue to be bound by Hong Kong laws, as the general criminal law, the Bill of Rights, civil law and ordinances which bind the Crown would apply to the 'State'.[25] The basis of this argument is dubious. There is no express provision of application to the Crown in most statutes in Hong Kong. For example, there is no such provision in statutes relating to fire services, third party motor insurance, personal data protection, town planning, building construction, environmental protection. It would be highly undesirable to leave the important question of applicability to the Crown to 'necessary implication'.[26] Even if the 'State' is prepared to comply with these laws which do not apply to it explicitly or by necessary implication, the effect of section 66 is that the State obeys the law not as a matter of necessity, but as a matter of grace, a proposition which, in the words of Lord Templeman, 'would reverse the result of the Civil War'.[27]

The SAR government may be on stronger ground if it argued that the presumption of immunity in section 66 should only apply to itself. Even so, it is debatable that this colonial principle, which is a historical aberration, should be preserved. There is no persuasive reason why the government should not be equally subject to the ordinary law of the land unless it is expressly exempted. The presumption of immunity effectively puts it above the law and is contrary to the modern notion of equality before the law. The SAR government argued that equality before the law never applied to statutes; statutes were selective and could confine its application to a specific sector or a specific group or a specific cause. This might be the situation, but the starting point must be that all statutes apply to everyone, citizens and government alike, unless there are justifications for the contrary. The new section 66 reverses this starting point unjustifiably. In this regard it is worth recalling A.V. Dicey:[28]

When we speak of the 'rule of law' as a characteristic of our country, [we mean] not only that with us no man is above the law, but (what is a different thing) that here every man, whatever be his rank or condition, is subject to the ordinary law of the realm and amenable to the jurisdiction of the ordinary tribunals. In England the idea of legal equality, or of the universal subjection of all classes to one law administered by the ordinary courts, has been pushed to its utmost limit. With us every official, from Prime Minister down to a constable or a collector of taxes, is under the same responsibility for every act done without legal justification as any other citizen. The reports abound with cases in which officials have been brought before the courts, and made, in their personal capacity, liable to punishment, or to the payment of damages, for acts done in their official character but in excess of their lawful authority. A colonial governor, a secretary of state, a military officer, and all subordinates, though carrying out the commands of their official superiors, are as responsible for any act which the law does not authorise as is any private and unofficial person.

Despite strong criticisms from the legal profession and from many quarters of the community, the amendment was passed by the Provisional Legislative Council (PLC) by an overwhelming majority on the second last day of its short and controversial life.[29] The resumed second debates were over in less than 30 minutes.[30]

Who decides to prosecute?

It is ironic that our law has laid down numerous safeguards to ensure procedural equality or, in more modern language, the equality of arms, between the contesting parties in litigation, yet it has done little if anything at all on the very question when an innocent person, at least in the eyes of the law, should be dragged into the complex web of criminal process. Section 15(1) of the Criminal Procedure Ordinance provides[31] that 'The Secretary for Justice shall not be bound to prosecute an accused person in any case in which he may be of opinion that the interests of public justice do not require his interference.' This statutory power is reinforced by Article 63 of the Basic Law.[32] It is not controversial that in deciding whether to prosecute, the Secretary for Justice will consider whether there is sufficient evidence to prove the charge, whether there is a reasonable prospect of securing a conviction, and whether it is in the public interest to prosecute.[33]

At the beginning of 1998, the Secretary for Justice Elsie Leung made two controversial decisions not to prosecute. In the first case, several senior members of Hong Kong Standard Newspaper Ltd were charged with, inter alia, an offence of conspiracy with Sally Aw, chairman of the corporation, to defraud advertisers of two of Aw's newspapers by inflating the circulation figures. As explained in Chapters 1 and 3, although named in the indictment Aw was not prosecuted. In early 1999 all the defendants were convicted. Aw is known to be close to the Chief Executive and the CPG. When questioned in the legislature Secretary Leung stated that she took no account of Aw's political background in deciding not to prosecute, and that the public would understand her decision once the evidence of the criminal proceedings against Aw's subordinates unfolded. The primary reason was a lack of evidence, which did not sound convincing. The most controversial part, however, was her second reason, that it would not be in the public interest because Aw was the head of a large organization; to prosecute her would bring down the organization and might result in a large numbers of unemployed, which would be extremely undesirable in a recession. This interpretation of public interest shocked the community, as it effectively means that the rich is immune from criminal prosecution.

The next case, which concerns the Xinhua News Agency, is more disturbing. Xinhua is directly under the State Council of the PRC. Its Hong Kong branch was set up in 1947. Legally it is registered as a newspaper under the Registration of Local Newspapers Ordinance,[34] but it is not registered as a company under the Companies Ordinance,[35] or as a firm under the Business Registration Ordinance,[36] or as a society under the Society Ordinance.[37] While it is formally a news agency, it is also the front organization for the Hong Kong and Macao Work Committee of the Chinese Communist Party – a party organ of ministerial rank – and acted as the mouthpiece of the Party in Hong Kong.[38] Indeed, after the signing of the Sino-British Joint Declaration, it functioned as the *de facto* embassy of the PRC in Hong Kong.

On 20 December 1996, an elected legislator Emily Lau wrote to Xinhua to enquire whether it had kept any of her personal data and if so, to supply her with copies of such personal data pursuant to the Personal Data (Privacy) Ordinance. Under section 19 of the Ordinance, Xinhua had to reply within 40 days of the request but did not do so until 10 months later, categorically denying having any of her personal data. Lau complained to the Privacy Commissioner, who found, in February 1998, a breach of section 19 and referred the matter to the Secretary for Justice. In March 1998, the Secretary decided not to prosecute. No explanation was given, apart from reiterating the general consideration of sufficiency of evidence and public interest. The case aroused widespread speculation that her decision was related to the sensitive status of Xinhua and that a state organ like it might be above Hong Kong law. Inadequate evidence could hardly be an explanation, given that the Privacy Commissioner has already found a breach. It might be said that this was only a trivial technical offence, but if so, this might be a serious blow to the enforcement of the Ordinance, as it would mean that no one has to take the statutory time limit to comply with a data access request seriously. It might be said that the offence had become stale, as the breach took place some time ago and might even be time-barred.[39] However, if this is the main consideration, the Secretary could easily have said so.

These two incidents highlight the competing roles of the Secretary for Justice in defending the integrity of the legal system and in maintaining public confidence in the administration of justice, and the inherent tension between her privilege not to disclose her reasons not to prosecute and her accountability to the public. Despite its statutory origin, the discretionary power of the Secretary to decide whether to take out prosecution has been held to be the equivalent of the exercize of the Royal Prerogative.[40] Until the handover, the exercise of this power was not subject to judicial review[41] even though the Attorney General is answerable to the Legislative Council.[42] When he was questioned in the Legislative Council for his decision not to prosecute Alan Bond in the 1980s the then Attorney General Michael Thomas defended his position:[43]

> There are good reasons why any Attorney General does not normally explain in public a decision not to prosecute in a particular case. It is rare for any public announcement to be made of that decision because it would reveal unfairly that someone had been under suspicion for having committed a criminal offence and even where that fact is known, to give reasons in public for not prosecuting the suspect would lead to public debate about the case and about his guilt or innocence. The nature of the evidence against the suspect would have to be revealed. Then some might say that was proof enough for guilt, and the suspect would find himself condemned by public censure. Sir, in our legal system the only proper place for questions of guilt or innocence of crime to be determined is in a Court, where the accused has the right to fair trial in

accordance with the rules of criminal justice, and the opportunity to defend himself. So, members will readily appreciate that it would be quite wrong for any Attorney General, having decided that the issue should not proceed to trial in the Courts, to say anything in public that might be taken to indicate a belief in the suspect's guilt, or which might lead to a public discussion of that very question.

The right of the Attorney General not to disclose the reasons for his decision not to prosecute was again reaffirmed in *R v Harris*, where the then Attorney General firstly decided not to prosecute an ex-Crown counsel (who happened to be the head of the anti-vice unit) for certain sexual offences, and later changed his mind to prosecute, apparently in response to immense public pressure. The Court of Appeal refused to speculate the reasons for the change of mind and upheld the Attorney General's right.[44] It emphasized that the court should be slow to be involved in the decision whether to bring a prosecution. Its supervisory power lay in staying the criminal proceedings, after they had been instituted, if the prosecution constituted an abuse of due process.[45]

No doubt protection of the right of the accused and the avoidance of a trial by media are powerful considerations supporting the Secretary for Justice's right to silence. These factors deserve the most careful consideration, but they should not be the only concern. Equally important is the time honoured principle that justice must not only be done, but must manifestly be seen to be done. Public confidence in the administration of justice will likely be eroded if silence is maintained in circumstances where there is a reasonable doubt on the propriety of the decision not to prosecute, for example, in the Xinhua case.[46] After surveying a number of cases from the last century, Peter Wesley-Smith concluded that while there was no question on the independence of the Secretary for Justice in routine matters, she perhaps did not enjoy the same degree of prosecutorial autonomy on a question as important as Hong Kong's relations with mainland China.[47] While it is arguable that a historical survey on how the prosecutorial discretion was exercized in the last century had no bearing on how the discretion is exercized today, it is certainly true that an inflexible attitude in maintaining silence is unlikely to dispel the legitimate doubt on the part of the public. Nor would silence be conducive to the maintenance of public confidence in the administration of justice, which is at least of equal importance, especially at this time of Hong Kong's history, when an explanation is warranted.

Independence and impartiality of the judiciary: when should judicial provence end and the executive's reign begin?

When a member of the public is aggrieved by a decision of government or a public authority, he is entitled to look to the court as the guardian of his rights. In a system that respects the rule of law, everyone can legitimately expect the court to discharge its functions independently and impartially, without any predisposition in favour of the government. By and large the Hong Kong judiciary has lived up to that expectation.

Independence and impartiality of the judiciary is so entrenched in the common law system that it has almost been mystified – it appears or assumes that the judiciary is an apathetic, neutral institution and personal values of judges are irrelevant to the outcome of any judicial decision. This is far from true, even when there is no constitution or a bill of rights.[48] In all judicial process, choices have to be made, and balance between conflicting interests has to be carried out. No doubt personal values of a judge will affect how these choices and decisions are made. When one of the parties is the government, a judge will have to decide at what point the executive has overstepped its boundary and called for an intervention by the judiciary. The dividing line between the executive and the judiciary is far from clear, and human factors might play a crucial role in determining where the boundary lies.

Land resumption

In *Fok Lai Ying v Governor in Council*,[49] the issue was whether the applicant was entitled to be heard before her land was resumed by the government for a public purpose. Under section 3 of the Crown Lands Resumption Ordinance, 'whenever the Governor in Council decides that the resumption of any land is required for a public purpose, the Governor may order the resumption thereof under this Ordinance.'[50] 'Resumption for a public purpose' is defined as widely as one can possibly imagine: it includes, *inter alia*, whatever the Governor in Council might decide to be a public purpose.[51] By section 19, a notice to resume any land stating that the land is required for a public purpose is deemed conclusive. At first instance, Mr Justice Cheung held that the Governor in Council was obliged to provide the applicant with an opportunity to make submissions before the resumption was ordered, and as no such opportunity had been provided, the order for resumption was quashed.

This decision was reversed on appeal. The Court of Appeal (comprising Vice-President Mr Justice Litton, Mr Justice Godfrey and Mr Justice Ching) stressed that a scheme of public works involved a variety of competing interests and affected many parties. To read into a few lines in the Crown Lands Resumption Ordinance a duty to afford an opportunity to those affected to make representations and thereby introducing 'a judge-made scheme of an amorphous kind' would be tantamount to legislative amendment. This was unwarranted, and the court affirmed that prior to a decision to resume land for a public purpose, the Governor was not bound to consult anyone other than the Executive Council. Delivering the judgment, Mr Justice Litton explained the correct approach to judicial review:[52]

> The concept of fairness in action cannot be invoked to destroy a statutory scheme. The justice of the common law, coming to the aid of an individual, cannot supply the omissions of the legislature in this way.... Administrative law governs the activities of all government departments. It is vitally important that any implication of law, arising from the express words of a statute, should not only be fair but also be practical in operation and easy to comprehend. Otherwise, administrative law would create not fairness but chaos.

The Privy Council disagreed with this approach. Having described the provisions of the Crown Lands Resumption Ordinance as 'singularly sweeping and on their face draconian', Lord Cooke re-asserted the primacy of procedural fairness:[53]

> The judgement of the Court of Appeal in this case and the judgement of a Full Bench of the High Court in the earlier *KOY* case[54] depend ultimately on the ideas that to superimpose on the statutory language requirements apt to lead to protracted exchanges or something akin to a public inquiry would be to frustrate the purposes of the Ordinance; and that to take away for public purposes all or some of a person's home is neither arbitrary nor unlawful if monetary compensation is furnished. Their Lordships are not to be taken as endorsing this approach. So far as it invokes a kind of *expressio unis* argument – derived from the presence in the [Crown Lands] Resumption Ordinance, the Town Planning Ordinance and the Roads (Works, Use and Compensation) Ordinance of limited express rights to be heard – it may not be reconcilable with *Doody*,[55] where a somewhat similar argument was

rejected and the natural justice principle of supplementation applied. So far as it invokes practical inconvenience, the opportunity of response to official arguments which the appellant seeks might seem a modest enough request.[56]

Repatriation of Vietnamese boat people

Between 1988 and 1992, there was a second wave of migrants from Vietnam to Hong Kong; about 71 300 residents of Vietnam arrived without any valid travel document during this period. In June 1988, a screening procedure was introduced. Vietnamese migrants who arrived without travel documents were detained pending screening to ascertain whether they were refugees within the meaning of the 1951 United Nations Convention and the 1967 Protocol. Those screened out, and a large proportion of them were, were detained pending repatriation. Section 13D(1) of the Immigration Ordinance conferred a discretion on the Director of Immigration to detain any persons 'pending removal from Hong Kong'.

In 1991, the Hong Kong Government introduced an Orderly Repatriation Programme for the compulsory repatriation of those economic migrants from Vietnam who refused volunteer repatriation. Particulars of those concerned were sent to the Vietnamese authorities to enable them to confirm the acceptance of repatriation.

In *Tan Le Lam v Superintendent of Tai A Chau Detention Centre*,[57] which was a test case, the four applicants were former residents in Vietnam of Chinese origin. They arrived in Hong Kong without any travel documents between 1989 and 1991. They were detained upon their arrival and were eventually screened out. From that point onward they were detained pending removal. When they were in Vietnam, they were treated by the Vietnamese authorities as non-nationals because of their Taiwanese nationality. Their particulars were forwarded to the Vietnamese authorities. There was evidence that the Vietnamese policy was to reject repatriation of those deemed non-Vietnamese nationals. However, no refusal was received from the Vietnamese authorities regarding any of the applicants. They were detained for a period between 22 to 44 months pending removal, between 35 and 68 months since they first arrived in Hong Kong. They applied for *habeas corpus*.

At first instance, Mr Justice Keith found that while the original detention pending screening was lawful, the purpose of the detention pending removal was spent when it became reasonably clear that they would not be accepted for repatriation. He ordered their release, describing their detention as 'extremely long' and 'when coupled with the length of their detention pending screening, the time which these applicants have been in detention is … an affront to the standards of the civilized society which Hong Kong aspires to be.'[58]

The order of *habeas corpus* was set aside by the Court of Appeal. Delivering the judgment, Mr Justice Litton emphasized that the jurisdiction of the court, even in a case of *habeas corpus*, was purely supervisory: it was not for the court to reach findings as to the underlying facts, in this case namely, whether or not the period of detention was reasonable or whether Vietnam would accept repatriation. The court's enquiry was confined to whether attempts were still being made for the repatriation of the applicants. If so, the application could only succeed if the applicants could demonstrate (and the burden was on them) that the Director of Immigration was *Wednesbury* unreasonable in reaching his conclusion that their removal would still be practical. Litton emphasized that repatriation of illegal immigrants was a bilateral process, requiring dialogues between the Hong Kong government and the immigration authorities overseas. When the legality of the detention of a particular Vietnamese migrant depended only in part upon the efforts of the local government in effecting his or her repatriation to Vietnam, the passage of time alone could not provide a guide to the legality of that detention. He added:

> … as to whether such purpose [of removal from Hong Kong] can, as a matter of hard fact, be achieved, the judgement of the Director of Immigration must carry great weight with the court. He is, after all, charged by the legislature with the responsibility of carrying out the policy set out in the Ordinance; so long as he is acting in good faith and within the scope and purpose of the Ordinance it is difficult to think of circumstances where a court could legitimately interfere…. Repatriation might involve at times delicate negotiations between governments. The foreign government is not a party to the proceedings. The court is in no position to weigh up its policies and attitudes judicially. If the circumstances of a particular group of Vietnamese migrants were in fact under discussion between the two governments, or thought in good faith by the Director to be under consideration by the Vietnamese authorities, the court generally cannot intervene: no court can declare with confidence that the purpose of detention is spent when, factually, dialogue and negotiations are still underway.

In other words, so long as there is no unambiguous refusal to accept for repatriation from the Vietnamese authorities, the detention of the applicants, no matter for how long, even indefinitely, would still be lawful; and the legality of the administrative detention without trial is not affected by the fact that the delay is due solely to the tardiness of the Vietnamese authorities. The applicants strenuously argued that the power to detain under section 13D(1) must be construed in such a way that detention pending removal should be limited to a period which is necessary for that purpose, relying on the famous *Hardial Singh* principle.[59] Litton distinguished *Hardial Singh* on the basis that that case involved the deportation of persons lawfully in the United Kingdom and their release pending deportation would cause no social problems, whereas the same could not be said of the Vietnamese migrants who had no existing way of life outside the detention centre. It was held that the *Hardial Singh* principle had no application to the statutory scheme of compulsory repatriation of Vietnamese migrants in Hong Kong.

The Privy Council refuted this approach. Lord Browne-Wilkinson stated:

> Their Lordships have no doubt that in conferring such a power to interfere with individual liberty, the legislature intended that such power could only be exercised reasonably and that accordingly it was implicitly so limited. The principles enunciated by Woolf J in *Hardial Singh* are statements of the limitations on a statutory power of detention pending removal. In the absence of contrary indications in the statute which confers the power to detain 'pending removal' their Lordships agree with the principles stated by Woolf J. First, the power can only be exercised during the period necessary, in all the circumstances of the particular case, to effect removal. Second, if it becomes clear that removal is not going to be possible within a reasonable time, further detention is not authorized. Third, the person seeking to exercise the power of detention must take all reasonable steps within this power to ensure the removal within a reasonable time.... Subject to any constitutional challenge (which does not arise in this case) the legislature can vary or possibly exclude the *Hardial Singh* principles. But in their Lordships' view, the courts should construe strictly any statutory provision purporting to allow the deprivation of individual liberty by administrative detention and should be slow to hold that statutory provisions authorize administrative detention for unreasonable periods or in unreasonable circumstances.

In marked contrast, individual liberty was not even mentioned in Mr Justice Litton's general approach to interpreting section 13D or in his discussion of the applicability of the *Hardial Singh* principles.[60] Instead, what has come out very prominently in his judgment is the paramount governmental interest in upholding the repatriation scheme.

The Privy Council also disagreed with the Court of Appeal on the role of the court. It was held that it was for the court, and not the Director of Immigration, to determine the facts relevant to the question whether the applicants were being detained 'pending removal', as this question went to the jurisdiction of the Director to detain or to the exercize of the discretion to detain. Their Lordships accepted that the legislature might, by clear words, confer power on the executive to determine its own jurisdiction, but where 'human liberty is at stake, very clear words would be required to produce this result.'[61] There was no such clear intention. Therefore, it was for the executive to prove to the court on a balance of probabilities that the facts necessary to justify the conclusion that the applicants were being detained 'pending removal'. Lord Browne-Wilkinson commented that the Court of Appeal's approach would cut at the very basis of the constitutional importance of *habeas corpus*. He laboured this point in strong language:

> If a jailor could justify the detention of his prisoner by saying 'in my view, the facts necessary to justify the detention exist' the fundamental protection afforded by a habeas corpus would be severely limited. The court should be astute to ensure that the protection afforded to human liberty by habeas corpus should not be eroded save by the clearest words.[62]

The Privy Council restored the order to release. However, soon after the defeat at the Privy Council, the Hong Kong government forced through an amendment to the Immigration Ordinance to put it beyond doubt that so long as there is no refusal from the Vietnamese authorities, the detention of any Vietnamese migrant would be deemed to be detention pending removal.[63]

Right of abode

Over the years many Hong Kong Permanent Residents[64] got married in China and have children there. Prior to 1 July 1997, the PRC authorities operated a one-way exit permit system under which a certain quota of persons living in mainland China were permitted to settle in Hong Kong. This permit system was handled entirely by the public security bureau in mainland China, and the Immigration Department in Hong Kong had no part to play in the issue or allocation of permits, though it was consulted on the size of the quota. Children born in China to Hong Kong Permanent Residents did not acquire any right of abode in Hong Kong before the changeover.

Under Article 24 of the Basic Law, children born outside Hong Kong to a parent who is a Hong Kong Permanent Resident is qualified to be a Hong Kong Permanent Resident. In anticipation of the coming into effect of the Basic Law on 1 July 1997, many of these children entered Hong Kong clandestinely or overstayed after entering with a visitor permit. After 1 July 1997 they approached the Immigration Department to seek recognition of their status as permanent residents of the SAR and the issuance of identity cards.

On 10 July 1997, the PLC enacted the Immigration (Amendment) (No. 3) Ordinance 1997.[65] The amendment introduced a certificate of entitlement scheme under which the status of a claimant of SAR permanent residents can only be established by holding a valid travel document and a valid certificate of entitlement affixed to such travel document, unless he can produce a valid SAR passport or a valid permanent identity card issued to him. The certificate of entitlement can only be applied for in the PRC. The certificate is affixed to the one-way exit permit at the immigration control point when he arrives in Hong Kong. This means even if a child can prove that he satisfies the requirements under Article 24 of the Basic Law to be a Hong Kong Permanent Resident, he is not eligible to make such a claim unless he is in possession of the necessary certificate of entitlement. Possession of the certificate becomes the sole and exclusive means of proof of the status of Hong Kong Permanent Residents. This requirement does not exist in Article 24 of the Basic Law. The amendment went through all three readings in one day and operated retrospectively from 1 July 1997.

As a result, all children already in Hong Kong on or before 10 July 1997 who were born on the mainland to a Hong Kong Permanent Resident became liable to immediate removal. For them, the condition required for possession of a certificate of entitlement is an impossible one. It is a fiction created to nullify their right of abode. Unfortunately, an immediate consequence of the amendment was that the children became illegal immigrants, and both they and their parents could be guilty of various immigration offences. The Bar was outraged by such retrospective legislation and called for an emergency meeting. After the meeting, over a hundred barristers signed up to act for these children on a *pro bona* basis to prevent them from being summarily removed. Eventually, legal aid was granted and the Immigration Department undertook not to remove any of them until the final determination of the judicial review. *Cheung Lai Wah v Director of Immigration* was lodged as a test case.[66] The applicants argued, *inter alia*, that the amendment was inconsistent with Article 24 of the Basic Law. One of the issues before the court was the retrospective operation of the amendment. It was argued that an unqualified constitutional right of abode in Hong Kong of those who were already in Hong Kong on or before 10 July 1997 was retrospectively taken away.

At first instance, Mr Justice Keith held that the amendment could be justified by Article 22(4) of the Basic Law. On the question of retrospectivity, the reasoning of the trial judge is most curious. In the first place, he held that since the right of abode of these children were already curtailed by Article 22 of the Basic Law, which came into effect on 1 July 1997, there was no retrospective denial of their right. As to the other argument based on Article 12(1) of the Hong Kong Bill of Rights, Mr Justice Keith said:[67]

> This argument proceeds on the assumption that art 12(1) of the Hong Kong Bill of Rights prohibits legislation which exposes persons to the possibility of prosecution for conduct which was not criminal at the time of the conduct. I do not construe art 12(1) in that way. I construe art 12(1) as prohibiting the prosecution of persons for conduct which was not criminal at the time of the conduct. After all, if a person cannot be prosecuted for such conduct, no question of him being exposed to the possibility of prosecution arises. Indeed, that is far more consistent with the language of art 12(1): 'No one shall be held guilty of any criminal offence ...'. I know that two commentators on the equivalent provision (art 7(1)) in the European Convention on Human Rights take a different view, but the travaux preparatoires of art 15(1) of the ICCPR are inconclusive. Accordingly, the challenge to the No 3 Ordinance on the basis of retrospectivity fails. What could be challenged successfully is any prosecution on the basis of a contravention between 1 and 10 July of s 38(1)(a) of the Immigration Ordinance.

In short, the legislature is free to enact retrospective provisions, but no one could be prosecuted for violating these retrospective provisions! This is the most curious kind of reasoning. As counsel for the applicants forcefully argued on appeal, 'if the judge were right, it would mean that the lawmakers could with impunity stigmatize as offences acts which were perfectly lawful at the time they occurred and deny these people the right to have the law declared invalid and their innocence vindicated in a court of law.'[68]

The Court of Appeal split on this issue. Chief Judge Chan held that there was no justification whatsoever for the retrospective provision and found it unconstitutional. Accordingly, those who arrived in Hong Kong before 10 July could not have their constitutional right of abode taken away. He re-affirmed that the courts have always viewed retrospective provisions with caution and disfavour, and would be slow to uphold retrospective provisions unless there is clear and express provision to that effect, especially when they affect accrued rights. He stated:[69]

> The retrospective provision in the present case does not fit in comfortably with reality. How can the Ordinance say that the appellants do not have the status of permanent residents and the right of abode when in actual fact they can clearly show that they have? How can it be said that between 1st and 9th July 1997, a person (whether he be in Mainland China or in Hong Kong) could apply for a certificate of entitlement when the necessary forms were not even in existence until the 10th July when the law was passed or even 11th July 1997 when the Director's Notice was issued? The Director could not possibly have issued any certificates during that period. If these appellants had applied for and had been issued permanent identity cards between 1st and 9th July 1997 before the amendment to the provisions of the Registration of Persons Regulations by the No 3 Ordinance, would they have been able to fall within section 2AA of the No 3 Ordinance? Presumably they would not. This is because the Ordinance was deemed to have taken effect on 1st July and these people did not have permanent identity cards on that date but only obtained them after that date. What then would their status be? What would happen to their accrued rights? As the authors of Bennion, *Statutory Interpretation*, 2nd edn, say at p. 215: 'Retrospectivity is artificial, deeming a thing to be what it was not. Artificiality and make-believe are generally repugnant to law as the servant of human welfare.'

This strong conviction against retrospective application of legislation provision was not shared by the other two judges. Mr Justice Mortimer, Vice-President, upheld the retrospective provision and was brief on this point:[70]

> The applicants' main argument that the effect of the Ordinance was to retrospectively deprive them of their accrued rights of abode as permanent residents present in Hong Kong on 1 July 1997 falls away, in my judgement, if the exercise of that right of abode is limited by Article 22(4) as I conclude. A retrospective provision in legislation is not per se unconstitutional or unlawful, or in breach of the Bill of Rights or the ICCPR, as applied in the Basic Law. In my judgement, it cannot be said that the Ordinance has by its retrospective provision arbitrarily deprived the applicants of an accrued right of abode when the exercise of the right of abode is constitutionally limited and the provisions of Ordinance No 3 are themselves consistent with the Basic Law. In these circumstances, I find it impossible to conclude that the relevant retrospective provisions are not valid and effective.

Mr Justice Nazareth, Vice-President, adopted a half-way house solution. Having held that the amendment was constitutional because of Article 22(4) of the Basic Law, he took the view that the amendment should not affect any person who had arrived in Hong Kong before 1 July 1997, but those who were here between 1 and 10 July 1997 would be caught by the amendment. Since Art 22(4) came into effect on 1 July 1997, the retrospective provision was sanctioned by Art 22(4) and accordingly it was not unconstitutional. As to Article 12 of the Bill of Rights, he agreed with Mr Justice Keith that 'The necessity from time to time to make retrospective legislation should not be absolutely barred simply because some persons might be exposed to criminal prosecution; rather they should have immunity from prosecution, as in fact they here appear to do.'[71] On further appeal, the Court of Final Appeal unanimously decided that the retrospective provision was unconstitutional.

Conclusion

The right to be heard, the right not to be detained for an inordinate and unreasonable period of time, and non-retrospective application of legislation to take away vested rights, are the hallmarks of the due process. They were challenged at the eve of the British administration and at the dawn of the new regime. In all three cases the Court of Appeal found that these fundamental principles have to give way in order not to frustrate important government policies: resumption of land in *Fok Lai Ying*, compulsory repatriation of Vietnamese migrants in *Tan Le Nam*, and orderly arrival of children born to Hong Kong Permanent Residents outside Hong Kong in *Cheung Lai Wah*. In *Fok Lai Ying*, the Court of Appeal refused to introduce a right to be heard in land resumption on the basis that to do so would amount to legislative amendment, which is not the role of the judiciary. In *Tan Le Nam*, the Court of Appeal found that an application for *habeas corpus* could only succeed if it can be shown that the Director of Immigration's decision that removal is practical is *Wednesbury* unreasonable. In *Cheung Lai Wah*, the issue was dealt with as a matter of technical statutory inter-pretation. *Wednesbury* unreasonableness and the principle that the function of the judiciary is to apply the law and not to legislate are of course familiar principles of the common law. However, when the judiciary has crossed the imaginary line dividing the judiciary from the executive, or when the executive has reached that elusive standard of *Wednesbury* unreasonableness and hence called for the intervention by the judiciary, is not a matter subject to scientific definition. The skilful use of technical and apparently neutral principles should not disguise the real issue inherent in any judicial scrutiny of executive conduct, namely, the proper demarcation between the judiciary and the executive. The different outcomes before the Court of Appeal and the Privy Council in *Fok Lai Ying* and *Tan Le Nam* amply demonstrate that the demarcation is fine and fluid. Independent or otherwise, the readiness of the judiciary to intervene in executive decisions, in the name of exercizing its supervisory function in judicial review, is affected by many factors, and not least by the prevailing political climate and the perception of individual judges on the proper role of the judiciary. A restrained perception of the role of the judiciary will result in affording greater leeway and ready acceptance of the need to uphold government policies, whereas a different perception of the role of the judiciary may require the most stringent justification from the executive before fundamental principles of the due process could be compromised. In the last three cases, what is of concern is the readi-ness of the judiciary to give up the fundamental principles of the due process when major government policies might be perceived to be at stake. In *Fok Lai Ying* and *Tan Le Nam*, the decisions of the Court of Appeal in these respects were reversed by the Privy Council. The reversal is less so on different interpretation or application of rules and principles, but of a more fundamental nature as to the proper role of the judiciary and the commitment to procedural justice. So far as the HKSAR is concerned, the Privy Council has now gone. The Court of Final Appeal is still at its early days. While its decision in *Cheung Lai Wah* was generally hailed as a strong confirmation of the rule of law and the independence of the judiciary, that decision soon led to one constitutional crisis after another. As examined in Chapters 1 and 3 certain parts of the judgment were strongly criticized by Beijing. Upon application by the SAR government the CFA was forced to give an unprecedented clarification of its judgment, clarifying that it did not intend to place itself above the NPC or its Standing Committee. The clarification was made solely on the ground that some quarters (namely Beijing) had misunderstood the judgment. Then in June 1999, despite strong opposition of the legal profession, the government invited the NPC Standing Committee to make an interpretation of the relevant articles in the Basic Law to reverse the decision of the CFA.[72]

It is not just the judiciary. The SAR government has not shown the respect for the rule of law either, when the upholding of the rule of law is likely to frustrate important government policies. The former government has no hesitation in forcing through an amendment to the Immigration Ordinance to undo the decision of the Privy Council in *Tan Le Nam*, and the present government is prepared to push through the Adaptation of Laws (Interpretative Provisions) Bill despite strong opposition from the community and the lack of any urgency for the amendment. In routine matters, there is little doubt that the rule of law will be respected and upheld. Yet the litmus test is not in routine matters, but in matters which mean a lot to the government. In this latter area, there is a grave doubt.

Notes

1. Lord Denning defined 'due process' in these terms: '... the measures authorised by the law so as to keep the streams of justice pure: to see that trials and inquiries are fairly conducted; that arrests and searches are properly made; that lawful remedies are readily available; and that unnecessary delays are eliminated.' Lord Denning, *The Due Process of Law* (London: Butterworths, 1980), p. v.
2. Adaptation of Laws (Interpretative Provisions) Bill 1998, Legal Supplement No. 3, C512 (22 February 1998).
3. Speech by the Acting Secretary for Justice, Mr Ian Wingfield, in the PLC on

7 April 1998 on the resumption of the Second Reading Debate on the Adaptation of Laws (Interpretative Provisions) Bill.

4. See S.A. de Smith, *Constitutional and Administrative Law* (Harmondsworth: Penguin, 5th edn, 1985), at p. 134; F.A.P. Bennion, *Statutory Interpretation* (London: Butterworths, 1997, 3rd edn), section 34.
5. *M v Home Office* (1994) 1 AC 377 at 395, per Lord Templeman.
6. *British Broadcasting Corporation v Johns* (1965) Ch 32 at 78.
7. *Ministry of Agriculture v Jenkins* (1963) 2 QB 317. The examples of Crown immunity here are taken from de Smith, supra.
8. *Mersey Docks and Harbour Board Trustees v Cameron* (1964) 11 HLC 464.
9. Art VII, Letters Patent.
10. See also Colonial Laws Validity Act. The only exception is that provided for in the Hong Kong Act 1985, which made provisions for Order in Council to be made authorizing the Hong Kong Legislative Council to amend and repeal UK Acts of Parliament applicable to Hong Kong in limited circumstances.
11. Arts 17 and 158, Basic Law.
12. (1611) 12 Co Rep 74. See also *Burmah Oil v Lord Advocate* (1965) AC 75.
13. For example, see *Tamlin v Hannaford* (1950) 1 KB 18; *British Broadcasting Corporation v Johns* (1965) Ch 32.
14. (1994) AC 377 at 395. See also *R v Home Secretary and Criminal Injuries Compensation Board, ex parte P* (1995) 1 All ER 870.
15. *British Broadcasting Corporation v Johns* (1965) Ch 32 at 79.
16. *Campbell v Hall* (1774) 1 Cowp 204, and the Colonial Laws Validity Act 1865, 28 & 29 Vict, c 63.
17. (1985) AC 374.
18. *R v Secretary of State for Foreign and Commonwealth Affairs, ex p Everett* (1989) QB 811.
19. *In re M* (1994) 1 AC 377.
20. Arts 13 and 14.
21. Arts 18 and 19. Foreign affairs and defence should be governed by national law which will be extended to the SAR through Annex III of the Basic Law.
22. See, for example, *Commonwealth v Cigamatic* (1962) 108 CLR 372; *Commonwealth v State of Tasmania* (1983) 158 CLR 1; *The Queen Alta v Can Transport Commission* (1978) 1 SCR 61; *Gauthier v The King* (1918) 56 SCR 176. I am grateful to Dr Berry Hsu and Dr Steve Tsang who kindly drew my attention to these authorities.
23. See, for example, *Commonwealth v State of Tasmania* (1983) 158 CLR 1.
24. *Gauthier v The King* (1918) 56 SCR 176.
25. Speech of Ian Wingfield, supra, at p. 3.
26. Not surprisingly, the ICAC found it necessary to issue a press statement that the Corrupt and Illegal Practices Ordinance (Cap 288) and the Prevention of Bribery Ordinance (Cap 201) will apply to everyone in Hong Kong.
27. *In re M* (1994) AC 377 at 395.
28. A.V. Dicey, *Introduction to the Study of the Law of the Constitution* (London: Macmillan, 10th edn, 1959), pp. 193–4.
29. 7 April 1998. For the controversy on the legality of the PLC, see Johannes Chan, 'The Jurisdiction and Legality of the Provisional Legislative Council' (1997) 27 HKLJ 374–87.

30. As a compromise, the SAR government promised to review about 90 ordinances which applied to the Crown before the changeover and consider whether they should apply to the State. This, however, does not address the concern that laws which did not apply to the Crown do not automatically mean that they should not apply to the State, which is now an enlarged concept.
31. Cap 221.
32. Article 63 provides that the conduct of criminal proceedings is the sole responsibility of the Department of Justice which is to be discharged free from any interference.
33. Department of Justice, *Prosecution Policy: Guidance for Government Counsel* (1998), paras 8–18.
34. Cap 268.
35. Cap 32.
36. Cap 310.
37. This is based on various searches which I caused to be made in July 1998. As far as the records of registered society under the Societies Ordinance are concerned, there was no record of registration of Xinhua News Agency, New China News Agency, Hsin Hua News Agency, or its various other names in both the English and the Chinese languages (with or without 'Hong Kong branch').
38. Discussions of having a formal PRC office in Hong Kong took place between the Chinese and the British Government after the Second World War with futile results, and the proper role of Xinhua News Agency was discussed within the British Hong Kong government in the late 1940s and early 1950s: see Peter Wesley-Smith, 'Colonial Exercise of Prosecutorial Discretion', (1998) 28 HKLJ 412 at 413–15; Steve Tsang, *Hong Kong: Appointment with China*, pp. 139–43; and Steve Tsang, 'Strategy for Survival: The Cold War and Hong Kong's Policy towards Kuomintang and Chinese Communist Activities in the 1950s' (1997) 25 *Journal of Imperial and Commonwealth History*, p. 294.
39. Under s 26 of the Magistrates' Ordinance, an information has to be laid within 6 months of the offence.
40. *R v Harris* (1991) 1 HKLR 389 at 394, per Silke VP. See also *R v Tsui Lai-ying* (1987) HKLR 857 and *Cheung Sou-yat v R* (1979) HKLR 630. It is assumed that the Secretary for Justice stands in the same position as the Attorney General before the changeover: see Declaration of Change of Titles (General Adaptation) Notice 1997.
41. *R v Inland Revenue Commissioners, ex parte Allen* (1997) STC 1141. For a useful review of authorities, see *Hallett v Attorney General (No 2)* (1989) 2 NZLR 96. For earlier decisions which suggested that the court should not become too closely involved in the question of whether a prosecution should be commenced, see *R v Connelly* (1964) AC 1254; *R v Humphrys* (1977) AC 1.
42. In *R v Tsui Lai-ying* (1987) HKLR 857 at 867 the court held that the accountability of the Attorney General in Hong Kong was on a different plane from that of his United Kingdom counterpart:

> This stems from the very nature of the two different systems of Government: ours being a non-ministerial system: the United Kingdom

a full parliamentary, ministerial system with accountability to Parliament being the core of its existence. But, in Hong Kong, the Attorney General is still susceptible to having his conduct questioned by members of the Legislative Council.

43. (1986-87) Legco Procs, p. 1271 (25 March 1987), quoted with approval by Silk VP in *R v Harris*, supra, at 395.

44. At 395–6.

45. The remark that the decision not to prosecute was not subject to judicial review must now be regarded as doubtful: see *R v Inland Revenue Commissioners, ex p Allen* (1997) STC 1141.

46. I should declare that I have been briefed, on a *pro bono* basis, to appear for Ms Lau in her private prosecution.

47. Peter Wesley-Smith, 'Colonial Exercise of Prosecutorial Discretion' (1998) 28 HKLJ 412–19.

48. There is obviously much more room for judicial creativity in applying a constitution or a bill of rights because of the nature of these instruments and personal values of judges might play a more important role in determining the outcome of a dispute in these areas. I have argued elsewhere that judicial attitude towards the Bill of Rights has resulted in a conservative body of case law which is resistant to international influences: Johannes Chan, 'Hong Kong's Bill of Rights: Its Reception of and Contribution to International and Comparative Jurisprudence' (1998) 47 ICLQ 306.

49. (1996) 7 HKPLR 63 (HCt); (1996) 7 HKPLR 78 (CA); (1997) 7 HKPLR 327 (PC).

50. Cap 124.

51. Under s 2, 'resumption for any purpose' includes 'resumption of any purpose of whatsoever description whether *ejusdem generis* with any of the above purposes or not, which the Governor in Council may decide to be a public purpose.'

52. At 87.

53. (1997) 7 HKPLR 327 at 341.

54. *Re KOY Investment Co Ltd* (1983) HKLR 28, where the Full Court held that the Governor was not bound before ordering a resumption to consult anyone other than the Executive Council. At first instance, Cheung J held that this case was outdated and could not stand the subsequent House of Lords' pronouncement of the primacy of a duty of fairness, which may require affording an opportunity to be heard, in *R v Secretary of State for the Home Department, ex p Doody* (1994) 1 AC 531.

55. *R v Secretary of State for the Home Department, ex p Doody* (1994) 1 AC 531.

56. Their Lordships also refused to accept that the availability of compensation meant that a compulsory acquisition is not arbitrary or unlawful. The appeal, however, was dismissed on facts, as their Lordships found that the appellant had indeed been afforded opportunity to make representation before the resumption order was made.

57. (1995) 1 HKC 566 (HCt); (1995) 5 HKPLR 149 (CA); (1996) 6 HKPLR 13 (PC).

58. (1995) 1 HKC 566 at 596.

59. *R v Governor of Durham Prison, ex p Hardial Singh* (1984) 1 WLR 704.

60. (1995) 5 HKPLR 156–160.
61. (1996) 6 HKPLR 13 at 28–29.
62. Ibid., at 29.
63. Immigration (Amendment) Ordinance 1996, Ord No 33 of 1996, *Government Gazette*, Legal Supplement No 1, p. A428 (31 May 1996).
64. By 'Hong Kong Permanent Residents' I refer only to those persons of Chinese origin who have acquired permanent resident status by 7 years' residence in Hong Kong. Those who acquired this status by way of British Dependent Territories citizenship are in a different category.
65. Ord No 124 of 1997, *Gazette of the HKSAR*, Legal Supplement No. 1, p. A301 (10 July 1997).
66. (1997) 3 HKC 64 (CFI); CACV No 203 of 1997 (CA). There were in fact four different cases chosen to represent four typical categories of applicants.
67. (1997) 3 HKC 64 at 89. Art 12(1) of the Bill of Rights provides that 'no one shall be held guilty of any criminal offence on account of any act or omission which did not constitute a criminal offence, under Hong Kong or international law, at the time when it was committed.'
68. At p. 28.
69. At pp. 29–30.
70. At p. 69.
71. At p. 54.
72. *Ng Ka Ling v Director of Immigration* (1999) 1 HKC 291 (sub nom *Director of Immigration v Cheung Lai Wah*).

7
Freedom of the Press and the Rule of Law*
Richard Cullen

Introduction

More than two years after Hong Kong became a Special Administrative Region (SAR) of the People's Republic of China (PRC) the rule of law continues to underpin its political structure.[1] But Hong Kong presents a case where the rule of law lacks what might be termed, a full set of foundations. Usually, when one encounters the rule of law, one discovers three fundamental political structure features: an independent judiciary; a free press;[2] and democratic–representative government. Hong Kong has enjoyed the first two over many decades but it has never experienced the third.

The SAR's new quasi-Constitution, the Basic Law does not forbid increased democracy before the year 2007 as the Basic Law can be amended. But Article 68 and Annex II of the Basic Law clearly assume that full democracy will not be introduced before then. The underpinnings of the rule of law there thus rely more heavily than is normal on a free press and an independent judiciary. It means it would be easier than in almost any other jurisdictions enjoying the rule of law to undermine it seriously through executive action.

The purpose of this chapter is to consider the range of factors impinging on freedom of the press in Hong Kong including, especially, the role of the judiciary in protecting press freedom. In fact, the judiciary, to date, has played a comparatively limited role in this regard. Accordingly, a range of other political and economic factors affecting media freedom is discussed below.

This chapter starts with an overview of the media in the SAR, which is followed by a summary of the current regulatory framework. It then examines the role of the judiciary and other non-judicial factors that influence press freedom. Certain illustrations of the impact of these factors are noted prior to the concluding remarks.

Overview of the media in Hong Kong

Hong Kong is one of East Asia's major media centres. Its claim to this rests on the vibrancy of its locally focused media and the large number of regional media operations located in its midst. Hong Kong enjoys possibly the highest per capita concentration of newspapers anywhere in the world. In 1993 there were 77 registered papers and 619 registered periodicals serving 6.3 million people. Many daily papers devote themselves to horses or starlets exclusively, so hardly qualify as newspapers, but the extent of newspaper publishing is still remarkable.[3] By mid-1997, there were still close to 20 true, general newspapers published daily.[4] In many western cities of comparable size there are, nowadays, only a handful of daily newspapers left. There are also two broadcast television stations in Hong Kong (using two separate channels each to broadcast multilingually), satellite television services, an interactive television service and an extensive cable television network, plus a wide range of radio broadcasters. Hong Kong is also a major user of the internet.

Various factors help to explain this phenomenon. Pre-eminently, expression has historically been less regulated in Hong Kong than virtually anywhere else in East Asia. Second, the press has served as a sort of surrogate 'parliament-in-print'. Hong Kong has only recently acquired a quite limited democratic input into its governance. It has, however, an abundance of wealthy persons keen to express their views. The relative ease of getting a licence to publish and the density of population (which makes circulation fairly straightforward) have made it comparatively easy to go into print. Also, there is no licensing system for reporters in Hong Kong. The local population, in their turn, have provided an eager market. Moreover, Hong Kong has been able to establish itself as the base for many publications circulating through the Chinese diaspora of over 50 million people.[5]

Regional print media operations have been drawn to Hong Kong because of the freedom to publish and also for other reasons. First, there is its location. It is both ideally placed for 'China watching' and is well located to cover all of East Asia and beyond. Within around six hours flying time from Hong Kong live 50 per cent of the world's population. Second, this part of the globe contains a higher proportion of what, until recently, were the fastest growing economies in the world. Third, it has excellent infrastructure including high quality communication links. The same factors have also helped make it one of the hubs for Asia's electronic media and home to one of Asia's largest film industries.

The media in Hong Kong can be divided into several broad groups.[6] The most obvious division is between the English language media (both press and broadcast) and the Chinese media. Generally speaking, its English language press remains reasonably robust although signs of increased self-censorship have emerged over the last several years. The two principal outlets are the daily newspapers, the *South China Morning Post* and the *Hong Kong Standard*. There is also a Hong Kong edition of *China Daily*, the flagship of the PRC English language paper. There are also some English language weeklies, most of which provide light reading. The leading periodical is the *Far Eastern Economic Review*. Other regional English language publications include the *Asian Wall Street Journal* and the *International Herald Tribune*. In April 1997, the *South China Morning Post* appointed a Chinese Consultant to assist the editor. The consultant, Feng Xiliang, was a founding editor of *China Daily* in Beijing. Prior to joining the *South China Morning Post*, he worked for *Window* magazine, a now defunct, English language, pro-Beijing weekly.

It is argued that self-censorship is more established within the English language electronic media than within the English language press.[7] Perhaps the most notorious example involved the dropping of the BBC international television service from Star TV soon after Rupert Murdoch acquired control. The removal of the BBC was designed to improve corporate relations with China.

Within the Chinese press, further broad divisions are apparent. First, there are the pro-Beijing papers, the most well-known being *Wen Wei Bao* and *Ta Kung Pao*. During the 1989 Tiananmen incident, several pro-Beijing papers were strongly critical of events in the PRC. Disciplinary measures soon followed; journalists and editors found themselves without jobs and measures to avoid any further incorrect reporting were introduced.[8] A further broad division within the Chinese press is between those papers that are largely politically independent and those which are essentially non-political. Recently papers have been divided by Beijing into four categories: (a) China owned; (b) friendly; (c) neutral; and (d) hostile.[9]

The jailing of Xi Yang, a reporter for *Ming Pao*, a leading Hong Kong daily paper, for 12 years in 1994 for stealing state secrets (while in the PRC) remains probably the most worrying single indicator of what the future might hold for the Hong Kong press and its personnel.[10] A more pervasive form of pressure comes from Hong Kong based PRC institutions directing their advertising towards preferred papers. Some self censorship is now a fact of life for a number of Hong Kong papers, although the degree of self censorship might have moderated since July 1997.[11] It would seem the press erred on the side of caution in the lead up to the change of sovereignty. The 'hands off' approach by Beijing since the changeover and some limited signs of increasing official liberalization on the mainland have seen the 'brakes come off' to some degree.[12]

Many problems facing the Hong Kong–Chinese press are attributable to economic forces. Competition is unrelentingly fierce and recent price wars have been especially savage (and have culled several publications). Prior to the handover, the English Language *Eastern Express* (run by the Oriental Press Group) and *Sing Tao Evening News*, a paper that had been published for some 58 years, folded.[13] More significantly, a quality analytical monthly, *The Nineties*, has recently closed down in Hong Kong (and Taiwan).[14]

As 1997 drew closer, the ownership of Hong Kong's media began to change. The new owners tend to be international entrepreneurs entering the China market and pro-China business people who saw the usefulness of the media as a component in 'business diplomacy'. This phenomenon has continued since the handover. Most recently, the SAR's number two broadcast television operator, Asia Television (ATV), has been the subject of a controversial takeover bid which includes PRC interests. The prospect of PRC interests controlling this operator (there are only two such operators in the SAR) is something which many find alarming. What is most concerning was the lack of information revealed about the likely ultimate ownership of ATV, when the purchase was being negotiated.[15]

Hong Kong's public broadcasting authority, Radio Television Hong Kong (RTHK) was also embroiled in controversy prior to the handover. RTHK runs a number of English language and Chinese language radio stations. It also produces regular television programmes which are shown on commercial television (both English and Chinese). Under British rule, RTHK developed into a government funded but independent broadcaster modelled on the BBC. The British floated the idea of privatizing RTHK prior to the handover. This idea was strongly criticized by Beijing. RTHK in government hands was seen as providing an important mouthpiece for the SAR government (the PRC model rather than the BBC model) while in private hands it might become a source of yet more strident criticism.

In the midst of this high pressure media world, new papers continue to emerge, most notably in recent times, *Pinguo Ribao* or *Apple Daily*, launched by tycoon Jimmy Lai, a PRC immigrant. The *Apple Daily* thrives on sensational but fairly thorough coverage and a notably independent stance – especially with respect to the PRC. It was launched in June 1995. Within two years it had become the second most popular Chinese language daily after the *Oriental Daily News*.[16] Through the post-handover period it has been locked in combat with a number of rivals and principally the *Oriental Daily News*.

The regulatory framework

In all jurisdictions, neither freedom of expression nor freedom of the press are absolute. The rights of the state, or the community or, some-times, minorities within the state, are often found to be in conflict with individual rights to publish or broadcast. Hong Kong is no excep-tion. Although the basic principles underpinning freedom of the press do apply in Hong Kong, a range of statutory instruments (and the Common Law) serve to restrict and limit this freedom.[17] In the first place media outlets, whether print or electronic based, need to be licensed. For publications in print, the relevant ordinance is the Registration of Local Newspapers Ordinance (1951).[18] For the elec-tronic media, important ordinances include: the Television Ordinance (1964);[19] the Broadcasting Authority Ordinance (1987);[20] and the Telecommunication Ordinance (1963).[21] The last contains provisions which allow the government to ban certain messages from transmis-sion or intercept them if it is in the public interest.

Under the Film Censorship Ordinance (1988)[22] the Film Censorship Authority enjoys wide-ranging powers, including the power to censor films for cinema or television distribution on grounds of moral offen-siveness or social divisiveness.[23] And the Immigration Ordinance (1972)[24] allows the government to deport persons where it is conducive to the public good or for reasons based on Hong Kong's relations with other jurisdictions.

A wide range of more general measures also apply to control expres-sion in the media. First, Hong Kong has no real Freedom of Information ('FOI') law. It does have an administrative access to infor-mation system in place but it is of limited effect compared to, for example, the fully developed American FOI law.[25] The result is that government can control information flows simply by 'sitting' on infor-mation in many cases. Second, there are what have been described as excessive restrictions on reporting of proceedings in court in Hong Kong.[26] Third, Hong Kong is subject to a localized version of the UK Official Secrets Act (1989) which prohibits damaging disclosure of any information obtained while in service by government servants related to national security or international relations.[27] Fourth, both the Public Order Ordinance (1967)[28] and the Crimes Ordinance (1971)[29] criminalize, often in sweeping terms, a wide range of political activities in certain circumstances.

In late 1996, it was proposed that the Crimes Ordinance be amended to add the crime of 'subversion' to this list. As Fu has explained in detail in Chapter 4, Article 23 of the Basic Law stipulates that Hong Kong should outlaw subversion. Subversion is a specific criminal offence under PRC criminal law (as is sedition) though it is not a charge commonly brought.[30] The proposed amendment caused heated debates. The colonial government had tried to make the definition of this new crime clearly restricted to the use of force for any alleged 'subversive' activity to be criminal. As it turned out, the Legislative Council (Legco) rejected the proposed amendment. In fact, there is no need to create a new crime of subversion to comply with Article 23. As Fu rightly argues in Chapter 4 the Common Law is more than adequately equipped to punish any subversive activity.

Further restrictions apply under the Prevention of Bribery Ordinance (1971)[31] and related Hong Kong anticorruption ordinances. Under the Emergency Regulations Ordinance (1922)[32] the government is granted the power to make any regulation necessary to maintain public order, suppress rebellion and maintain essential services provided it is established that a public emergency exists.[33] The Police Force Ordinance (1922)[34] also has extensive search and seizure provisions. These were used in October 1989 to seize news videotapes from Hong Kong television stations. In 1995, the Hong Kong government provided, in Part 12 of the Interpretation and General Clauses Ordinance (1966),[35] that henceforward, any seizure of (widely defined) 'journalistic materials' would require an order from a judge.

Another Ordinance affecting the media is the Control of Obscene and Indecent Articles Ordinance (1987).[36] It replaced earlier legislation but is hardly less problematic. The difficulty of drawing a line between acceptable and unacceptable materials in this area is notorious as so much depends on individual assessments. The Post Office Ordinance (1926)[37] is also relevant as it prohibits the posting of obscene or indecent materials. Moreover, the Common Law, in 1962, appears to have created the offence of 'conspiracy to corrupt public morals'.[38]

The restrictions outlined above are largely in the public law domain. The media in Hong Kong is also subject to private law actions seeking redress for defamation, although such actions have been comparatively lacking in impact compared to jurisdictions like Australia or England and Wales. Hong Kong still retains an action for criminal defamation in the Defamation Ordinance (1887).[39] All media operators also are subject to laws related to advertising and copyright.

The judiciary and the media

The general approach of the judiciary in Hong Kong towards its role in mediating the relationship between government and citizens is one of restraint. This is not to say that the judiciary is 'tame' or ineffective. But a comparative review of the approach the Hong Kong judiciary has often applied in cases brought under the Bill of Rights Ordinance (1991)[40] (BORO) shows a distinct difference to the approach of senior courts when applying new Bills of Rights in, for example, Canada and New Zealand.[41] In Hong Kong, the courts have, generally, shown a marked deference to the government and to the legislature.[42] Despite this comparative lack of activism, there has been much litigation based on the BORO (which came into effect on 8 June 1991) most of it focused on criminal law and administrative law.[43]

The first major BORO case, *R v Sin Yau-ming*,[44] indicated, in 1991, that the Hong Kong courts might have been set, in contrast to past practice, to follow a more activist approach when applying the BORO.[45] The general approach in Sin Yau-Ming was subsequently criticized in the Judicial Committee of the Privy Council (JCPC). In *Attorney-General v Lee Kwong-kut*,[46] Lord Woolf, speaking for the JCPC, cast doubt on the appropriateness of complex protection of rights tests in the Hong Kong context. He argued that it might be appropriate to use such tests in cases involving real difficulty but, usually, the correct position could be established without resort to complex tests. He also noted that, although foreign precedents may be relevant generally the local context would need to be considered to resolve their specific relevance in a particular case. He also urged caution and reiterated the advisability of showing due deference to the legislature. He was worried that the BORO might, unless it was applied with circumspection, foster excessive litigation, causing the BORO to be brought into disrepute. This assertion has been strongly criticized as being both damaging to Hong Kong jurisprudence and internally inconsistent. Lord Woolf, it is said, recognized the need for balancing interests between the individual and society but his dismissal of the two-stage test established in *Sin Yau-ming's* case removed a method for trying to achieve balance without suggesting a proper replacement.[47]

In 1995, in *R v Town Planning Board, ex parte Kwan Kong Co Ltd*,[48] Mr Justice Waung took the approach of the JCPC to its logical conclusion. In that case he concluded that the BORO had no special status and, therefore, it ought to be applied with restraint. Moreover, the use of foreign authorities should be avoided. This interpretation, which questioned the authority of *Sin Yau-ming's* case, has been described as bold and startling.[49]

Numbers of commentators do have powerful reservations about the use of Bills of Rights as platforms for judicial activism. In Canada, there has been strong criticism of the way in which the Charter of Rights and Freedoms (1982) (Charter) has been applied.[50] These reproaches raise a number of points including: the undemocratic nature of the judiciary; the lack of competence and/or training of judges to deal with matters best left to the broad political process; and the lack of general resources enjoyed by courts to deal with complex social, economic and political questions. These are serious concerns. Certainly criminal defendants have benefited from the Charter in Canada. And corporate Canada even more so. But the Charter has also tended to increase divisions within society in some respects and it has generated a vast increase in litigation. Within a few years of its inception it was described as 'a dripping roast for lawyers'.[51]

The SAR is, however, in quite a different political position to Canada. The SAR enjoys a distinct sort of freedom – one without real democracy. It is for this reason that undue deference by the Hong Kong judiciary towards the executive and towards the legislature raises special concerns. An overactive judiciary in a political environment such as prevails in Canada can prove a real danger insofar as it cramps the style of popularly elected government for the benefit of special interests. In Hong Kong, a judiciary (or press) without real independence has to be a cause for serious concern.

The press in court

A somewhat notorious pre-handover case concerning press freedom in Hong Kong related to the book, *Spycatcher*. This book revealed certain details about the operation of Britain's intelligence services. The Hong Kong government at the behest of the British government, sought, in 1987, to suppress its publication in Hong Kong. An injunction was granted on the grounds of protecting national security and preventing a breach of confidence and a breach of fiduciary duty.[52]

In 1995, a practice of the Hong Kong Correctional Services Department, which related to press freedom, was taken to court. The Department was in the habit of removing those sections devoted to horse racing from local newspapers distributed to prison inmates. The purpose of this censorship, apparently, was to discourage illegal betting in prisons. In *Chim Shing Chung v Commissioner of Correctional Services*,[53] the High Court declared that the practice infringed the right of inmates to receive information under Article 16(2) of the BORO. The Court of Appeal overturned this decision.[54] It found that the reservation in Part 3 of the BORO applied. This reservation makes members of the armed forces and persons detained in penal establishments subject to certain restrictions notwithstanding the general protections in the BORO. The court also noted that the infringement of liberties involved was justifiable in this case even without the reservation.

In 1995, in *Cheung Ng Sheong Steven v Eastweek Publisher Ltd*,[55] the Court of Appeal did endorse the importance of maintaining a free press, when it found that jury awards of damages in defamation actions were more than usually subject to review on appeal. The court was concerned that such awards could sometimes be excessive in a given case – and their very size could produce a chilling effect on expressions of opinion in the press. Unlike in the USA, Hong Kong does not make celebrities or those who enter public life subject to a rule which says that, when they are engaged in (widely defined) public activities, they can only sue in defamation where they can prove both actual damage and actual malice with convincing clarity.[56] An attempt to make a move in this direction in 1996 at first instance in Hong Kong[57] was overturned by the Court of Appeal.[58]

One of the most significant cases related to freedom of the press involved a leading, quality daily newspaper, *Ming Pao*. The newspaper was in the course of investigating an alleged cartel organized to depress prices at government land auctions. Reporters from the newspaper who attended an auction were interviewed by investigators from the Independent Commission Against Corruption (ICAC). The following day, the newspaper published articles reporting that the ICAC had spoken to *Ming Pao* reporters and that an investigation of possible fixed-bidding was underway. The publisher and senior editorial staff of the newspaper were charged with breaching section 30 of the Prevention of Bribery Ordinance for disclosing details of a suspected offence under that Ordinance. Section 30 is designed to allow the

ICAC to maintain secrecy during investigations so that suspects are not 'tipped off', especially through stories in the media.

The magistrate at first instance found that there was no case to answer. He said that there could only be a section 30 offence where there was a particular suspect or an allegation of bribery against a specified person and neither had been shown to exist in this case. He also found that section 30 was inconsistent with Article 16 of the BORO, which protects freedom of expression. The Attorney-General appealed. In 1996, in *Ming Pao Newspapers v Attorney-General*,[59] the Court of Appeal overruled the magistrate. The court found that the restriction in section 30 was applicable to these facts and that it was not struck down by the BORO. The restriction served the purposes of both enhancing the fight against corruption and protecting the rights of any person being investigated, prior to their being charged.

The defendants appealed to the JCPC, which found for the newspaper but not based on the application of the BORO.[60] It vindicated the magistrate's view that section 30 could not take effect until some specific person was the subject of an investigation. In this case there was no evidence that, when the articles were published, the ICAC had progressed beyond commencing a general investigation. No specific suspects had been identified. For the JCPC, this decided the matter but the argument based on the BORO was subject to some further, obiter, comments. The court stressed the importance of the right of freedom of expression and the need to limit any restrictions on that freedom to a minimum. Moreover, any such restrictions had to be proportional to the ends being sought. The JCPC then applied this test to section 30 and concluded that it did not offend the BORO. It emphasized, once again, that local Hong Kong conditions had to be taken into account and section 30 did not seem to exceed what could be considered reasonable. It was a provision which was acceptable as a means to enhance the effectiveness of investigations into corruption. The findings of the JCPC with respect to the BORO in this case have been strongly criticized for failing to explain the evidence on which these claims were based.[61]

The Oriental Press Group Ltd, a related company, certain executives and a former chief editor of the *Oriental Daily News*, Wong Yeung-ng, were charged with contempt of court. The case, *Secretary for Justice v Oriental Press Group Ltd and Others*, was heard in mid-1998.[62] The charges arose out of a dispute between the *Oriental Daily News* and the *Apple Daily*. The former was refused leave to take a legal dispute with the latter further by a judge of the High Court. The *Oriental Daily News* subsequently subjected the judge to round-the-clock surveillance. The newspaper also published a series of attacks on the judiciary and on a particular tribunal which relied, *inter alia*, on conspicuous racial slurs. The diatribes were as vicious as they were relentless.[63] The defendants argued at their trial that the contempt action, if successful, would be exceedingly harmful to press freedom.[64] The High Court convicted Mr Wong and sentenced him to four months imprisonment for 'scandalizing the court'. The Oriental Press Group was fined approximately £400 000 and the defendants suffered an adverse costs award also.[65] Mr Wong's sentence is reckoned to be the longest modern term of imprisonment imposed on a media person for contempt in the common law world.[66]

Summary

The judiciary in Hong Kong, although very much within the common law tradition, has certain characteristics which set it apart. First, there is the local context. An overwhelmingly Chinese society, Chinese values not surprisingly dominate. Indeed, in many ways, Hong Kong retains more traditional values than the PRC, where countless campaigns against 'feudal superstition' have taken their toll on some practices. The Chinese tradition on individual rights, established over several millennia, is that those rights are always circumscribed significantly by the interests of society – and the state.[67] A concomitant of this view is the adherence to a fundamentally authoritarian political culture over the same period. Until comparatively recently, there has been a total absence of any democratic experience in any Chinese polity. Next, the judiciary in Hong Kong remains bound to a common law tradition (which has faded significantly elsewhere) not to become involved in public debate.[68] Third, Hong Kong is now an SAR, a highly privileged enclave within the largest one party state in the world. The potential difficulties and sensitivities which this arrangement creates are clear to everyone in the SAR including judges.

The judiciary's approach to protecting individual rights immediately after the introduction of the BORO showed signs of activism. Since then activism has been in retreat. We seem now to have reached a position where, when one alleges an infringement of a right, there is a strong possibility the court will assume legislative validity unless 'unreasonableness' can be demonstrated. This is virtually an inversion of the rule used for Charter interpretation in Canada; a rule which the judiciary in Hong Kong initially embraced. It would seem that freedom of the press questions are subject to the same approach; they enjoy no special status.

That the judiciary seems to have taken one step forward and one step backward in its approach to protecting individual rights is, perhaps, not surprising. The factors pushing the court in this direction are significant. Many commentators in other jurisdictions like Canada would applaud such judicial restraint. In Hong Kong, where so much reliance is placed on the courts (and the press) to preserve the SAR's widely enjoyed freedoms, this impulse to restraint is a cause for real and continuing concern.

Prevailing influences

Political and economics influences

The role of the judiciary in relation to freedom of the press in Hong Kong has so far been rather limited. A range of other factors have played an important part in the development of the media and their interaction will continue. This section attempts to identify certain of these influences. Some are directly related to the media and others are wider in their impact.

More than two years after the change of sovereignty the general political position in the SAR is markedly less anxious than many had predicted. A 'hands off' approach is being applied by Beijing. The most striking changes have been economic and these have resulted from the Asian financial tempest rather than from the handover. The media has carried on as before. The SAR government comes under constant attack and the reporting of mainland politics remains much as before. That is, although the mainstream press tends to tread lightly in some areas, for example by avoiding personal attacks on high profile mainland figures, policy analysis seems to be as direct as ever. What might be termed the cross-border political climate has proved to be less problematic than many had expected.[69] On the mainland, there are signs that the death of paramount leader Deng Xiaoping has resulted in some easing of the political atmosphere. Mainstream political dissidents are being controlled as closely as ever but academic and intellectual discussion is now somewhat more open.[70]

Reporters know the highly dangerous zones.[71] Writing about the SAR and it governance from within Hong Kong seems subject to little impediment.[72] Writing about the mainland and its governance is more problematic, especially from within the mainland. One notorious example of pre-handover self censorship at the *South China Morning Post* involved the axing of a cartoonist who specialized, *inter alia*, in biting personal attacks on senior PRC leaders.[73] Advocating the overthrow of the mainland system of governance or independence for Taiwan or Tibet (or Hong Kong) are high on the list.[74] Revealing (loosely defined) state secrets and any reporting on national security or military related topics are well up there also. Reporting in Chinese generally is more risky than reporting in English. Reporting from *within* the mainland rather than from the SAR also increases the risk. It would seem that mainland citizens (or former citizens) are more likely to be badly treated within the mainland than those who are not.[75] The *Ming Pao* reporter Xi Yang, who was jailed several years ago for revealing state secrets was reporting from the mainland. In 1994, Gao Yu was imprisoned for six years for her work published in the generally pro-Beijing, Hong Kong magazine *Mirror*.[76]

There is no doubt that self censorship is practised by the Hong Kong media. There is no doubt that it is practised in western media outlets either.[77] The threat of arrest and possible punishment within the PRC for reporters operating from there on behalf of the Hong Kong media certainly has had a chilling effect on some reporting[78] but the continuing diversity of the Hong Kong printed media, especially, has thus far provided a significant check against any wholesale chilling effect.[79] The market pays well for bold, investigative reporting.

One problem that has arisen since the handover is the comparative lack of access which reporters now find they have to the SAR government. The last British Governor, Chris Patten was a professional politician prior to coming to Hong Kong. During his tenure he made a major effort to provide increased access to government for the media. That relatively easy access is no longer available.[80]

On a day to day basis, the relationship between the press and the judiciary has a special dynamic of its own. The interaction between judges and reporters can have a real impact on the transparency and effectiveness of the judicial process. Judges have significant power over the way cases are heard. There is no sign that there has been any inordinate increase in the use of either closed court orders or contempt orders since the handover. This area is worth watching as a possible 'litmus test' of any general change in attitudes within the judiciary over time, however.

The changes in ownership of media outlets continue to be watched carefully and they continue to give rise to real concerns. But the SAR is blessed with access to information on a scale that brooks few equals. Every international paper of any note is sold and it enjoys full access to the international electronic media. It is massively wired into the Internet. And it still has record-breaking numbers of papers per head.

Finally, the Hong Kong media remains significantly less concentrated than in many western jurisdictions.

The trend, however, is towards concentration of the print media in Hong Kong.[81] This is due, primarily, to the demise of various titles, which have fallen victim to price wars and changing readership trends. There is also a tendency towards changing ownership. Rupert Murdoch sold the highly profitable *South China Morning Post* prior to the handover. He also purchased Star TV from its former local owners. ATV, the second terrestrial television broadcaster, recently came under control of a consortium including mainland interests.[82] *Ming Pao* has changed ownership twice over the last few years. Control of the *Hong Kong Standard, Sing Tao Daily* and *Tin Tin Daily* also might pass from Sally Aw. Two features of these changing ownership patterns warrant scrutiny. First, media ownership is passing, more and more, not to specialist media operators but to people with a general business background involving, *inter alia*, business with the mainland. Second, there are now signs that mainland interests are buying into the Hong Kong media with some vigour. These changes do not automatically spell erosion of freedom of the press, but it does indicate an increased potential for such erosion.

Case studies

A number of issues related to the media have arisen recently in the SAR. Not all are linked directly to the question of freedom of the press but they all touch on this matter. In early 1998, Rupert Murdoch apparently decided it would be better if a publisher which he controls, HarperCollins, were not to publish the Hong Kong memoirs of former Governor Patten entitled *East And West*.[83] The claim is that Murdoch told the publisher to try and tone down comments on China in the book. The general view is that the Murdoch group gained little in China from this episode while the British interests of the group suffered.[84]

After the handover a local government body the Provisional Urban Council (PUC) was put in place under Beijing's stewardship. The PUC quickly distinguished itself for its clumsy approach on many issues. In early 1998 its poor reputation plumbed new depths when it attempted some coarse political censorship. Christine Loh, a sacked 1995 Legco member, featured in a film about the handover, which was due to be shown at the Hong Kong Film Festival in April 1998. The PUC enjoyed ultimate control over the Festival. A subcommittee of the PUC recommended that the film containing the Loh segment not be shown as the festival would occur prior to the May 1998 Legco elections in which Loh would be a candidate. By a margin of 17 votes to 16 the PUC over-turned the subcommittee decision. The crassness of this attempt at censorship for transparent political reasons[85] ensured it generated significant publicity which, in turn, doubtless played a part in convincing a majority on the PUC to back away from the initial abuse of power by the subcommittee.[86]

Xu Simin, publisher of *Mirror* magazine in Hong Kong has been a critic of RTHK's independence for some time.[87] In March 1998 he launched an attack on the broadcaster while attending a session, in Beijing, of the Chinese People's Political Consultative Conference (CPPCC), of which he is a member. Xu claimed that some RTHK programmes went too far in their criticism of both the PRC and SAR governments. He was upset that a publicly funded broadcaster should do so. He also complained that RTHK had vilified the SAR Chief Executive, Tung Chee-hwa.[88] Xu's attack prompted a hostile reaction within Hong Kong.[89] Many voiced their support for RTHK. Shortly after Xu's remarks Tung expressed the SAR government's commitment to freedom of speech and freedom of information.[90] At about the same time, mainland officials made a veiled attack on Xu. It would appear that Beijing was especially sensitive to any attempt being made to add momentum to his attack by launching it from Beijing. The Chairman of the CPPCC, Li Ruihuan, stressed in a statement made shortly after Xu's attack that the CPPCC was not a forum to monitor SAR politics.[91]

In December 1996, high profile Hong Kong politician and democracy activist, Emily Lau, requested certain information from the Hong Kong office of Xinhua (the New China News Agency). It is widely believed that Xinhua was (and still is) in the habit of keeping files on various people in Hong Kong, including democracy activists. Lau took the view that Xinhua maintained a file on her. She sought access to that file under the newly enacted *Personal Data (Privacy) Ordinance* (1995).[92] As a potential gatherer of personal data Xihua was subject to the Ordinance. It failed to respond within the 40 days as required by the Ordinance. This provides grounds for a possible prosecution. In the event the Secretary for Justice decided, on advice, not to prose-cute.[93] It caused a furore. Lau has now launched a private prosecution against the current director of Xinhua (who was not the director when she lodged her original request). She was given permission by a magis-trate to issue a private summon.[94] Xinhua's director has moved to try and block the prosecution in the courts.[95]

In the mean time, the SAR government has moved to bestow what is commonly still known as 'Crown privilege' on certain mainland bodies operating in the SAR including Xinhua. The government argued that they were only providing the same benefits for these mainland entities as British Crown entities had previously enjoyed. The privilege, briefly, confers immunity on qualifying bodies from SAR laws unless those laws expressly, or by clear implication, apply to them. The PLC passed the controversial legislation in early April 1998. The exempting legislation applies retrospectively, from 1 July 1997 (other than in cases involving criminal offences).[96] It does not affect Lau's private prosecution.

Cross-border politics can and do affect the commercial welfare of media groups in Hong Kong. One of the more notorious cases was the attempt by Jimmy Lai's Next group to list itself on the Hong Kong stock exchange. Next owns two of Hong Kong's most successful Chinese publications, the *Apple Daily* and the weekly *Next* magazine. The listing looked apt to achieve a marked success. Sun Hung Kai International, a leading local investment bank, was lined up as the underwriter. Then, on the eve of the listing, Sun Hung Kai advised it was withdrawing from the process. No replacement could be found and the listing never went ahead. Publications of the Next Group have always taken a highly independent and critical stance on PRC politics. It is widely believed that its failure to list was the result of pressure applied from Beijing.[97] Prior to this attempt, Lai had severed his links with the Giordano casual clothing empire he had built. Giordano stores encountered trouble on the mainland, following certain stories appearing in the *Apple Daily*. The aim of the severance was to reduce the threat to Giordano's commercial success. Another pressure point is advertising. Newspapers (or other media outlets) on Beijing's 'hostile' list are most unlikely to find their pages filled with advertising from enterprises with close PRC links.[98]

One aspect of the operation of the media in Hong Kong which is well recognized (though less often widely discussed) is the involvement of organized crime. Triad links to film production and also within television broadcasting appear to be a fact of life.[99] The fortunes which have launched certain Hong Kong media forays are widely believed to have been derived from less than savoury commercial activity.

Despite the continuing pressures of competition, the Asian economic meltdown and other burdens, Hong Kong continues to thrive as a media hub. Singapore and Malaysia are still significantly less important in this regard.[100] Close to 200 media organizations have offices and virtually all the major international press groups, major international electronic media groups and many international publishers retain bases in the SAR.[101] Two years after the handover it is still the location of choice if you are in the media business and you have an interest in East Asia.

Conclusion

Two of the key safeguards of Hong Kong's remarkable mix of commercial and political freedom are the independent judiciary and freedom of the press. Hong Kong has to be especially vigilant to ensure that these safeguards are not undermined. A fully democratic government is not in prospect under the Basic Law as it currently stands until 2007 at the earliest.[102] The possibility of amending the Basic Law in order to introduce a fast-track to a fully democratic Legco is matter of wide debate following the May 1998 Legco elections, where a record turn-out of voters returned many pro-democracy activists.[103] Presently, however, this is no more than a topic of political debate.

The Hong Kong judiciary has demonstrated, more than one year into the new era, that it remains independent. But its deference to the executive and to the legislature also continues. This deference is rooted in British judicial tradition. Chinese cultural attitudes have tended to reinforce this hesitancy. Today this deference is also driven by a reasonable recognition of the new political reality: the SAR is governed ultimately by China. The Hong Kong judiciary is now in the process of finding its role within this new actuality. It is a key agent in maintaining Hong Kong's freedoms. Most local people want the judiciary to exercise prudence. They are worried and constantly watchful, however, lest this prudence slide into passivity.

This review has demonstrated that there are very real concerns, especially with respect to maintaining press freedom. These concerns arise from a variety of sources including: changes in media ownership; declining numbers of outlets; the extent of self-censorship; judicial deference; overt attacks on freedom of the press; apparent lack of government even handedness; lack of access to official information; and the attitude of government. Despite these concerns it is also clear that two years after the handover its press remains one of the freest and most informative, and Hong Kong is still the premier choice of international media operators seeking a base in East Asia.

One abiding concern has recently been in the spotlight – how much of a threat to media freedom in Hong Kong is the media itself? One side of this concern is the menace of self censorship. The other, in many ways even more difficult to deal with, is what might be termed media recklessness. Although many in Hong Kong supported the recent decision of the High Court in the *Oriental Daily News* case to jail the former editor of that paper for contempt, the wider implications of the decision still give cause for anxiety. The precedent of the SAR government using the law to punish the press has been created.[104] As explained, this case did not involve a verbal attack on China but a deliberate and direct attack on the SAR judiciary. A clear lack of self restraint was involved. All media operators must feel at least somewhat more nervous. A practical step for Hong Kong to minimize future use of this precedent is for the media to develop an institutionalized form of self restraint by creating a press council to hear complaints and decide on their merits.

In summary, the SAR looks set to remain a (comparatively) very wealthy, highly educated enclave with strong traditions in law, politics and social interaction drawn from the Anglo-common law world (blended with Chinese tradition) within a fast changing country. The more one reflects on the future of the SAR within the PRC, the more one is struck by the fact that, as in the past, its destiny will ultimately rest more on the Hong Kong Chinese than anyone else. A heavy burden rests on its political, business, judicial, intellectual and civil service élite to ensure its remarkable substructure of political and social tolerance and exceptional commercial energy are retained and developed. Nowhere will this burden be greater than in maintaining the freedom of the press. Perhaps the greatest political hazard is that its élite would take its significant political achievements – especially its vibrant and free media – for granted. This danger is heightened by the financial and economic turmoil which has beset the region since 1997. Faltering economies can rapidly fall victim to social disruption and, in turn, to exhortations for increased controls on the media – in the interest of social stability.

Notes

* The chapter is based in part on findings in H.L. Fu and Richard Cullen, *Media Law in the PRC* (Hong Kong: Asia Law and Practice, 1996), especially Chapter 12; Richard Cullen, 'Freedom of the Press in Hong Kong', *Internationales Asienforum* (1997) no.27; and Richard Cullen, 'Media Freedom in Chinese Hong Kong', *Transnational Lawyer* (1998) no.11, pp. 383–418. I wish to thank Dr H.L. Fu, Gren Manuel of the *South China Morning Post* and Lucia Palpal-Latoc of the *Hong Kong Standard* for their

valuable input. The views expressed are my own.

1. Ghai, Yash, 'Praise is not enough', *SCMP*, 22 March 1998.
2. For reasons of length this chapter deals with freedom of the press rather than of expression generally. Freedom of the press encompasses freedom of the media generally not just of the print media.
3. Michel Bonnin, 'The Press in Hong Kong – Flourishing but Under Threat', *China Perspectives*, (September 1995) p. 48. See also Perry Keller, 'Freedom of the Press in Hong Kong: Liberal Values and Sovereign Interests', *Texas International Law Journal* (1992) no.27, p. 371.
4. Goddard *et al.*, *Hong Kong Journalists Association Annual Report 1997* (HKJAAR97) (Hong Kong Journalists Association, Hong Kong, 1997) Section 1, p. 6.
5. A. Lin Neumann, 'Freedom Under the Dragon', *The Committee to Protect Journalists Newsletter* (1997) p. 1.
6. See, Joseph Man Chan and Chin-Chuan Lee, 'Shifting Journalistic Paradigms: Editorial Stance and Political Transition in Hong Kong', *The China Quarterly*, no.117 (1989).
7. Bonnin, op. cit.
8. Bonnin, op. cit. and Chin Chuan Lee and Joseph Man Chan, 'Thunder of Tiananmen: The Hong Kong Press in China's Orbit', in Chin Chuan Lee (ed.), *Voices of China: The Interplay of Politics and Journalism* (New York: Guilford Press, 1990).
9. *HKJAAR97*, note 6, Section 1, p. 5.
10. Xi Yang was released on parole and returned to Hong Kong in January 1997. When he was arrested *Ming Pao*, took a strongly independent line in its reporting about the mainland and protested most strongly against his arrest. By the time of his release the paper was thanking Beijing for its 'leniency'. HKJAAR97, note 6, Section 1, p. 7.
11. Jean-Philippe Beja, 'The Goose's Golden Eggs Lose Their Shine', *China Perspectives*, no.15 (January 1998) p. 4.
12. Neumann, op. cit. p. 9 note 7, (quoting Philip Bowring).
13. The demise of the English language *Eastern Express* prior to the handover seems explicable in economic terms. It was a major loss. The same applies to the closure of *Sing Tao Evening News*. HKJAAR97, Section 3, p. 2 note 6.
14. Kevin Kwong, 'Political Monthly runs out of steam', *Sunday Morning Post*, 5 April 1998.
15. G. Schloss and S. Beck, 'Complex plot in ATV stake saga', *SCMP*, 4 May 1998.
16. *HKJAAR97*, Section 3, p. 3.
17. A review of media regulation in Hong Kong (in Chinese) can be found in (Liang Weixian and Chen Wenmin (eds)), *Chuanbofa Xinlun (Media Law in Hong Kong)* (Hong Kong: Commercial Press, 1995).
18. *Laws of Hong Kong*, Cap. 268.
19. *Laws of Hong Kong*, Cap. 52.
20. *Laws of Hong Kong*, Cap. 391.
21. *Laws of Hong Kong*, Cap. 106.
22. *Laws of Hong Kong*, Cap. 392.
23. Ibid., Part 3.
24. *Laws of Hong Kong*, Cap.115.

25. See *Hong Kong Bar Association Annual Statement 1995/96* (Hong Kong: Hong Kong Bar Association, 1996) p. 68; and HKJAAR97, Section 2, p. 10.
26. Peter Wesley-Smith, *Constitutional and Administrative Law in Hong Kong* (2nd edn) (Hong Kong: Longman, 1994), p. 384. See also HKJAAR97, Section 2, p. 9.
27. Wesley-Smith, *Constitutional and Administrative Law*, p. 379.
28. *Laws of Hong Kong*, Cap. 245.
29. *Laws of Hong Kong*, Cap. 200.
30. Fu and Cullen, *Media Law in the PRC*, Chap. 7.
31. *Laws of Hong Kong*, Cap. 201.
32. *Laws of Hong Kong*, Cap. 241.
33. For further discussion, see Wesley-Smith, *Constitutional and Administrative Law*, pp. 397–8.
34. *Laws of Hong Kong*, Cap. 232.
35. *Law of Hong Kong*, Cap. 1.
36. *Laws of Hong Kong*, Cap. 390.
37. *Laws of Hong Kong*, Cap. 98.
38. *Shaw v DPP* (1962) Appeal Cases, 220.
39. *Laws of Hong Kong*, Cap. 21, section 5.
40. *Laws of Hong Kong*, Cap. 383.
41. James Allan and Richard Cullen, 'A Bill of Rights Odyssey for Australia: The Sirens are Calling' *University of Queensland Law Journal*, no.19 (1997), pp. 171.
42. For detailed discussions of the Hong Kong judiciary's approach to BORO litigation see Yash Ghai, 'Sentinels of Liberty or Sheep in Woolf's Clothing? Judicial Politics and the Hong Kong Bill of Rights' *Modern Law Review*, no.60 (1997) p. 459; and Johannes M.M. Chan, 'Hong Kong's Bill of Rights: Its Reception of and Contribution to International and Comparative Jurisprudence' *International and Comparative Law Quarterly*, no.47 (1998) p. 306.
43. See Johannes Chan, 'The Hong Kong Bill of Rights, 1991–95: A Statistical Overview' in Johannes Chan and George Edwards (eds), *Hong Kong's Bill of Rights: Two Years before 1997* (Hong Kong: Hong Kong University Law Faculty, 1995).
44. *Hong Kong Public Law Reports*, (1991) p. 88.
45. Chan, 'Hong Kong's Bill of Rights', p. 308.
46. *Hong Kong Public Law Reports*, no.3 (1990), p. 72.
47. Ghai, 'Sentinels of Liberty', op. cit., p. 469.
48. *Hong Kong Public Law Reports*, no.5 (1995), p. 261.
49. Ghai, 'Sentinels of Liberty', op. cit., p. 471.
50. See, for example, Michael Mandel, *The Charter of Rights and the Legalization of Politics in Canada* (Wall & Thompson, Toronto: 1989); Joel Bakan, *Just Words: Constitutional Rights and Social Wrongs* (Toronto: University of Toronto Press, 1997), and Allan and Cullen, op. cit., p. 171.
51. Mandel, ibid.
52. *Attorney-General (UK) v South China Morning Post* (1987) Court of Appeal, Civil Appeal No. 114 of 1987. An attempt to suppress the same book in the courts in Australia failed.
53. *Hong Kong Public Law Reports*, no.5 (1995), p. 570.

54. *Hong Kong Public Law Reports*, no.6 (1996), p. 313.
55. *Hong Kong Public Law Reports*, no.5 (1995), p. 428.
56. *New York Times v O'Sullivan* (1964) 376 US, 254. See also H.L. Fu and Richard Cullen, 'Defamation Law in the People's Republic of China', *Transnational Lawyer*, no.11 (1998) p. 1.
57. *Hong Kong Polytechnic University v Next Magazine Publishing Ltd* (Digested in *Current Law Hong Kong 1997* (Hong Kong: Sweet & Maxwell Asia, 1998) para. 275.
58. *Hong Kong Polytechnic University v Next Magazine Publishing Ltd* (Digested in *Current Law Hong Kong 1997* (Hong Kong: Sweet & Maxwell Asia, 1998) para. 271.
59. *Hong Kong Public Law Reports*, no.5 (1995), p. 13.
60. *Hong Kong Public Law Reports*, no.6 (1996), p. 103.
61. Ghai, 'Sentinels of Liberty', op. cit., p. 459.
62. (1998) 2 Hong Kong Cases, 627.
63. Ibid, 629–31.
64. C. Parsons, 'Free press "hangs in the balance"', *SCMP*, 18 May 1998.
65. (1998) Hong Kong Cases, 627, at 681–6.
66. C. Parsons, 'Four-month term for editor wins broad approval', *SCMP*, 1 July 1998. Also see below.
67. Stanley Lubman, 'Studying Contemporary Chinese Law, Limits, Possibilities and Strategy', *American Journal of Comparative Law*, no.39 (1991), p. 293.
68. Ghai, 'Sentinels of Liberty', op. cit., p. 479.
69. Beja, 'The Goose's Golden Eggs', op. cit., p. 13.
70. See Willy Lam, 'The Beida barometer', *SCMP*, 29 April 1998; and Willy Lam, 'Liberals urge work on Deng thought', *SCMP*, 25 April 1998.
71. A pre-handover survey by the Chinese University of Hong Kong showed that although individual reporters did not seem to see themselves constrained by these zones, they saw their colleagues constrained (the so-called 'third-party effect'). The survey revealed that 50 per cent of reporters experienced hesitation in criticizing the Chinese government and almost 37 per cent in criticizing large corporations. See *HKJAAR97*, Section 4, p. 8.
72. Ibid. Less than 6 per cent were said to feel any hesitation in criticizing the Hong Kong government. This survey was conducted before the handover.
73. The cartoon strip, entitled, *The World of Lily Wong*, by Larry Feign was taken over by the *Independent* of London. It was offered world-wide. No newspaper in Hong Kong took up the offer.
74. The so-called distinction between 'reporting' and 'advocacy' was regularly drawn before the handover by PRC officials like Lu Ping, but has been comprehensively criticized as a distinction without a difference. The official PRC line is that while reporting of sensitive matters (such as Tibet separatism) may be permissible, advocacy would not be. The distinction was drawn in *Dennis v United States* (1951) 341 US 494 and then abandoned six years later as unjust and unworkable in *Yates v United States* (1957) 354 US 298. See also, Fu and Cullen, *Defamation Law in the PRC*, op. cit., 138ff.
75. A number of these areas of difficulty are set out in more detail in ibid., Chap. 12.
76. Neumann, 'Freedom Under the Dragon', op. cit., p. 9.

77. *HKJAAR97*, Section 4, p. 6. See also C. Jensen, *20 Years of Censored News* (London: Turnaround 1998).
78. *Ming Pao* reporters felt especially constrained in their writing while their colleague, Xi Yang was in jail on the mainland (see *HKJAAR97*, Section 4, p. 9). After dissident Wang Dan was exiled to the US foreign reporters who went to visit the home of his parents in Beijing were apparently detained and threatened.
79. In this regard, it has been argued that the *Apple Daily* has played a key role. This paper has enjoyed unprecedented circulation success by taking a fiercely independent stance, especially in its reporting on the Chinese government. This has both provided a diversity of viewpoints plus the *Apple Daily* benchmark has provided a certain 'shelter' for other papers. *HKJAAR97*, Section 3, p. 5.
80. Neumann, op. cit. notes 7 and 9. See also A. Li, 'Martin Lee finds Tung hard to meet', *SCMP*, 24 July 1998.
81. *HKJAAR97*, Section 3, p. 1.
82. It is said the Murdoch also has some connections with the consortium. See: Mukui Munish, 'Beijing group closes in on ATV', *Hong Kong Standard*, 26 March 1998; and G. Schloss, 'ATV buyer denies plot by mainland', *SCMP*, 28 May 1998.
83. D. Wallen, 'Murdoch "trying to censor Patten book"', *SCMP*, 23 February 1998; and J. Dugdale, 'Politics by the book', *SCMP*, 28 February 1998.
84. 'Rupert and the Dragon', *The Economist*, 7 March 1998, p. 69.
85. The subcommittee included several potential rivals of Loh in the then looming Legco elections.
86. See G. Ku, 'Loh "rivals" lose festival film vote' and 'Editorial', *SCMP*, 4 February 1998.
87. *HKJAAR97*, Section 1, 9.
88. Chris Yeung, 'Broadcaster stays open to debate', *SCMP*, 22 March 1998.
89. Michael Wong and Ceri Williams, 'RTHK is a Hong Kong issue Tung assures worried critics', *Hong Kong Standard*, 7 March 1998.
90. Ibid.
91. L. Choy, 'Xu's attack on RTHK dismissed', *SCMP*, 8 March 1998.
92. *Laws of Hong Kong*, Cap. 486.
93. C.K. Lau, 'A split for justice's sake', *SCMP*, 26 March 1998.
94. Audrey Parwani, 'Xinhua to face court', *SCMP*, 1 May 1998.
95. C. Buddle and G. Manuel, 'Xinhua tries to halt privacy case', *SCMP*, 21 May 1998.
96. G. Manuel and A. Li, 'Mainland bodies win transferred privileges', *SCMP*, 8 April 1998.
97. Neumann, 'Freedom Under the Dragon', p. 5.
98. *HKJAAR97*, Section 4, p. 4.
99. G. Schloss, 'ATV executive receives threat over sackings', *SCMP*, 25 July 1998.
100. Garry Rodan, 'Asia and the International Press: The Political Significance of Expanding Markets', in Vicky Randall (ed.) *Democratization and the Media* (London: Frank Cass, 1998) p. 144.
101. Ibid.
102. Simon Macklin, 'Call for clear definition of Xinhua's role', *South China*

Morning Post, 29 April 1998.

103. S. Lannin, 'Direct elections in 2000: Lee', *Hong Kong Standard*, 26 May 1998.

104. T. Hamlett, 'Legal dinosaur roused from welcome slumber', *Sunday Morning Post*, 5 July 1998.

8
Prospects for the Rule of Law: the Political Dimension

Leo F. Goodstadt

Commitment to the rule of law has become an article of faith for Hong Kong. Since the establishment of the Special Administrative Region (SAR), no major speech by its senior officials has seemed complete without a passage explaining the importance of this idea to the territory's wellbeing. The media have had a special role to play in encouraging public respect for this concept and in highlighting allegations of departures from its principles,[1] as Richard Cullen has discussed in the last chapter. This state of affairs was not one which could have been taken for granted before the British departure. The legal system and its future had been the subject of protracted negotiations with the Chinese government which were not made easier by the two sides' very different views as to what the rule of law should mean and the priority it should command. For China 'to allow the fundamental legal precepts of English civilization to remain behind' was an 'extraordinary concession',[2] particularly as China's leaders might well have shown the same unyielding mistrust towards British advocacy of the rule of law as they did towards the British colonial administration's proposals for modest democratic reforms.

This chapter examines how China came to allow Hong Kong's legal system to survive and the rule of law to play such an important role in the affairs of the SAR. The analysis begins by examining the 'Hong Kong environment' and the potential political and other dividends for the post-colonial leadership from its public commitment to the rule of law. Next comes a review of the 'Chinese environment' and the way in which legal reforms were an important element in the nation's post-1978 modernization programme. The analysis then proposes a model to identify the circumstances under which Sino-British negotiations were able (or otherwise) to persuade China's

180

leaders to tolerate Hong Kong systems and institutions, even when very alien or suspect. Because of the serious constitutional implications of the Court of Final Appeal's controversial definition of its powers to interpret the Basic Law in January 1999, the negotiations over its establishment are selected for review to illustrate how the model operated. This chapter concludes with an assessment of the rule of law's prospects in the SAR.

The Hong Kong environment

In the post-colonial era, Hong Kong's leaders have had three main motives in invoking the rule of law:
• to resist demands for political reform;
• to support business interests;
• to capitalize on community sentiments.

Resisting reform

The SAR government found the rule of law of special value in maintaining the power of officialdom in the face of demands for political reform. This tactic was a continuation of the colonial administration's defence of the lack of democracy. The classic example of this use of the rule of law dates back to 1982 and an essay by the then Attorney General, John Griffiths. He claimed first that 'Britain's great gift to the world' was not democracy (because 'that system has not always proved easy to transplant') and secondly 'that the greater contribution has been the transplantation of ... the Rule of Law.'[3] He proclaimed the special merits of the Colony's legislators and policymakers, guided by the rule of law, specifically because they were not elected, and he even found in the colony and its political institutions unreconstructed from the Victorian Empire a 'version of Athenian democracy'.[4]

A decade later, the last British Governor, Chris Patten, took a different line in the belief that 'democracy and the rule of law together constitute a liberal democracy, which combines the best of what ... was passed down to us from Greece and Rome.'[5] For him, this formula provided the best attainable form of government in terms of its economic as well as its political potential. However, he could not wean even all his senior official advisers from the grave reservations about the merits of elections which accompanied their traditional sense of attachment to the rule of law.[6] Furthermore, Patten's plea that a First World community like Hong Kong needed a democratic legislature to underwrite an open and accountable administration met with fierce opposition from within the local establishment no less than from the Chinese government.[7]

There was an historical consistency, therefore, in the post-colonial administration invoking the rule of law to reject the sort of political reforms which Patten had espoused. On a visit to London in 1998, the Chief Secretary defined the British legacy flatteringly and with a reference to the rule of law but not to democracy.[8] More directly Chief Executive Tung Chee-hwa declared that 'it is still too early to say when universal suffrage should be implemented in Hong Kong', though he offered the consolation that 'democracy includes ... the rule of law.'[9] Invocation of the rule of law to counter calls for democratic reform became a prominent feature of the new administration's response to the 1998 Legislative Council elections. These were a considerable triumph for the 'pro-democracy' candidates[10] and, to quote the Chief Secretary, 'laid to rest once and for all the patronising canard that Hong Kong people are only interested in money, and not politics'.[11] The Chief Executive declared: '... people equate democracy with universal suffrage and, yes, this is quite right. But let me say this, that democracy is also about the rule of law....'[12] The Chief Secretary admitted that 'Hong Kong people believe that democracy is the backbone of an open and plural society like Hong Kong.'[13] But she also insisted: 'I think we ought to distinguish between democracy and whether the Legislative Council should be returned by popular vote. To a very large extent, Hong Kong is already a democratic society. We have the rule of law.'[14]

In support of business

The post-colonial leadership found the rule of law similarly helpful in the context of protecting business interests. Once again, this approach employed a line of argument which the colonial administration had deployed. During the closing years of the colonial era, the Hong Kong government had sought to convince China's leadership to preserve the legal system by pointing out the contribution of the rule of law to the creation of a flourishing business environment. For example, in one speech, Patten stated: 'We need to keep [the economy's] competitive edge, that capacity to attract international business.... We shall only succeed in this if we can ensure that the integrity and credibility of our legal system cross the threshold of 1997 without a blemish.' He detailed the colonial administration's programme to assist business by winning the Chinese government's co-operation on legal issues but pointedly avoided any reference to political reform.[15]

For the post-colonial administration, there was no need to convince China's leaders of the priority to be attached to business interests. They had already endorsed a Basic Law to govern the SAR which 'represents only a tentative and cautious advance towards democracy and participation but sets out a liberal and extensive framework for the market economy' because its underlying theory was 'that capitalism requires a rational and autonomous legal system'.[16] In 1998, however, that 'liberal and extensive framework' faced a major challenge when Hong Kong suffered its first negative economic growth in over 35 years.[17] The new administration adopted unprecedented measures to reverse the downward pressure on property and share prices, and officials retreated from the principle of leaving supply and demand free to determine prices with property and share markets allowed to find their own levels.

In seeking to explain this break with Hong Kong's bedrock policies, the SAR government turned to the rule of law. The Chief Executive had laid the foundations for this approach when, soon after the British departure, he described the preservation of the rule of law as more critical for the territory's future success than even the free market economy.[18] Once the recession had gathered momentum, he deployed the concept when justifying government measures to protect property interests and presented it as a substitute for price competition: 'While we are conscious of competitiveness from a cost point of view, competitiveness is also about the rule of law.'[19] The Financial Secretary, Donald Tsang, used the same argument in justifying the decision to use the equivalent of US$15 billion from the Exchange Fund to intervene in the stock market to stabilize share prices:[20] 'In Hong Kong, a free market means being able to rely on the rule of law upheld by an independent judiciary.'[21]

Responding to the community

While officialdom and the business community had obvious reasons to value the rule of law in protecting their special interests, local leaders also appreciated the reality that the rule of law was a principle declared by all shades of political opinion to be crucial to Hong Kong's wellbeing. One observer claimed, 'if Hong Kong society has a defining ideology, it may be the rule of law. The commitment of people to the law ... may be greater than their commitment to democracy. It certainly serves as a powerful substitute.'[22] The post-colonial establishment was not prepared to promise the community any rapid progress towards more representative government. It could instead present the rule of law as an effective restraint on abuse of power. Early in the history of the SAR, no less an authority than its first Secretary for Justice, Elsie Leung, defined the concept in reassuring, almost text-book terms, which could appeal to the community's broadest interests:

> Amongst the underlying values and ideals of the common law is the fundamental concept of the rule of law. There are several vital prin-ciples under this concept, all of which are alive and well in the SAR. One is that laws operate separately from the political system; they are published and are accessible; and they provide a degree of certainty and predictability as to how disputes are to be resolved. A second principle is that everyone, no matter how high, is subject to the law, and that a person can only be punished for conduct that is a breach of the law. A third principle is that of equality before the law: no one gets better or worse treatment under the law because of his or her status, wealth, race and so on. A fourth principle is that the settlement of disputes is in the hands of judges who are inde-pendent of the executive and who are not subject to pressure from any source in carrying out their duties. The Government of the SAR is committed to maintaining the rule of law.[23]

The attachment of the community at large to the rule of law was very evident from a number of scholarly studies.[24] These demonstrated that the rule of law enjoyed widespread acceptance because it seemed to meet the needs of both the community and the individual in an increasingly prosperous and sophisticated post-industrial society. This research also revealed that the public's respect for the rule of law was not based on a naive idealism about how the law operated in practice. Hong Kong could hardly avoid an awareness of the shortcomings of its legal system, both institutional and individual. Details of the institu-tional defects of the legal system were provided most authoritatively by Sir Ti-liang Yang, the last substantive Chief Justice under British rule and an unsuccessful candidate for Chief Executive. He expressed concern that the Common Law, imported from England, was remote from the experience of China and largely alien to the bulk of the community. He saw its adherence to the English language as a further obstacle to access to justice. The judiciary and the administration of justice generally were the last institutions to be localized by the colo-nial administration, and Yang regarded them as tainted by racism.[25]

The weaknesses attributable to individuals were also widely known. Legal malpractice and judicial misconduct had long been recorded in considerable detail, including greed, malpractice and corruption among legal practitioners;[26] a 'rude and bullying attitude' in the Court of Appeal;[27] and a judicial tendency towards 'excessive deference to executive policies and legislative sovereignty, and ... only a half-hearted commitment to fundamental human rights'.[28] Even the rule of law itself had been criticized as imperial baggage. 'Much is made of the blessings of the rule of law brought by the British to Hong Kong', stated one scholar, 'At that time the rule of law was merely the "rule by might".'[29] Indeed, the initial establishment of Hong Kong's legal institutions was far from smooth, as Christopher Munn recounts in Chapter 2. Nevertheless, for all the system's defects and disappointments, 'the rule of law is definitely a foremost British legacy for Hong Kong and is rightly perceived as such' by the community.[30]

Expectations and apprehensions

The community's attitude towards the rule of law reflected its expectations and apprehensions. It expected the rule of law to play a beneficial role in the public life of Hong Kong and it had reason to be apprehensive about both the Chinese government's attitude to the rule of law and its record on human rights.

Hong Kong expectations

The community had come to recognize that the rule of law helped to create patterns of behaviour essential to the wellbeing of a modern, urban society. A striking example of its role in shaping public conduct was provided by the Legislative Council's handling of the departure from the Public Service of the Director of Immigration, Laurence Leung, whose abrupt resignation in 1996 provoked a spate of rumours that he had been compelled to retire for scandalous reasons.[31] The Legislative Council felt obliged to set up a Select Committee to investigate the matter, which behaved impeccably. Sensation and scandal were not permitted to distort an incident which had the potential to discredit the Civil Service and cause new embarrassments in relations with the Chinese government just prior to the handover. Its report avoided speculation which could not be thoroughly tested and its findings displayed a sophisticated appreciation of the difficulties which the colonial administration had faced in handling this case. In short, the Select Committee showed very powerfully how the rule of law had created a culture whose code of conduct promoted open government but reduced the opportunities for political exploitation of public scandals.

Chinese apprehensions

Before the British departure, Hong Kong's attachment to the rule of law was reinforced by an awareness of the very different conditions which prevailed under the Chinese. For fundamental ideological reasons, Chinese officials could not share the Hong Kong view of this concept because their legal system rejected 'such bourgeois notions as the rule of law, the separation of powers, the independence and impartiality of the judiciary; the dominance of law over politics, individual rights, and limited government'.[32] The Hong Kong community could not ignore these ideological differences when Beijing stood accused of 'widespread and well-documented human rights abuses ... tight restrictions on freedom of speech, the press, assembly, association, religion, privacy, and worker rights'.[33] There was an apprehension in Hong Kong that, given their domestic record, China's leaders would be unconcerned by the erosion of either civil liberties or the integrity of the legal system after 1997.[34]

The Chinese environment

On the analysis presented so far, it is reasonable to suggest that the community at large had a deeper attachment to the rule of law than government and business leaders, who valued it mainly because of its potential contribution to the defence of their special interests. In terms of the 'Hong Kong environment', the rule of law can be said to have survived the end of British colonialism at least as much because of political convenience combined with economic expediency as because of principle. The question remains: why did China's leaders tolerate in Hong Kong a legal system against which they had serious ideological objections within the 'Chinese environment', especially when they took such an unrelenting line on political reform? There were, after all, several parallels between the two issues. For example:

- The Chinese government attacked the British side for reneging on diplomatic agreements and seeking to transfer power directly to the legislature in respect of both the legal system and political reform.[35]
- Some Chinese officials saw the colonial administration's advocacy of the rule of law as linked to the same 'British plot' to leave behind disruption as its proposals for political reform.[36]
- The colonial administration's advocacy of the rule of law and its 1992 proposals for more democratic electoral arrangements both represented the aspirations of a majority in the community.[37]

Thus, the unresolved rancour over the colonial administration's modest steps towards a more representative legislature was an intriguing contrast to China's willingness to reach a negotiated settlement on a key building block for the post-1997 legal system (the Court of Final Appeal).

China's national interest

In the Chinese government's management of negotiations over Hong Kong issues prior to 1997, the defence of 'national interest' was its starting point, and its response to British proposals can be seen as generally reflecting three primary Chinese concerns:[38]

- *Sovereignty*. The Chinese government would oppose any British initiatives that it suspected could impinge on China's total rights over the territory; or allowed Hong Kong equal participation in discussions over future arrangements for the territory; or appeared to transfer power directly from the United Kingdom to Hong Kong.
- *Imperialism*. The Chinese government would oppose any measures that it feared might enable the United Kingdom to undermine Hong Kong's prosperity and stability or to extend its control or influence after the colonial era.
- *Prosperity*. The Chinese government would consider concessions to enhance Hong Kong's ability to contribute to China's future prosperity provided that they would not enable the United Kingdom to limit China's sovereignty or exploit the territory excessively.

The missing factor

In addition, another factor, the 'Chinese environment', needs to be taken into account. This term goes beyond the impact on China's Hong Kong policies of such major events as 4 June 1989, or a change of prime ministers. It involves more than such well-canvassed considerations as the role of 'face' or the avoidance of confrontation in Chinese society. This fourth factor refers to the frame of reference which Chinese leaders and officials brought to their decision making on Hong Kong issues, embracing their current political and economic challenges as well as their past experience of political management at home and abroad.[39]

Before the handover, however, little attention was paid to the practical implications of this specific Chinese perspective either by the British side or by commentators generally,[40] in spite of repeated warnings from the Chinese government's supporters in Hong Kong about the urgent need to do so.[41] It would be wrong to argue that this neglect caused disagreements over routine technical issues to become full-blown diplomatic disputes. Nevertheless, failure to comprehend the full Chinese background within which Chinese leaders and their officials were evaluating Hong Kong policies and proposals can be shown to have intensified the Chinese side's opposition on crucial issues.

The importance of this factor varied from one issue to another. In general, failure to take comprehensive account of the Chinese context proved an aggravating factor in three types of situation.[42]

- *When a Hong Kong project ran counter to the Chinese leadership's own experience of what constituted sound administration and prudent policy.*[43] Thus, the colonial administration assumed its costly new airport would encounter no serious Chinese resistance[44] because prior to its formal announcement in October 1989, the official *Xinhua News Agency* had reprinted Bank of China proposals to assist its funding[45] and Chinese officials had voiced no objections in private briefings. Hong Kong officials had first failed to grasp the inability of China's post-Tiananmen leadership to focus on the issue in the summer and autumn of 1989.[46] They then failed to follow up constructive talks between the Governor Sir David Wilson and the then Premier Li Peng in January 1990 with financial presentations to Chinese officials which specifically addressed their Marxist–Maoist preconceptions about colonialism, their fears of costly showpieces and their experience of local administrations' mismanagement of major projects within China.

- *When the colonial administration was reluctant to explain publicly why a proposal was subject to attack by competing Hong Kong business interests.* Thus, Chinese suspicions of a plot to reward the Keswicks for their support of the new Governor, Chris Patten, by awarding Container terminal No. 9 to a consortium led by their Jardine Group were fanned by complaints from the business community that the tendering process had been altered to favour British interests. The colonial administration was reluctant to counter these charges directly with a public discussion of how existing terminal operators levied the highest charges in the world,[47] and it failed to make the case for expanding port ownership out of a fear of alienating business leaders and thus losing this traditional source of support.

- *When the Hong Kong bureaucracy felt unable to engage its Chinese counterparts in substantive discussions.* Thus, when the Chinese government demanded a full inventory of the colonial administration's assets, Hong Kong officials did not realize that such inventories were part of a well-developed, national policy designed to prevent misappropriation of state property throughout China[48] rather than a move to embarrass the British. Consequently, since the colonial administration itself had never complied with such an inventory, it failed to see why the Chinese could have a legitimate need for an exercize which it feared would be unrealistically costly and time-consuming.[49]

By contrast, the 'Chinese environment' proved a positive factor:

- when a Hong Kong policy or proposal was in line with developments within China;
- when the colonial administration was able to achieve a degree of consensus with the business community and rally its help in explaining Hong Kong's case to China's leaders; and
- when the Hong Kong bureaucracy displayed ingenuity in engaging its Chinese counterparts in the search for solutions.

Overall, the 'Chinese environment' proved a benevolent factor in negotiations over the whole range of legal issues.[50] Its positive impact will be assessed in more detail by its contribution to resolving the dispute over the Court of Final Appeal.

China's legal reforms

During the era of Deng Xiaoping, the first element in the 'Chinese environment' favourable to the survival of the rule of law in Hong Kong was the leadership's awareness of the need for a modern, effective and credible legal system, particularly since so many senior officials had suffered harsh, arbitrary and unlawful punishment during the Cultural Revolution (1966–76). Between 1949 and 1976, the nation's laws and legal institutions had first been made subservient to the Communist Party and then swept aside by the mass political campaigns culminating in the Cultural Revolution.[51] At the height of the Cultural Revolution, human rights and all conventional state administration were suspended. After the death of Mao Zedong in 1976, followed by the arrest of his closest associates ('the Gang of Four') and the discrediting of the Cultural Revolution, China's leadership faced two urgent tasks:[52]

- First, the Communist Party needed to bolster its legitimacy with a new source of authority to replace the tarnished doctrines and the personality cult of the Maoist era. China's leaders, thus, had a vested interest in the creation of a credible legal system, and among the first acts of the post-Mao leadership was a campaign to seek to replace the 'rule of man' with the 'rule of law' through strengthening 'socialist legality'.

- Second, the leadership needed to put in place structures and institutions which would allow a return to orderly and efficient administration, and replace the voluntarism and anti-establishment tendencies which Mao had sought to foster. This process gave the law and legal processes a new importance.

The economic reforms and 'open door' policies introduced after 1978 created additional pressures to rely on law rather than ideology. The Chinese government found it useful to draw on international practice in creating a modern framework for the foreign trade and investment on which its economic reforms relied very heavily. At a later stage, China's policymakers proved willing to borrow from foreign regulatory frameworks in such other fields as social welfare.[53] As economic growth gathered momentum and Communist Party discipline declined, the leadership turned increasingly to the legal system as a remedy for the bureaucratic insubordination, abuse of office and endemic corruption, which had become the most serious issues confronting it in the 1990s.[54]

Overall, then, China's legal culture was being 'modernized' during the period of Hong Kong's transition to 1997. Although the process of legal reform was not motivated by liberal principles and was marred by serious abuses, it was pragmatic, aware of the political dangers of a legal and judicial vacuum, influenced by western practices and responsive to external pressures. To China's leaders, the law and the courts reinforced state authority and promoted political stability and economic prosperity, in sharp contrast to the 'anarchy' which they perceived democratic reforms to bring in their wake, especially after 4 June 1989.[55] This was the 'Chinese environment' which would shape official attitudes during Sino-British negotiations on legal issues.

Defining the SAR's legal system

The process of identifying the cornerstones of Hong Kong's legal system in preparation for the British departure began with the Joint Declaration. This agreement provided for continuity of the legal system. Article 3 (3) declared:

> The Hong Kong Special Administrative Region will be vested with executive, legislative and independent judicial power, including that of final adjudication. The laws currently in force will remain basically unchanged.

As with much of the Joint Declaration, this provision was couched in broad but vague terms and would require further clarification. What, for example, would the phrases 'currently in force' and 'basically unchanged' mean in practice? What institutional arrangements would be necessary to exercize 'final adjudication'?[56] Articles 80 to 96 of the Basic Law later added more detail, but gaps and omissions remained which Hong Kong hoped would be clarified ahead of the handover through discussion with the Chinese government. In particular, the Basic Law had not defined the detailed arrangements by which the Court of Final Appeal would be constituted.

The Court of Final Appeal

Negotiations over the Court of Final Appeal (CFA) began in 1988, but the serious Sino-British disputes which followed 4 June 1989, meant that this issue received limited attention from either officials or the public. A formal Sino-British agreement on the CFA emerged eventually, almost as a footnote to the flurry of diplomatic activity in connection with the 1991 visit to China by the British Prime Minister, John Major, to sign the Memorandum of Understanding on the new airport. The airport deal took the limelight, and its commitment to closer working relations between the colonial administration and Chinese officials seemed to promise a fresh start. The colonial administration assumed that the breakthrough on the CFA was of minor importance by comparison. Its expectation that, whatever the fine print, the agreement on the CFA would be welcomed by Hong Kong and its legislature as part of the process of normalizing relations with the future sovereign was to prove ill-founded.

Electoral sensitivities

It was the outcome of the 1991 elections to the Legislative Council which created the crucial test of the acceptability of Sino-British arrangements for the CFA. Sino-British negotiations had been an important electoral issue, and voting patterns could be interpreted as evidence of public dissatisfaction with the results of the diplomatic process.[57] In any case, the new Legco was not prepared to co-operate with the colonial administration without first considering the attitudes of the community and specific constituencies. Even the government appointed members proved no more supportive than their elected colleagues mainly because the system of appointment to Legco was to end in 1995.[58] Appointed members who wanted a political future would have to develop their own constituencies if they were to continue their political careers by contesting the 1995 elections. Thus, the colonial administration's traditional, easy majorities disappeared during this final stage of the switch from appointed to elected membership. Most senior officials had not foreseen the difficulties which this development would create in their relationship with the legislature.[59] The bureaucracy initially lacked both the lobbying apparatus and the parliamentary experience to cultivate the new legislature effectively and fend off attacks by the legal profession and the media on the CFA agreement as another example of a 'British sell-out'.[60]

A second-best solution

The 1991 agreement was rejected by Legco principally because of the legal profession's disquiet over the number of foreign members of the Court and the definition of 'acts of state'. The colonial administration was in a quandary. It could not hope to induce the Chinese government to amend the agreement to accommodate its local critics because compromise on these points had previously been rejected. When in 1994, the colonial administration sought a return to the negotiating table, Chinese officials indicated that a deal would only be possible on terms less favourable than had been acceptable in 1991. But by mid-1995, the atmosphere had changed, and the Chinese government was now prepared to endorse legislation for a CFA on what appeared to be much the same terms as 1991 except that the Court should not begin to function until after the British departure.[61] The colonial administration felt able politically to accept this deal for two reasons.

- First, its officials had become much more experienced in political lobbying and felt confident of their ability to mobilize majorities in Legco even in the face of determined opposition.
- Second, by 1995, the legislature contained a significant (though not a majority) block which would not vote against measures supported by the Chinese government. Consequently, the Court of Final Appeal Ordinance (Cap. 484) was passed in July 1995 by a comfortable majority.

Shaping a deal

The Chinese government's decision to modify its position substantially between May 1994 and May 1995 can be attributed to two main factors:
- The first was the intense lobbying of senior Chinese officials by Hong Kong's legal profession and business representatives. The colonial administration ensured that before visiting the Chinese capital, tycoons and business delegations were briefed extensively

on how to explain the potential commercial and financial costs to the territory of a legal vacuum after 1997.

• The second was the use made by Hong Kong officials of their personal contacts with individuals who were influential members of the new political establishment which the Chinese government was creating for Hong Kong.[62]

These contacts allowed the colonial administration to appear to retreat on an important matter of principle without jeopardizing its political credibility. It had previously insisted that there could be no dealings with the Preliminary Working Committee (PWC), established in 1993, or the future Provisional Legislative Council (PLC) because these bodies had not been authorized either by the Joint Declaration or the Basic Law and were intended explicitly to oppose both the colonial administration and the more representative legislature to be elected in 1995. Nevertheless, Hong Kong officials created a variety of opportunities at which to discuss the CFA (and a range of other issues) with members of the PWC's Legal Sub-Group on a selective and individual basis. As a result, the final agreement on the arrangements for establishing the Court was 'coincidentally' very close to the Sub-Group's eight-point proposal on the subject, which the Chinese government could represent as constituting a major concession over British non-recognition of bodies set up by China.[63]

A further concession which the Chinese side believed it had won was to prove more illusory. The formal 'Agreement between the British and Chinese Sides on the Question of the Court of Final Appeal in Hong Kong' contained the following provision:

The Chinese and British sides agree that the *team designate* of the Hong Kong Special Administrative Region shall, with the British side (including relevant Hong Kong Government departments) participating in the process and providing its assistance, be responsible for the preparation for the establishment of the Court of Final Appeal on 1 July 1997 in accordance with the Basic Law and consistent with the provisions of the Court of Final Appeal Ordinance.[64] (Emphasis added.)

The colonial administration knew that the Chinese government intended the term 'team designate' to include the PLC, and so it faced the danger of being attacked for abandoning its commitment to have no dealings with this body. It decided that the political risk from including this reference in the text was manageable:

- First, the Governor's Policy Address in October 1995 would pledge full co-operation with separate components of the Team Designate in language carefully contrived to exclude the PLC.
- Second, the colonial administration would ignore any Chinese demands for the term to be interpreted to include the PLC once that body had been established.

The colonial administration won this gamble. The community did not regard the reference to the Team Designate as evidence of a fresh British betrayal of Hong Kong's interests. Furthermore, the Chinese side was unable to compel the colonial administration to collaborate with the PLC.

The deal on the CFA was secure, although the Court itself was to become the source of the first serious post-colonial clash between Hong Kong and the Chinese authorities when, in January 1999, it claimed the right to interpret and enforce the Basic Law. This decision was denounced by the Chinese side as arrogating to Hong Kong 'some aspects of the jurisdiction of an independent sovereign state, which is ridiculous ... and practically turning Hong Kong into an independent political entity'.[65] In addition, the Court's decision was impugned for not regarding an individual's Basic Law right to enter Hong Kong by claiming permanent resident status as subordinate to such consider-ations as the effect on social services and employment of substantial immigration from elsewhere in China.[66] This criticism illustrated how Chinese officials had failed to comprehend that, in Hong Kong, the rule of law was expected to protect the individual's rights regardless of the administration's priorities or the community's convenience. In the event, Hong Kong opinion rallied solidly behind the Court decision once the rule of law was seen as under threat.[67]

Conclusions

Even more important for the survival of the rule of law than the lobby-ing and ingenuity in finding ways to work with Chinese officials to break an apparent impasse over questions of principle was the 'Chinese environment'. In a sense, Hong Kong's lobbyists were preach-ing to the converted in their discussions with Chinese leaders on the rule of law generally and the CFA in particular. The Chinese Communist Party saw legal reform as a source of stability and pros-perity for the nation as a whole, and stability and prosperity were its watchwords in Hong Kong. It had long since taken the decision in principle to look beyond Marxist–Leninist legal doctrines and to use western models in developing a modern legal system to promote trade and investment with the outside world.

The future Hong Kong SAR was expected to play a crucial role in China's commercial and financial relations with the global economy. In addition, the colonial administration succeeded in mobilizing active support for the rule of law not just from the obvious groups like the legal profession but also business interests, political parties of all persuasions and, most important of all, the new Hong Kong élite which the Chinese government had created. Thus, China's leadership was prepared to accept Hong Kong's rule of law (despite its colonial features) and to compromise on the CFA (despite the 1991 rebuff to its sovereignty by Legco). Nevertheless, the official denunciation of the CFA's view of its relationship to the Basic Law in 1999 underlined the threat posed by the conflict between Chinese and Hong Kong concepts of the rule of law.

China's decision to tolerate the continuation of Hong Kong's legal culture is not in itself enough to ensure its survival. Hong Kong's tragedy has been its inability to convince Chinese leaders that survival of the rule of law depends just as much on the representativeness of its political institutions as on the composition of its highest judicial body. Without a democratically-elected legislature, the rule of law lacks the open and accountable government essential to its wellbeing, and it becomes vulnerable to threats from within Hong Kong itself. Unless an administration is answerable to a democratic legislature, maintenance of the rule of law can swiftly become a matter of expediency and dependent on the good will of officialdom. This threat is increased by doubts about the depth of the business world's commitment to this concept[68] since business interests have been such a powerful influence in shaping both the institutions and the policies of the SAR.

On the evidence presented in this chapter, the rule of law has been deployed already by Hong Kong's post-colonial administration more for political convenience than as a matter of principle. It might be argued that in this regard, post-colonial officials have been no more cynical than their colonial predecessors, under whom Hong Kong made considerable progress. That argument applied to the post-colonial world of the Basic Law reduces the concept to mere political rhetoric, which brings its own dangers.

- First, invocation of the rule of law to counter criticism of the lack of democracy under British rule was self-serving and unconvincing, for the rule of law may ameliorate the absence of democracy but

cannot replace it. Nevertheless, the argument reflected the constitutional reality that the colonial administration was 'accountable to
a democratic government [in Britain] which treasures freedom and
the rule of law'.[69] In addition, the colonial administration had to
avoid oppressive or irresponsible policies after 1945 if only because
these would have strengthened the threats to British rule from anti-
colonial liberals overseas as well as from supporters of the Chinese
Communist Party.[70]

- Second, invocation of the rule of law to counter criticism of the SAR
  government's economic measures is deeply troubling. The rule of
  law is not an instrument of economic policy, and it offers no guarantee of a policy's commercial or financial soundness. Of itself, it
  does not create wealth. At best, the rule of law may enable, though
  not ensure, its creation. To pretend otherwise is 'to put the rule of
  law on a precarious ledge, for if it could be shown that the rule of
  law, bereft of any moral or democratic values, is in fact not essential to [Hong Kong's] economy, the whole edifice of the Basic Law
  ... will be in danger of collapse.'[71]

Within Hong Kong, critics have protested that its retreat from even
the modest degree of democracy achieved by the end of the colonial
era has been followed by an erosion of the rule of law.[72] When these
protests intensified in early 1999 because of the SAR government's
tactics to allay Chinese official indignation about the CFA, the Chief
Secretary sought to reassure the community with a ringing pledge:
'The rule of law to Hong Kong is not a cliché or a slogan. It is the very
foundation on which the community has been built. It has protected
our freedom and underwritten our progress and prosperity.'[73]
Nevertheless, its ultimate survival will need more than official reassur-
ances. Vested interests, and not just the public at large, will have to
display a commitment to the rule of law which goes beyond rhetoric
and expediency and is based on genuine respect for its principles.

Notes

1. See, for example, the exchanges between Legislative Councillor Margaret
   Ng and Secretary for Justice Elsie Leung, *SCMP*, 15 and 29 October 1998.
2. Jamie Allen, *Seeing Red. China's Uncompromising Takeover of Hong Kong*
   (Singapore: Butterworth-Heinemann Asia, 1997), pp. 256–7.
3. 'The Constitution of Hong Kong: The Hub of the Wheel of State', *Hong
   Kong 1983* (Hong Kong: Government Printer), p. 9.
4. Ibid., p. 5.
5. Chris Patten, *East and West* (London: Macmillan, 1998), p. 175 *et seq.*

6. For example, Baroness Dunn, one of Hong Kong's most distinguished public and political figures, in her essay, 'The Way We Are', *Hong Kong 1996* and *A Pictorial Review of The Past Fifty Years* (Hong Kong: Government Printer), pp. 2–4.
7. For example, the long-standing hostility to political reform expressed by Sir S.Y. Chung, official adviser first to the colonial administration, then the Chinese government and finally the post-colonial administration recorded in Sally Blythe and Ian Wotherspoon, *Hong Kong Remembers* (Hong Kong: Oxford University Press, 1996), p. 53.
8. *Government Information Service* (hereafter *GIS*), 28 October 1998.
9. *GIS*, 3 April 1998.
10. Election details are provided by David Newman and Alvin Rabushka, *Hong Kong Under Chinese Rule: the first year* (Stanford: Hoover Institution, 1998).
11. *GIS*, 9 June 1998. Five years earlier, 78 per cent of the respondents in an opinion poll commissioned by the *Hong Kong Standard* (10 and 12 April 1993) had supported more democracy immediately even at the risk 'that Hong Kong will be less prosperous'.
12. *GIS*, 28 May 1998.
13. *GIS*, 9 June 1998.
14. *GIS*, 27 May 1998.
15. 'The Implementation of the Joint Declaration: An Overview' in Wang Gungwu and Wong Siu-lun (eds), *Hong Kong's Transition A Decade After the Deal* (Hong Kong: Oxford University Press, 1995), p. 158.
16. Yash Ghai, 'The Rule of Law and Capitalism: Reflections on the Basic Law', in Raymond Wacks (ed.), *Hong Kong, China and 1997: Essays in Legal Theory* (Hong Kong: Hong Kong University Press, 1993), pp. 348, 356. To be fair to the post-colonial administration, the rule of law's role is part of a much wider debate over the relationship between democracy and free markets than Hong Kong's electoral arrangements. See David Beetham's summary of the issues in 'Market Economy and Democratic Polity', in Robert Fine and Shirin Rai (eds), *Civil Society: Democratic Perspectives* (London: Frank Cass, 1997), pp. 77–8.
17. See the Financial Secretary, Donald Tsang, *GIS*, 28 May 1998.
18. *GIS*, 31 July 1997.
19. *GIS*, 22 June 1998.
20. T.L. Yang, *GIS*, 26 October 1998.
21. *GIS*, 1 October 1998. Revealingly, Joseph Yam, Chief Executive of the Hong Kong Monetary Authority did not find it necessary to invoke the rule of law in his definition of free markets when he defended government intervention. *GIS*, 26 March 1999.
22. Quoting Yash Ghai. 'Tung Constrained', *Economist*, 28 March 1998. Nevertheless, there is real anxiety about post-handover developments. Emily Lau, for example, promptly rejected such optimism in a letter to the editor in the *Economist* of 11 April 1998, offering a succinct summary of cogent reasons to believe that the rule of law itself was at risk.
23. Speech at the 15th LawAsia Biennial Conference, *GIS*, 30 August 1997. As Gordon White, Jude Howell and Shang Xiaoyuan have noted in the context of China itself, this sort of definition 'derives most clearly from the Anglo-American liberal tradition of political theory' and is 'virtually

indistinguishable from a standard conception of a liberal democratic polity'. *In Search of Civil Society: Market Reform and Social Change in Contemporary China* (Oxford: Clarendon Press, 1996), pp. 3–4.

24. Kuan Hsin-chi, Lau Siu-kai and Wan Po-san, 'Legal Attitudes', in Lau Siu-kai *et al.* (eds), *Indicators of Social Development: Hong Kong 1988* (Hong Kong: The Chinese University, 1991); Kuan Hsin-chi, 'Legal Culture: The Challenge of Modernization,' in Lau Siu-kai *et al.* (eds), *Indicators of Social Development: Hong Kong 1990* (Hong Kong: The Chinese University, 1992); Berry Hsu, *The Common Law In Chinese Context* (Hong Kong: Hong University Press, 1992), chapters 6 and 7.

25. Emily Lau, *Far Eastern Economic Review* (hereafter *FEER*), 20 April 1989; Yang's 'Address at the Opening of the Legal Year,' *GIS*, 13 January 1992; and Lau Chi Kuen, *Hong Kong's Colonial Legacy* (Hong Kong: The Chinese University Press, 1997), 130–46.

26. Margaret Ng, 'The Legal System: Turbulence and Shadows,' in Choi Po-king and Ho Lok-sang (eds),*The Other Hong Kong Report 1993* (Hong Kong: The Chinese University Press, 1993), pp. 15–16; Emily Lau, *FEER*, 6 October 1988.

27. Johannes Chan, 'To Change or Not to Change: The Crumpling Legal System', in Nyaw Mee-kau and Li Si-ming (eds), *The Other Hong Kong Report 1996* (Hong Kong: The Chinese University Press, 1996), p. 24.

28. Johannes Chan, 'Human Rights: From One Era to Another', in Joseph Y.S. Cheng (ed.), *The Other Hong Kong Report 1997* (Hong Kong: The Chinese University Press, 1997), p. 145. Yang himself caused considerable controversy with the views he conveyed to Chinese officials on the Bill of Rights. Christine Loh, 'Human Rights in a Time Warp', in Nyaw and Li, *The Other Hong Kong Report 1996*, op. cit., p. 97.

29. Yash Ghai, *Hong Kong's New Constitutional Order* (Hong Kong: Hong Kong University Press, 1997), p. 2.

30. Ming K. Chan, 'The Legacy of the British Administration of Hong Kong: A view from Hong Kong', *The China Quarterly*, No. 151 (1997), pp. 567, 570, 580.

31. Legislative Council, *Report of the Select Committee to Inquire into the Circumstances Surrounding the Departure of Mr Leung Ming-yin from the Government and Related Issues. Volume I: Report and Minutes of Proceedings* (June 1997), pp. 26–7.

32. Peter Wesley-Smith, 'Law in Hong Kong and China: The Meshing of Systems', *The Annals*, Vol. 547 (1996), p. 107.

33. The Bureau of Democracy, Human Rights, and Labor, *China Country Report on Human Rights Practices for 1997* (US Department of State, 30 January 1998), p. 1. This official American indictment came from the Clinton administration often accused of being too complaisant about the Chinese record on human rights.

34. Jacques deLisle and Kevin P. Lane, 'Cooking the Rice without Cooking the Goose: The Rule of Law, the Battle over Business, and the Quest for Prosperity in Hong Kong after 1997', in Warren I. Cohen and Li Zhao (eds), *Hong Kong Under Chinese Rule: The Economic and Political Implications of Reversion* (Cambridge: Cambridge University Press, 1997), pp. 34–5.

35. *Ta Kung Pao*, 7 March 1993.

36. See Michael Yahuda, 'The Foreign relations of Greater China', in David Shambaugh (ed.), *Greater China: The Next Superpower?* (Oxford: Oxford University Press, 1995), p. 41.

37. Public opinion polls in July and August 1997 found a majority preferred Chris Patten's electoral arrangements to the post-colonial administration's proposals and also favoured a large increase in the number of directly elected seats. *ACR Opinion Poll, 26–28 August 1997* (Hong Kong: Asian Commercial Research Ltd, 1997), p. 6.

38. An excellent analysis of the Chinese government's approach is to be found in Steve Tsang, *Hong Kong. An Appointment with China* (London: I.B. Tauris, 1997), chapter 7.

39. Wang Jisi has made a powerful case for much greater attention to the 'Chinese mindset' in analyzing China's international behaviour. 'International Relations Theory and the Study of Chinese Foreign Policy: A Chinese Perspective', in Thomas W. Robinson and David Shambaugh (eds), *China's Foreign Policy. Theory and Practice* (Oxford: Clarendon Press, 1994), pp. 498–505.

40. With such exceptions as Michael Yahuda's well-considered summary of the 'cultural' conflict between the two sides in *Hong Kong. China's Challenge* (London: Routledge, 1996), pp. 8–13.

41. Leung Chun-ying, for example, preached this message in public as well as in private. See his essay, 'The transition and Unexpected Changes', in Wang and Wong, *Hong Kong's Transition*, op. cit., pp. 143–4. Such views tended to be dismissed as partisan support for China's negotiating position.

42. The analysis which follows does not purport to provide a full account of the complex and protracted negotiations over the airport, Container Terminal 9 or government assets, but seeks no more than to illustrate where failure to be fully aware of the 'Chinese environment' added to the difficulty of managing disputes.

43. This concern was a salient theme in one lengthy interview on the new airport with Lu Ping, Director of the Hong Kong and Macao Affairs Office, as China's desire to oversee the colonial administration. *Wen Wei Po*, 26 May 1991.

44. The official then responsible for the project, Anson Chan, was still stating publicly that the project had 'the support of the Chinese Government' and that the 'Chinese authorities had always welcomed the territory's infra-structural projects' on the eve of a bitter denunciation of the new airport by Jiang Zemin. *SCMP*, 3 December 1989.

45. 28 September 1989 in Chinese and 29 September 1989 in English. Sir David Wilson announced the Hong Kong Government's intention to build the replacement airport on 12 October 1989.

46. Sir Percy Cradock, *Experiences of China* (London: John Murray, 1994), p. 238.

47. On competition in Hong Kong's port services, see Leonard K. Cheng and Yue-Chim Richard Wong, *Port Facilities and Container Handling Services* (Hong Kong: City University of Hong Kong Press, 1997).

48. For example, 'Regulations on Management of State Property', *New China News Agency* (*NCNA* hereafter), 29 July 1994, art. 10 (2).

49. The British Civil Service completed such an inventory for the United

200 of 228 Judicial Independence and the Rule of Law in Hong Kong

Kingdom within six months of the Labour Party taking power in 1997: 'The 550-page National Asset Register ranges from art to equipment, land and buildings.' *The Times*, 24 November 1997.

50. Overviews of the negotiating record are provided by the Chief Secretary, *GIS*, 4 October 1996 and *Hong Kong 1997* (Hong Kong: Information Services Department, 1997), p. 40.

51. Wang Chenguang, 'Future Directions of the Chinese Law,' in Joseph Y.S. Cheng (ed.), *China in the Post-Deng Era* (Hong Kong: The Chinese University Press, 1998), p. 171.

52. These developments are summed up very well by Shiping Zheng, *Party vs State in Post-1949 China. The Institutional Dilemma* (Cambridge: Cambridge University Press, 1997), pp. 161–90. However, the legal philosophy to which the leadership turned after 1976 was derived from Leninism and Maoism, not liberalism. See my 'China's New Constitution: Maoism, Economic Change and Civil Liberties', *Hong Kong Law Journal*, Vol. 8 (1978), p. 307.

53. Michael Yahuda, 'How much has China learned about interdependence?' in David S.G. Goodman and Gerald Segal (eds), *China Rising. Nationalism and Interdependence* (London: Routledge, 1997), pp, 13–14.

54. This topic is analyzed very thoroughly by Melanie Manion, 'Corruption and Corruption Control: More of the same in 1996', in Maurice Brosseau, Kuan Hsin-chi and Y.Y. Kueh (eds), *China Review 1997* (Hong Kong: The Chinese University Press, 1997). The desire of senior cadres to arrange exemption from legal sanctions for themselves or their offspring does not mean that the Chinese Communist Party as an organisation was insincere in attacking malpractices.

55. For the Chinese Communist Party's invocation of the rule of law in this context, see Jiang Zemin, 'Report at the 15th National Congress of the Communist Party of China', *NCNA*, 12 September 1997.

56. Sections II and III of the Chinese government's Annex I to the Joint Declaration did not satisfactorily resolve these issues.

57. Ian Scott, 'An Overview of the Hong Kong Legislative Council Elections of 1991', in Rowena Kwok *et al.* (eds), *Votes Without Power: The Hong Kong Legislative Council Elections 1991* (Hong Kong: Hong Kong University Press, 1992), p. 17. This author also draws attention to civil liberties as part of the background to the elections.

58. Chan, however, regards the appointed members as the Governor's 'anti-democratic' placemen ('The Legacy of the British Administration of Hong Kong', p. 578).

59. One exception was the Financial Secretary, Sir Piers Jacobs. Blythe and Wotherspoon, *Hong Kong Remembers*, pp. 225–6.

60. This account of the demise of the original agreement focuses on the political and presentational problems involved, but this does not imply that the terms of the agreement were to be commended. The legal profession's criticisms deserved considerable respect both in 1991 and 1995. The question for the government was whether legislating for a second-best Court of Final Appeal was better than leaving the issue to a post-1997 legislature. Rhoda Mushkat usefully summarises the debate in 'The joint declaration and the CFA agreement', *Hong Kong Law Journal*, Vol. 26 (1996), pp. 277–81.

61. Jonathan Dimbleby, *The Last Governor. Chris Patten & the Handover of Hong Kong* (London: Little, Brown and Company, 1997), pp. 273–86.
62. For example, two professional lawyers: Elsie Leung, NPC Deputy and future Secretary for Justice and Maria Tam, former Legislative and Executive Councillor and future member of the PLC (very briefly) and CPPCC.
63. For which the colonial administration was criticized, for example, 'By taking on board some of the recommendations of the PWC about the composition of the powers of this court, the British government has *de facto* recognized the status of the PWC.' Anthony B.L. Cheung, 'The Civil Service in Transition', in Stephen Y.L. Cheung and Stephen M.H. Sze (eds), *The Other Hong Kong Report 1995* (Hong Kong: The Chinese University Press, 1995), p. 71.
64. *GIS*, 9 June 1995.
65. *NCNA*, 7 February 1999.
66. *China Daily*, 11 February 1999.
67. The Chief Secretary was refreshingly candid on this issue. *GIS*, 17 March 1999.
68. Ghai, *Hong Kong's New Constitutional Order*, pp. 470–1.
69. Joseph Y.S. Cheng, 'Preliminary Suggestions on the Political System of the Hong Kong Special Administrative Region', in Joseph Y.S. Cheng (ed.), *Hong Kong in Transition* (Hong Kong: Oxford University Press, 1986), p. 54.
70. Taciana Fisac and Steve Tsang (eds), *China Ante el Reto de la Modernizacion*, (Madrid: Edicions Bellaterra, 1999), chapter 10.
71. Ghai, 'The Rule of Law and Capitalism', p. 356.
72. See Margaret Ng 'Rule of Law. Post-handover Rule of Law – A New Interpretation' in Chris Yeung (ed.), *Hong Kong China: the Red Dawn* (Sydney: Prentice Hall, 1998).
73. *GIS*, 11 March 1999.

Index